PSYCHOANALYTIC MEDIATIONS

SEMEIA STUDIES

Steed V. Davidson, General Editor

Editorial Board:
Pablo R. Andiñach
Fiona Black
Denise K. Buell
Gay L. Byron
Masiiwa Ragies Gunda
Monica Jyotsna Melanchthon
Yak-Hwee Tan

Number 84

PSYCHOANALYTIC MEDIATIONS BETWEEN MARXIST AND POSTCOLONIAL READINGS OF THE BIBLE

Edited by

Tat-siong Benny Liew and Erin Runions

SBL PRESS

Atlanta

Copyright © 2016 by SBL Press

All rights reserved. No part of this work may be reproduced or transmitted in any form or by any means, electronic or mechanical, including photocopying and recording, or by means of any information storage or retrieval system, except as may be expressly permitted by the 1976 Copyright Act or in writing from the publisher. Requests for permission should be addressed in writing to the Rights and Permissions Office, SBL Press, 825 Houston Mill Road, Atlanta, GA 30329 USA.

Library of Congress Cataloging-in-Publication Data

Names: Liew, Tat-siong Benny, editor. | Runions, Erin, editor.
Title: Psychoanalytic mediations between Marxist and postcolonial readings of the Bible / edited by Tat-siong Benny Liew and Erin Runions.
Description: Atlanta : SBL Press, [2016] | Series: Semeia studies ; number 84 | Includes bibliographical references and index.
Identifiers: LCCN 2016021818 (print) | LCCN 2016022695 (ebook) | ISBN 9781628371413 (pbk. : alk. paper) | ISBN 9780884141679 (hardcover : alk. paper) | ISBN 9780884141662 (ebook)
Subjects: LCSH: Bible—Criticism, interpretation, etc. | Bible—Psychology. | Marxist criticism. | Bible—Postcolonial criticism.
Classification: LCC BS645 .P785 2016 (print) | LCC BS645 (ebook) | DDC 220.601/9—dc23
LC record available at https://lccn.loc.gov/2016021818

Printed on acid-free paper.

Contents

Abbreviations vi

Introduction: Psychoanalytic Mediations
    Erin Runions and Tat-siong Benny Liew 1

Part 1: Theoretical Reflections

Conversations in Africa: Postcolonial and Marxist Hermeneutics, and a Psychoanalytical Fulcrum?
    Jeremy Punt 19

Imperial Fetish: On Anti-imperial Readings of the Bible
    Roland Boer 45

Freud, Adorno, and the Ban on Images
    Roland Boer 65

Part 2: Textual Engagements

The End-or Medium
    Jione Havea 81

Haunting Silence: Trauma, Failed Orality, and Mark's Messianic Secret
    Tat-siong Benny Liew 99

The Gospel of Bare Life: Reading Death, Dream, and Desire through John's Jesus
    Tat-siong Benny Liew 129

Psychoapocalypse: Desiring the Ends of the World
  Tina Pippin 171

Part 3: Responses

Response: Disseminations (and/or Sublimations) of the
  Death Drive
  Theodore W. Jennings Jr. 195

Response: The Ideology of Universalization
  Christina Petterson 203

"Den Himmel überlasesen wir / Den Engeln und den Spatzen":
  A Tupiniquim Response
  Fernando Candido da Silva 211

Contributors 227

Ancient Sources Index 231
Modern Authors Index 237

Abbreviations

Primary Sources

Agr.	Tacitus, *Agricola*
A.J.	Josephus, *Antiquitates judaicae*
Ant.	Sophocles, *Antigone*
Bell. civ.	Appian, *Bella civilia*
B.J.	Josephus, *Bellum judaicum*
Ep.	*Epistulae*
Flacc.	Philo, *In Flaccum*
Hist.	Polybius, *Histories*; Tacitus, *Historiae*
Hist. Rome	Dio Cassius, *History of Rome*
Jul.	Suetonius, *Divus Julius*
Luct.	Lucian, *De luctu*
Phaed.	Plato, *Phaedo*
Phar.	Lucan, *Pharsalia*
Phil.	Cicero, *Orationes philippicae*
Sat.	Juvenal, *Satirae*
Spect.	Martial, *Spectacles*

Secondary Sources

ASV	American Standard Version
BibInt	*Biblical Interpretation*
CEB	Common English Bible
HSCP	*Harvard Studies in Classical Philology*
HTR	*Harvard Theological Review*
HvTSt	*Hervormde teologiese studies*
JAAR	*Journal of the American Academy of Religion*
JBL	*Journal of Biblical Literature*

JES	*Journal of Ecumenical Studies*
JETS	*Journal of the Evangelical Theological Society*
JRS	*Journal of Roman Studies*
JSHJ	*Journal for the Study of the Historical Jesus*
JSJSup	Supplements to the Journal for the Study of Judaism
JSNT	*Journal for the Study of the New Testament*
JTSA	*Journal of Theology for Southern Africa*
NASB	New American Standard Bible
Neot	*Neotestamentica*
NIV	New International Version
NRSV	New Revised Standard Version
NTS	*New Testament Studies*
Postscripts	*Postscripts: A Journal of Sacred Texts and Contemporary Worlds*
PMLA	Proceedings of the Modern Language Association
R&T	*Religion and Theology*
RBS	Resources for Biblical Study
Res	*Res: Anthropology and Aesthetics*
RevExp	*Review and Expositor*
RSV	Revised Standard Version

Introduction: Psychoanalytic Mediations

Erin Runions and Tat-siong Benny Liew

The essays in this volume question whether and how psychoanalytic readings might mediate between the important materialist grounding of Marxism and the poststructuralist analysis of exclusion and oppression in postcolonialism. Taken together, these essays consider how the unconscious workings of the very real material exploitations of capitalism and colonialism (ancient and modern) are variously worked out in the biblical text and its afterlives, via fetish or antifetish, storytelling, silence, dream work, and fantasy.

Why this volume, and why now? a reader might ask. Are Marxism and psychoanalysis still going concerns in humanities scholarship? Hasn't Marxism been questioned as too universalist, modernist, and teleological? Hasn't psychoanalysis given way to affect studies? Perhaps. But the traumatic effects of capitalist colonialism are still with us. Moreover, neocolonial, teleological narratives are alive and well in ongoing imperialism(s), from occupying armies to the advance of global capital. Such narratives continue to create the material, global conditions of racism and classism, war and displacement, incarceration and poverty, as well as labor abuses and inequities in access to food and medicine. This volume is concerned with recognizing and countering such ongoing oppressions of imperial dynamics whether encoded in, valorized, or resisted by the Bible.

Certainly over the last few decades Marxist and postcolonial theories have been major resources in biblical studies for analyzing and countering ongoing oppressions. Marxist criticism remains the strongest voice in the critique of capitalism and in trying to understand the material realities behind the biblical texts (e.g., Miranda 1974; Gottwald 1979; Mosala 1989; Boer 1996; 2009; Yee 2003; Boer and Økland 2008; Reed 2010; Blanton 2014), while postcolonial theory has been hugely important for drawing attention to the ongoing effects of colonialism and neocolonialism (e.g., Donaldson 1996; Liew 1999; Dube 2000; Runions 2001, 2003, 2005; Sugirtharajah 2002, 2012; Segovia 2000; Kim 2006; Moore 2006; Davidson 2011).

Yet there has been a divide in the field between those who favor postcolonial approaches and those who favor the more Marxist liberationist approaches. Discussion about these differences was precipitated by R. S. Sugirtharajah's (2002) attempt to distinguish postcolonial criticism from liberation theologies; Sugirtharajah is critical of liberation theology for being somewhat conservative in its adherence to the truth claims of the Bible. Several scholars have taken issue with Sugirtharajah's dismissal of liberation theology, especially its Marxist roots (e.g., Boer 2007; Jobling 2007). The issue emerged again in the festschrift for Sugirtharajah, edited by Tat-siong Benny Liew (2009). For instance, Gerald West (2009) argues that postcolonialism might be a co-option and commodification of local liberationism from diasporic contexts. Sharing West's South African context, Jeremy Punt (2009) uses the term "academic double agent" to reflect on the lack of interest in postcolonialism in his postcolonial country. The problem between Marxist liberationist and postcolonial approaches to the Bible, according to Fernando Segovia (2009), is a difference of emphasis on materialist or discursive analyses of power relations. This debate prompted the current volume.

This division in biblical studies reflects, to some degree, the larger debate around postcolonialism, which has turned on a similar set of concerns, although nontheological. As has been well recognized, Marxism has been important to the development of postcolonial theory and continues as an important impetus in much postcolonial work. Yet despite shared concerns about relations of capital, power, and empire, postcolonial and Marxist theorists have often disagreed on appropriate theoretical starting points. On the one hand, Marxist theorists have tended to be wary of the poststructuralist framework within which postcolonialism works, seeing it as not sufficiently materialist in nature, too focused on textualism and culture, reliant on its own commodification through Western academic institutions, and inadequate for grounding a politics (e.g., Ahmad 1992; Dirlik 1997; San Juan 1998; Parry 2004; Chibber 2013). On the other hand, postcolonial theory is wary of Marxisms commitment to modernism, its orientalism, its Eurocentrism—as, for instance, in Karl Marx and Frederick Engel's support of the invasion of Mexico and its annexation to California (Engels 1975; cf. Bosteels 2012, 5–6)—and its tendency to subsume various power differentials to one that is based on class (e.g., Young 1990; Prakash 1992; Scott 2014).[1]

Psychoanalysis has been, in the larger world of literary/cultural studies, a surprising meeting place between these two inquiries that have not always been friendly with each other. Both Marxist theorists and postcolonial theorists have used psychoanalytic concepts to give voice to their own. One only need mention Louis Althusser's (1971) Lacanian formulation of ideological interpellation and Homi Bhabha's (1997) use of the Freudian uncanny to indicate this overlap. Marxist and postcolonial theorists have both turned to psychoanalysis to show how the creation and management of desire are indispensable to the creation and maintenance of ideologies, which sustain totalitarianism, global capitalism, globalism, and empire.[2] Psychoanalysis has been an important tool in understanding how the traumas of colonialism manifest both materially and psychically (e.g., Fanon 2004, 2008; Bhabha 1994; Boheemen-Saaf 1999; Durrant 2004; Cho 2008; Anderson, Jenson, and Keller 2011; Scott 2014). Critics from both approaches have looked at how critiques and modifications of traditional oedipal psychoanalysis have been able to address questions of gender and sexuality that might otherwise be occluded in Marxism and postcolonialism (e.g., Kipnis 1993; Spivak 1999; Campbell 2000; Clough 2000; Hochschild 2003; Bate 2004; Floyd 2009).

Psychoanalysis is a valuable resource for bridging these two modes of thought for several other reasons as well. It allows for the working of the unconscious and the affective in systems of power. It confounds straightforward notions of subjectivity and temporality; it troubles notions of autonomy, identity, and progress that can sometimes ground resistance struggles but contribute to disappointment and demobilization when

---

1. For essays from both sides of the debate and in between, see McClintock, Mufti, and Shohat 1997. Many postcolonial theorists acknowledge their reliance on Marx and the importance of a materialist analysis even while critiquing him; see, for example, Prakash 1992; Spivak 1988; 1999; Bartolovich and Lazarus 2002; Lowe 2015. For an account of the Marxist influence in the Subaltern Studies group, see Spivak's biting review (Spivak 2014) of Chibber 2013.

2. For examples of those who work with Marxist theory and psychoanalysis, see Marcuse 1966; Adorno 1982; Laclau and Reiter-McIntosh 1987; Miklitsch 1998; Žižek 1989, 1991, 2000; Tomsic 2015. For examples of those who work with both postcolonial studies and psychoanalysis, see Seshadri-Crooks 2000; Khanna 2003; Gilroy 2005; Tuhkanen 2009; Silva 2015.

conflict emerges or when things do not go as planned.³ Perhaps most importantly for this volume, it offers a hermeneutic of suspicion that allows for greater attention to the colonial formations of the biblical text. These essays do not psychoanalyze characters and communal dynamics in the way that some psychoanalytic readings of the Bible do (e.g., Halperin 1993; Zeligs 1974; Rashkow 1993, 2000; Kessler and Vandermeersch 2001; Benyamini 2012), as much as investigate symptoms of hidden or disavowed power dynamics of larger systems, especially those concerning the material conditions of (neo)colonial relations. Many of the essays in this volume look at a text's silences, ruptures, oversights, overemphases, and inexplicable elements as symptoms of a set of oppressive material relations that shaped and continue to haunt the text in the ascendancy of the text in the name of "the West." These essays, taken together, show that the tools of psychoanalysis can be important in understanding the material oppressions that have given rise to the need for Marxist or postcolonial analysis, even though not all the essays use all three kinds of analysis or use them in equal proportions.

In a way, then, this collection of essays illustrates an adaptation of Leo Bersani's consideration of psychoanalysis as "an inspiration for modes of exchange" or "a new relationality" (2008, 4).⁴ Yet, we should not see psychoanalysis as simply a dialectic resolution to the tensions between Marxism and postcolonialism. In many ways, these three approaches form a symbiotic triad. Both psychoanalysis and postcolonialism are thoroughly informed by the Marxist emphasis on materiality. In addition, Alain Badiou (2009) has suggested that (post-Althusserian) Marxism and (Lacanian) psychoanalysis are both attempts in politically and affectively charged sit-

---

3. This is not to say that there has been no resistance or rejection of psychoanalysis among Marxist and postcolonial critics. See Wolfenstein 1993 for both an account of the differences between as well as an argument for the combination of Marxism and psychoanalysis. For examples of two postcolonial critics who critique psychoanalysis and yet see its potential for postcolonial theorization and practice, see Nandy 1995 and Said 2003. See also Rashkow 2012 for a general introduction to how psychoanalysis may be informative to biblical studies.

4. This is an adaptation because Bersani (2008, 4) thinks the modes of exchange inspired by psychoanalysis "can only take place outside of psychoanalysis," and the context of Bersani's statement is a discussion about human encounters in general and interpersonal intimacy in particular. To the contrary, this volume is attempting to bring about an exchange between two schools of thought (Marxism and postcolonialism) *through* or at least *alongside/with* psychoanalysis.

uations to address an acute crisis of the subject, though he seems to have forgotten, despite his mention of "colonial wars" (xi, 260) that postcolonialism can easily be understood as a similar attempt. Further, as many of the essays in this volume also point out, neither Marxism nor psychoanalysis can be free of the colonial contexts and inheritances in which they are formed. They are haunted by colonial oppression. Thus both need an intersectional postcolonial critique, including critical analyses of race, ethnicity, class, citizenship, gender, and sexuality. In this postcolonial world and in the world of postcolonial biblical criticism, the specters of Marx *and* Sigmund Freud may still come together to enable new connections and conversations.

The volume is divided into two sections: theoretical reflections and textual readings. The first section offers metacritical considerations of the uses, misuses, and nonuses of Marxism, psychoanalysis, and postcolonialism in biblical interpretation. The second section comprises analyses of biblical and cultural texts that speak back to imperial domination by reading the texts in relation to their historical or contemporary contexts.

The first section begins with Jeremy Punt's essay, "Conversations in Africa: Postcolonial and Marxist Hermeneutics, and a Psychoanalytic Fulcrum?" Punt outlines the challenges in using any of these three theoretical approaches in South Africa. While Marxism can offer an important analysis of material and postcolonial causes of oppressive power systems, neither Marxist nor postcolonial criticism, as it turns out, has been particularly useful in South African biblical criticism. Marxism has seemed too universal and too Western to be particularly compelling; it presupposes a modernist political subjectivity in ways that potentially reinscribe the bourgeoisie autonomous and imperialist subject. Postcolonialism, while moving away from Western epistemologies, is still Western and has been developed in Western-influenced academic settings; it is heavily textual in orientation and often fails to pay close enough attention to particular local histories, peoples, and material bases. Moreover, because of its roots in and reliance on poststructuralism, it may not offer adequate space for imaginative construction, or as Punt puts it, "a proper romantic modality" (31). Yet, Punt suggests, if a materialist anticolonial analysis is to be imagined, perhaps psychoanalytic theory could be helpful in deconstructing notions of subjectivity and power, desire and need, so that the way they are analyzed does not always return to Western paradigms, in which, for example, the non-Western subject is primarily defined by need. Moreover, psychoanalysis could help to understand how in the postcolonial period there is no unambivalent authentic "Other," untouched by the processes of colonization and globalization. In this way, both the theorizing and the practice of biblical criticism could move beyond the identity politics that sometimes end up sustaining the norms they seek to subvert.

The next two theoretical contributions are by Roland Boer. Both of these essays can be seen as part of Boer's project to develop a seemingly aporetic Marxist theology, based in his home away from home, China. The first of these contributions, "Imperial Fetish: On Anti-imperial Readings of the Bible," argues that the theological impetus to critique empire from within the United States is a kind of fetishizing "affirmation of empire through a negative critique." It has only emerged, he suggests, as the empire has begun to crumble. Along the way, Boer exposes the colonial roots of the idea of the "fetish"—a notion born in the Portuguese colonial encounter in Africa and developed theologically through the notion of the biblical ban on idolatry—which is taken up by both Freud and Marx. For Freud, the fetish stands in for the penis and blocks the fear of castration. Applying this to United States biblical criticism, Boer suggests that the theological language of the "kingdom of God," which is meant to surpass empire, is simply a substitution for it as well as a protection from recognizing the failures of the United States empire. If for Marx the fetish represents the transfer of power from human relations to elements of capital, so that "capital itself 'becomes a very mysterious being'" (56). Boer argues that critiques of empire among biblical scholars are fetishistic in a Marxist sense as well: they transfer power to empire.

The conclusion to Boer's first essay is best understood in combination with his second essay. At the end of the first essay, Boer suggests that the way to resist fetishism is not to disavow it, but rather to embrace it—to say, "I am castrated and that is exactly what I want." Rather than try to replace the penis or capitalism, one should recognize the lack within the system and work to block the transfer of power from one thing/person/imperial system to another. Thus Boer opts for a radical political iconoclasm, the background for which he develops in his second essay, "Freud, Adorno, and the Ban on Images." In addition to reminding us of the Frankfurt school's early attempts to bring Marxism and psychoanalysis together (see Jay 1996), Boer's second essay suggests that the biblical ban on images works to protect monotheism by preventing any idea that perhaps God is just one more idol. For Freud, the ban produces superior abstraction; for Theodor Adorno, however, this ban should prevent even the reification of abstract ideas or objects in capitalism. Like Adorno, Boer wishes

INTRODUCTION: PSYCHOANALYTIC MEDIATIONS

to embrace the ban on images that emerges from the biblical critique of idolatry. In Adorno's negative dialectics, this ban on images and/or reification opens onto the contemplation of the nonconceptual and nonidentical. Yet, Boer argues, reification of the abstract is almost impossible to avoid at some level, even for socialism; the implication is that it might be impossible to avoid theologizing as well (although Boer does not say as much, there is a hint that perhaps Adorno's political iconoclasm of the nonconceptual and nonidentical might be a way of thinking the theological). At the end of the day, Boer proposes, if we must reify at the level of abstract thought (i.e., theology), perhaps we should do it via socialism.

In the second section of the volume, the first engagement with the biblical text provides another starting point for thinking through the relation of Marxism to imperial power. In "The End-or Medium," Jione Havea retells the narrative of the medium of Endor in 1 Sam 28 through the contemporary postcolonial Oceania islander's oral medium of *talanoa*. Havea translates the text via Oceanic communal retelling; this community includes, for Havea, the incarcerated. He thus suggests, but not through propositional argumentation, that *talanoa* is a mediation that is perhaps more appropriate for dealing with the power dynamics of colonialism in Oceania—and in the academy—than Freudian psychoanalysis. *Talanoa*, like the medium of Endor, sits in the liminal spaces between life and death and between the more dominant, if rejected, powers, including failing king and former prophet—or, Marxism and postcolonialism. *Talanoa* is a *medium*, like the medium of Endor, that is able to "open the two worlds, and the two subjects, toward one another." Like psychoanalysis, *talanoa* can aid recognition of the varying work of fear, desire, torment, and taboo in these subhegemonic encounters through a kind of "talking cure." This intervention, like that of the medium of Endor, might be overlooked, invisible, and misrecognized, but it is productive in confounding rather than supporting recourse to militarized nationalism in resistance to empire, such as that of the Israelites against the Philistines, or traditional Marxist nationalist movements. The medium of Endor offers another way. Her silenced voice urges crossing borders; it is "less nationalist and more transitional and migrational" (94). Read this way, *talanoa* models "crossing borders [that] requires one to swim in the tides of tongues and risk being lost in translation." The offer of *talanoa* as a theoretical resource, like the meal offered by the woman of Endor, is meant to be generous, openhearted, and strength giving; we would do well not to exploit, discard, and demonize it—or other forms of Oceanic culture—as Saul and his men do to the woman of Endor after they eat at her table.

The next two textual readings, by Tat-siong Benny Liew, move to historic empire as the scene for the writing of the gospels—Mark and John respectively. The first essay, "Haunting Silence: Trauma, Failed Orality, and Mark's Messianic Secret," rereads the women's silence in the face of the empty tomb as a certain kind of agency in the face of colonialism. Their silence, and the silence of Mark's "messianic secret," does not represent a failure of the Jesus movement or a failure of discipleship, as many have supposed, but rather a response to colonial trauma. As Freud indicates, trauma can make orality fail. The so-called messianic secret is "itself a messy secret that is nevertheless telling" (121). Further, trauma can and does haunt the colonized, disturbing memory and representation, presenting what Bhabha has called the uncanny or unhomeliness in colonization. Liew, drawing on Marx, Freud, Jacques Derrida, and Avery F. Gordon, reads the experience of the empty tomb as a kind of haunting: "Those singular and yet repetitive instances when home becomes unfamiliar, when your bearings on the world lose direction, when the over-and-done with comes alive, when what's been in your blind field comes into view" (Gordon 2011, 2). At the same time, the women's *ekstasis* at the empty tomb indicates that there may be traumatic enjoyment in the haunting terror of the empty tomb; something like Lacan's *jouissance*, it is a recognition that even if there is a frightening absence in the loss of Jesus's body, Jesus's memory is kept alive to galvanize those disoriented and fragmented by the trauma of occupation.

Liew's second essay, "The Gospel of Bare Life: Reading Death, Dream, and Desire through John's Jesus," looks at Jesus's awareness of his impending death in John. Liew reads the focus on death in John as a kind of dream work to deal with the fact that Jews were living under a constant threat of death in Roman imperialism. Throughout the essay Liew makes the connection to the threat of death faced by African Americans within the United States empire (as highlighted by the Black Lives Matter movement of this century). Ancient Jews and contemporary African Americans are treated as what Giorgio Agamben has called bare life: namely, those who can be killed with impunity, those who are within the bounds of empire but are living within a zone of death. Within the Roman Empire, colonized peoples like the Jews were likely to be killed for punishment or a combination of punishment and entertainment, thus bolstering the empire's sense of power. Jews were what Abdul JanMohamed calls "death bound subjects." The dream work of the Gospel of John internalizes, reworks, and confronts this fact, suggests Liew, not only by focusing on death but also by taking control over death. Jesus is "willing to step right up to and into death" (150), thus making it into something new and creating community that goes beyond death. At the same time, there is ambiguity in this reworking, since John's Jesus maintains a subject position of subjugation: Jesus is obedient to his Father, who mirrors the hierarchical authority of Rome. John's dream work, like the colonial reality, both look to "paternal and paternalistic authorities who reward obedience with life and reprove disobedience with death" (162). Confronted with this ambivalence, the essay concludes, readers might do well to mourn the death of Jesus and let it go, rather than incorporate it in a melancholic relationship that would reinscribe these ambiguities.

The final essay in the volume, "Psychoapocalypse: Desiring the Ends of the World," by Tina Pippin, focuses on analyzing contemporary culture. While other essays in the volume have suggested how unconscious processes manifest in text and story to cope with the traumas of colonialism, this essay looks at how fantasy also supports the processes of colonialism. Pippin gives a critical reading of the colonial apocalyptic desires in Roland Emmerich's film *2012* (2009). Apocalyptic fantasies, she argues, narcissistically imagine a place for the self even as they imagine the end of the world. While utopian longings can make room for a newer, better world, they often imagine a remaking of the dominant order in hyperbolic terms for the remnant few. Moreover, the shocking nature of their violence often dulls people's senses and prepares them to accept the status quo. As Pippin puts it, "Here lies the powerful hold of apocalyptic … : to imagine death so that one may hope to live, or as a way of hanging on tighter to life, but also as a way of learning to let go, to let the apocalyptic powers win, now and in the future" (184). Apocalypse is a way of coping, but it often ends up valorizing and amplifying existing power dynamics. In the case of *2012*, the film imagines a catastrophic environmental disaster that ends with the resettlement of Africa by mostly white people from G8 countries; it is the fantasy of global capital. One way to resist the lure of apocalypse, Pippin suggests, via China Miéville, is to imagine multiple ends to the world rather than one singular end, thus reducing its hold as a narcissistic defense against fear and revealing apocalypse as the screen on which the multiple twists and turns of dream work are projected.

The volume ends with three responses that come from different geographical locations and from very different reading perspectives. All are strongly Marxist in their orientation and have varying appreciations of psychoanalysis and postcolonialism. Theodore W. Jennings Jr., writing from North America, draws out the workings of desire in the essays. Christina Petterson, in Australia, questions the project of the volume, asking whether the essays make too easy equations across historical periods and types of experience and whether they take class seriously. Fernando Candido da Silva, from Latin America, writes a complex Mestizo critique about colonial and capitalist fetishisms, including of the Bible and biblical criticism, as they are revealed and concealed in this volume. Their responses demand much from the authors and from the readers, asking us to draw out in our own turns the complexities, gaps, and muted thematics. Readers of this volume will decide if the desire for psychoanalytic mediations is meaningful and if the endeavor successful. They will have to judge if they find within these pages any "extorted reconciliation." This is the term used by Adorno (1991), who not only attempted to put together Marxism and psychoanalysis but also spent almost a decade in the United States empire, to refer to an imposition that compromises the integrity of a nuanced and complex text. Having said that, it is not really our goal to bring about reconciliation—not between Marx and Freud, not between postcolonialism and psychoanalysis, not between postcolonialism and Marxism, and not even between the Bible and its readers. Instead, our goal is perhaps at once more modest and more ambitious; we want to bring about new interpretations of the Bible as well as ongoing conversations and counteractions against global—yes, neocolonial—capitalism.

Works Cited

Adorno, Theodor W. 1982. "Freudian Theory and the Pattern of Fascist Propaganda." Pages 118–37 in *The Essential Frankfurt School Reader*. Edited by Andrew Arato and Eike Gebhardt. New York: Continuum.

———. 1991. "Extorted Reconciliation: On Georg Lukács' *Realism in Our Time*." Pages 216–40 in vol. 2 of *Notes to Literature*. Translated by Shierry Weber. New York: Columbia University Press.

Ahmad, Aijaz. 1992. *In Theory: Classes, Nations, Literature*. London: Verso.

Althusser, Louis. 1971. "Ideology and Ideological State Apparatuses (Notes towards an Investigation)." Pages 121–73 in *Lenin and Philosophy and Other Essays*. Translated by Ben Brewster. New York: Monthly Review.

Anderson, Warwick, Deborah Jenson, and Richard C. Keller, eds. 2011. *Unconscious Dominions: Psychoanalysis, Colonial Trauma, and Global Sovereignties*. Durham, NC: Duke University Press.
Badiou, Alain. 2009. *Theory of the Subject*. Translated by Bruno Bosteels. London: Continuum.
Bartolovich, Crystal, and Neil Lazarus. 2002. *Marxism, Modernity, and Postcolonial Studies*. Cambridge: Cambridge University Press.
Bate, David. 2004. *Photography and Surrealism: Sexuality, Colonialism and Social Dissent*. New York: Tauris.
Benyamini, Itzhak. 2012. *Narcissist Universalism: A Psychoanalytic Reading of Paul's Epistles*. New York: T&T Clark.
Bersani, Leo. 2008. "The It in the I." Pages 1–31 in *Intimacies*. By Leo Bersani and Adam Phillips. Chicago: University of Chicago Press.
Bhabha, Homi K. 1994. *The Location of Culture*. London: Routledge.
———. 1997. "The World and the Home." Pages 445–55 in *Dangerous Liaisons: Gender, Nation, and Postcolonial Perspectives*. Edited by Anne McClintock, Aamir Mufti, and Ella Shohat. Minneapolis: University of Minnesota Press.
Blanton, Ward. 2014. *A Materialism for the Masses: Saint Paul and the Philosophy of Undying Life*. New York: Columbia University Press.
Boer, Roland. 1996. *Jameson and Jeroboam*. Atlanta: Scholars Press.
———. 2007. "Marx, Postcolonialism and the Bible." Pages 166–83 in *Postcolonial Biblical Criticism: Interdisciplinary Intersections*. Edited by Stephen D. Moore and Fernando F. Segovia. London: T&T Clark.
———. 2009. *Political Myth: On the Use and Abuse of Biblical Themes*. Durham, NC: Duke University Press.
Boer, Roland, and Jorunn Økland, eds. 2008. *Marxist Feminist Criticism of the Bible*. Sheffield: Sheffield Phoenix.
Boheemen-Saaf, Christine van. 1999. *Joyce, Derrida, Lacan, and the Trauma of History: Reading, Narrative, and Postcolonialism*. New York: Cambridge University Press.
Bosteels, Bruno. 2012. *Marx and Freud in Latin America: Politics, Psychoanalysis, and Religion in Times of Terror*. New York: Verso.
Campbell, Jan. 2000. *Arguing with the Phallus: Feminist, Queer, and Postcolonial Theory: A Psychoanalytic Contribution*. New York: Zed.
Chibber, Vivek. 2013. *Postcolonial Theory and the Specter of Capital*. London: Verso.
Cho, Grace M. 2008. *Haunting the Korean Diaspora: Shame, Secrecy, and the Forgotten War*. Minneapolis: University of Minnesota Press.

Clough, Patricia Ticineto. 2000. *Autoaffection: Unconscious Thought in the Age of Teletechnology*. Minneapolis: University of Minnesota Press.
Davidson, Steed. 2011. *Empire and Exile: Postcolonial Readings of the Book of Jeremiah*. New York: T&T Clark.
Dirlik, Arif. 1997. *The Postcolonial Aura: Third World Criticism in the Age of Global Capitalism*. Boulder, CO: Westview.
Donaldson, Laura, ed. 1996. *Postcolonialism and Scriptural Reading*. Atlanta: Society of Biblical Literature.
Dube, Musa W. 2000. *Postcolonial Feminist Interpretation of the Bible*. St. Louis: Chalice.
Durrant, Sam. 2004. *Postcolonial Narrative and the Work of Mourning: J. M. Coetzee, Wilson Harris, and Toni Morrison*. Albany: State University of New York Press.
Engels, Friedrich. 1975. "The Movements of 1847." Pages 520–29 in vol. 6 of *Marx and Engels Collected Works*. Moscow: Progress.
Fanon, Frantz. 2004. *The Wretched of the Earth*. Translated by Richard Philcox. New York: Grove.
———. 2008. *Black Skin, White Masks*. Translated by Richard Philcox. New York: Grove.
Floyd, Kevin. 2009. *The Reification of Desire: Toward a Queer Marxism*. Minneapolis: University of Minnesota Press.
Gilroy, Paul. 2005. *Postcolonial Melancholia*. New York: Columbia University Press.
Gordon, Avery F. 2011. "Some Thoughts on Haunting and Futurity." *Borderlands* 10.2:1–21.
Gottwald, Norman K. 1979. *The Tribes of Yahweh: A Sociology of the Religion of Liberated Israel, 1250–1050 B.C.E.* Maryknoll, NY: Orbis.
Halperin, David J. 1993. *Seeking Ezekiel: Text and Psychology*. University Park: Pennsylvania State University Press.
Hochschild, Arlie Russell. 2003. *The Managed Heart: Commercialization of Human Feeling*. Berkeley: University of California Press.
Jay, Martin. 1996. *The Dialectical Imagination: A History of the Frankfurt School and the Institute of Social Research, 1923–1950*. Berkeley: University of California Press.
Jobling, David. 2007. "'Very Limited Ideological Options': Marxism and Biblical Studies in Postcolonial Scenes." Pages 184–201 in *Postcolonial Biblical Criticism: Interdisciplinary Intersections*. Edited by Stephen D. Moore and Fernando F. Segovia. London: T&T Clark.

Kessler, Rainer, and Patrick Vandermeersch, eds. 2001. *God, Biblical Stories and Psychoanalytical Understanding*. New York: Lang.
Khanna, Ranjana. 2003. *Dark Continents: Psychoanalysis and Colonialism*. Durham, NC: Duke University Press.
Kim, Uriah Y. 2006. *Decolonizing Josiah: Toward a Postcolonial Reading of the Deuteronomistic History*. Sheffield: Sheffield Phoenix.
Kipnis, Laura. 1993. *Ecstasy Unlimited: On Sex, Capital, Gender, and Aesthetics*. Minneapolis: University of Minnesota Press.
Laclau, Ernesto, and Amy G. Reiter-McIntosh. 1987. "Psychoanalysis and Marxism." *Critical Inquiry* 13:330–33.
Liew, Tat-siong Benny. 1999. *Politics of Parousia: Reading Mark Inter(con)textually*. Leiden: Brill.
―――, ed. 2009. *Postcolonial Interventions: Essays in Honor of R. S. Sugirtharajah*. Sheffield: Sheffield Phoenix.
Lowe, Lisa. 2015. *The Intimacies of Four Continents*. Durham, NC: Duke University Press.
Marcuse, Herbert. 1966. *Eros and Civilization: A Philosophical Inquiry into Freud*. Boston: Beacon.
McClintock, Anne, Aamir Mufti, and Ella Shohat, eds. 1997. *Dangerous Liaisons: Gender, Nation, and Postcolonial Perspectives*. Minneapolis: University of Minnesota Press.
Miklitsch, Robert, ed. 1998. *Psycho-Marxism: Marxism and Psychoanalysis Late in the Twentieth Century*. Durham, NC: Duke University Press.
Miranda, José Porfirio. 1974. *Marx and the Bible: A Critique of the Philosophy of Oppression*. Translated by John Eagleson. Maryknoll, NY: Orbis.
Moore, Stephen D. 2006. *Empire and Apocalypse: Postcolonialism and the New Testament*. Sheffield: Sheffield Phoenix.
Mosala, Itumeleng J. 1989. *Biblical Hermeneutics and Black Theology in South Africa*. Grand Rapids: Eerdmans.
Nandy, Ashis. 1995. *The Savage Freud and Other Essays on Possible and Retrievable Selves*. Princeton: Princeton University Press.
Parry, Benita. 2004. *Postcolonial Studies: A Materialist Critique*. London: Routledge.
Prakash, Gyan. 1992. "Postcolonial Criticism and Indian Historiography." *Social Text* 31/32:8–19.
Punt, Jeremy. 2009. "Postcolonial Theory as Academic Double Agent? Power, Ideology and Postcolonial Biblical Hermeneutics in South Africa." Pages 274–95 in *Postcolonial Interventions: Essays in Honor*

of R. S. Sugirtharajah. Edited by Tat-siong Benny Liew. Sheffield: Sheffield Phoenix.

Rashkow, Ilona N. 1993. *The Phallacy of Genesis: A Feminist-Psychoanalytic Approach*. Louisville: Westminster John Knox.

———. 2000. *Taboo or Not Taboo: Sexuality and Family in the Hebrew Bible*. Minneapolis: Fortress.

———. 2012. "Psychology." Pages 447–63 in *The Blackwell Companion to the Bible and Culture*. Edited by John F. A. Sawyer. Malden, MA: Blackwell.

Reed, Randall W. 2010. *A Clash of Ideologies: Marxism, Liberation Theology and Apocalypticism in New Testament Studies*. Eugene, OR: Pickwick.

Runions, Erin. 2001. *Changing Subjects: Gender, Nation and Future in Micah*. Sheffield: Sheffield Academic.

———. 2003. *How Hysterical: Identification and Resistance in the Bible and Film*. New York: Palgrave.

———. 2005. "Refusal to Mourn: U.S. National Melancholia and Its Prophetic Precursors." *Postscripts* 1:9–45.

Said, Edward. 2003. *Freud and the Non-European*. New York: Verso.

San Juan, E., Jr. 1998. *Beyond Postcolonial Theory*. New York: St. Martin's.

Scott, David. 2014. *Omens of Adversity: Tragedy, Time, Memory, Justice*. Durham, NC: Duke University Press.

Segovia, Fernando F. 2000. *Decolonizing Biblical Studies: A View from the Margins*. Maryknoll, NY: Orbis.

———. 2009. "Tracing Sugirtharajah's Voice from the Margin: From Liberation to Postcolonialism." Pages 215–39 in *Postcolonial Interventions: Essays in Honor of R. S. Sugirtharajah*. Edited by Tat-siong Benny Liew. Sheffield: Sheffield Phoenix.

Seshadri-Crooks, Kalpana. 2000. *Desiring Whiteness: A Lacanian Analysis of Race*. New York: Routledge.

Silva, Daniel F. 2015. *Subjectivity and the Reproduction of Imperial Power: Empire's Individuals*. New York: Routledge.

Spivak, Gayatri Chakravorty. 1988. *In Other Worlds: Essays in Cultural Politics*. New York: Routledge.

———. 1999. *A Critique of Postcolonial Reason: Toward a History of the Vanishing Present*. Cambridge: Harvard University Press.

———. 2014. "Postcolonial Theory and the Specter of Capital." *Cambridge Review of International Affairs* 27:184–98.

Sugirtharajah, R. S. 2002. *Postcolonial Criticism and Biblical Interpretation*. Oxford: Oxford University Press.

———. 2012. *Exploring Postcolonial Biblical Criticism: History, Method, Practice*. Chichester: Wiley-Blackwell.
Tomsic, Samo. 2015. *The Capitalist Unconscious: Marx and Lacan*. New York: Verso.
Tuhkanen, Mikko. 2009. *The American Optic: Psychoanalysis, Critical Race Theory, and Richard Wright*. Albany: State University of New York Press.
West, Gerald O. 2009. "What Difference Does Postcolonial Biblical Criticism Make? Reflections from a (South) African Perspective." Pages 256–73 in *Postcolonial Interventions: Essays in Honor of R. S. Sugirtharajah*. Edited by Tat-siong Benny Liew. Sheffield: Sheffield Phoenix.
Wolfenstein, Eugene Victor. 1993. *Psychoanalytic-Marxism Groundwork*. New York: Guilford.
Yee, Gale A. 2003. *Poor Banished Children of Eve: Woman as Evil in the Hebrew Bible*. Minneapolis: Fortress.
Young, Robert J. C. 1990. *White Mythologies: Writing History and the West*. London: Routledge.
Zeligs, Dorothy F. 1974. *Psychoanalysis and the Bible: A Study in Depth of Seven Leaders*. New York: Bloch.
Žižek, Slavoj. 1989. *The Sublime Object of Ideology*. New York: Verso.
———. 1991. *For They Know Not What They Do: Enjoyment as a Political Factor*. New York: Verso.
———. 2000. *Enjoy Your Symptom! Jacques Lacan in Hollywood and Out*. 2nd ed. New York: Routledge.

Part 1
Theoretical Reflections

Conversations in Africa: Postcolonial and Marxist Hermeneutics, and a Psychoanalytical Fulcrum?*

Jeremy Punt

Introduction: On the Back Foot

In South African biblical studies, postcolonial work finds itself in an unenviable position. It is often overlooked, notwithstanding the focus and concern of a postcolonial hermeneutical approach to include and give voice to the muted voices of the colonized, the voiceless, the marginalized, or the oppressed. Postcolonial investigations of disproportionate power relationships at the geopolitical as well as subsidiary levels, and at social and personal levels of the powerful ruler and the subaltern, remain un(der)utilized. So, too, do investigations of the interrelationship and debunking of (apparent) distinctions and contrasts between center and periphery.[1] Postcolonial biblical interpretation's focus on relationships of power and hegemony—in other words, on domination and subordination, and hence useful for investigating the wide-ranging but often inter-

---

* This article is a revised version of a paper I read at the Annual Meeting of the Society of Biblical Literature (African Biblical Hermeneutics), San Francisco, 22 November 2011.

1. The operative breadth of postcolonial studies covers the wide range of imperial-colonial formations since the empires of antiquity up to the present reach of global capitalism; as for underlying framework or foundational contexts, both economic and political environments are included, up to and including capitalism and modernity (Segovia 2005, 70–72). Some scholars, while affirming the imperialism-colonialism distinction, question the doublet's alignment with center and periphery and perceive center and periphery rather as mutually constitutive relations (Marchal 2008, 4–5, 128 n. 8).

connected areas of gender, race, sexuality, and economics in and around biblical texts[2]—lies largely fallow.

Postcolonial work may need to shoulder some of the blame, given how in attempts at self-definition it has not always owned up to its own subjection to cultural and epistemic imperialism and the internalization of Western discursive formations in its terminology and intellectual categories. Moreover, when nationalist discursive strategies reappraise the value and difference of Africa, colonialist or imperial tendencies tend to take a second bow. Prevailing oppositionality tends to reaffirm binary oppositions of Western making and generates contrasts such as a collective African spirit versus an individual Western consciousness; communal ownership in Africa versus capitalism and its inherent greed; and sexual expression in Africa unencumbered by "guilt-producing oedipalizing mechanisms" (Carusi 1991, 97) versus Western sexual pathologies. Oppositional thinking often betrays the internalization of imperialist categories, even when the classic response of indigenous authors is to embark on self-defense and reinvestment of culture and the past with value.[3] As Annamaria Carusi explains, "This type of oppositionality can occur only where Western epistemic systems have become so powerful that they achieve universal value, to the extent that the colonized body identifies its difference in terms of the imperialist's binaries" (1991, 97–98).

---

2. As Fernando Segovia states, "Postcolonial criticism seeks to analyze how the imperial-colonial phenomenon bears on constructions of the other-world, the this-world, and their relationship as advanced in the texts themselves, as construed in the established tradition of readings and readers in the West, and as offered in the contemporary production of readings and readers in the world at large" (Segovia 2005, 24). Similarly, according to Sabine Milz, "Postcolonial critical discourse has, in crucial ways, 'foregrounded the links between cultural forms and geopolitics … [and] considered the modalities of race, nation, gender, and ethnicity, in relationship to the global activity of hegemonic cultural, political and economic forces'" (Milz 2006, 2, citing Suzie O'Brien and Imre Szeman 2001, 606).

3. Ironically, this is true at a time when anthropological theory divests itself from "culture" for its excessive coherence and orderliness, as well as restrictedness and totalizing notions (Brett 1996, 220). Mark Brett explores the distinction between culture and ethnic identity or people groups, holding to the culturally permeable nature of people groups but also pointing out that people and not culture are the moral agents. This of course is not to deny the double challenge facing postcolonial writers in attempting both to resurrect their culture and to combat preconceptions about their culture.

Even if for different reasons, Marxist readings have also not succeeded in generating either an active following or a sustained discourse, at least not in African biblical studies.[4] This is clearly the case when Marxist interpretation is taken as a sociological approach to literature that investigates the material conditions of its origin, with literature seen as the result and therefore also reflection of historical forces. Focusing on the conflict between dominant and repressed classes at a specific period in history and invoking the key concept of ideology, a dominant and widespread worldview is often taken as the articulations of the dominant class. In the African context, Marxist categories are used in invoking a precolonial identity with reliance on a Marxist view of consciousness.[5] Such attempts, however, tend to become self-contradictory because identity may be constructed here also according to the very terms of the bourgeois imperialist subject, even if enveloped in a disclosure of return and recovery (Carusi 1991, 99).[6]

While the above does not augur well for their effective operationalization any time soon, both postcolonial and Marxist sentiments are palpable over a broad spectrum in Africa, daily politics included. In South Africa recent accusations about the political ineptness of the leader of the SA Communist Party (October 2011) were once again testimony to the prevalence, if often contestation, of such concerns.[7] This contribution primarily

---

4. Important exceptions should be noted, however; see, for example, Mosala 1989; West 1995, 1998. For a reference to other biblical scholars who avail themselves of Marxist thought in their work and, interestingly, how the Bible was found useful by Marxist theorists, see Boer 2007.

5. "But original African culture, which would include perhaps a mode of subject-specification different from Western culture, has been eradicated and hybridized to a virtually irrecoverable degree" (Carusi 1991, 99–100). In the end, any claim to an authentic indigeneity may in the contemporary world prove self-defeating.

6. A particular problem for liberation-focused hermeneutics and theologies of the Two-Thirds World were (are) their shared assumptions with metropolitan, academic culture, availing themselves of the same intellectual structure and modernist assumptions, mobilizing the same Western theories and methodologies, using an overly Christocentric framework, and in the process being absorbed by the West. See Sugirtharajah 1999, 11–12.

7. The national deputy president of the ruling party's (ANC) Youth League, Mr. Ronald Lamola, with youthful self-confidence told a gathering in Kimberley that the country's president Mr. Jacob Zuma's term as the party's president would end at the ANC's elective conference in 2012. Voicing also his disappointment about National Higher Education Minister and SA Communist Party leader Dr. Blade Nzimande's call

addresses the nature of the possible/probable relationship between postcolonial and materialist or Marxist approaches in biblical studies, as well as what may constitute possible connections between them[8]—thinking about psychoanalytic links or bridges in particular. Although not pursuing it as such, this discussion does touch on larger debates such as those about appropriate hermeneutical strategies in Africa or the quest for an African hermeneutic.[9]

Tracing Division and Alignment: Marxist and Postcolonial Work

While Aijaz Ahmad (1992) proposed that postcolonial and materialist cultural studies are fundamentally incompatible projects, others argue that the relations are of a much more complex nature than mere incompatibility (Chrisman 2003, 51; Parry 1993). Briefly tracing the relationship between two reluctant partners is complicated but is an essential

---

on the Young Communist League not to support the ANCYL marches for economic freedom scheduled for the end of October 2011, Lamola is reported as having said: "Nzimande has turned Chris Hani's SACP into an Oxford Dictionary ... a party that just does nothing but merely comes up with new words such as tenderpreneur. Chris [Hani] would be disappointed in Nzimande because he would have supported our march" (Mokoena 2011).

8. A few caveats are in order: No attempt is made, nor is the possibility suggested, to exhaustively describe poststructuralism, postcolonialism, or even Marxism, or present them as monolithic; no attempts are made to present detailed accounts of the work of earlier theorists (e.g., Marx, Freud, Lacan) or those of subsequent periods. For possible cultural reasons (favoring African theology), political sentiment (with a focus on black theology, albeit mostly limited to Southern Africa), or religious inclination (associations of Marxist reading and political regimes, or postcolonial interpretation and philosophical moorings) for disillusionment with both Marxist *and* postcolonial interpretative reception in South Africa, see Punt 2003, 2004, 2006. Looking at possible links between postcolonial and Marxist approaches is not to either deny the integrity of each of these competing discourses or search for some all-inclusive position (see Segovia 2000, 33).

9. The flip side of the hermeneutical-theory coin is the relevance of methods for the text: the question about relevance, appropriateness, and effects, both for postcolonial and Marxist biblical studies. What does it mean to use a postcolonial optic for interpreting a text that originated in a different geopolitical context, or to use of Marxist categories for a text produced in a very different political economic system? The enduring relevance of such questions, "for good or (all too often) ill, today" (Boer 2007, 73), increases their importance.

starting point in the ongoing debate between Marxist critics and postcolonial critics.

Broader Contexts: (Post)Structuralism and (Post)Modernism

Western-style anthropological studies of marginalized cultures across the world have been increasingly questioned since the 1950s,[10] exemplified by the demystification and political understanding of racism. As a strategy of scapegoating rather than prejudice, racism was recognized as a device that enabled colonial powers to legitimate their hold on power amid the violent reaction to it among the colonized.[11] The 1970s saw other developments in colonialist discourse, but focused attention on imperialism was still off limits in the world of literary studies. Changes started to happen when the centrality of colonialist debate was established by stressing both the effect(s) of imperialism on the colonies and the former colonies' literary response to contest or correct Western views (Gugelberger 1994, 581–82). To generalize and simplify a longer and more complicated history, in the end the intellectual theory and practice of postcolonial studies was (and still is) informed by the dialectic between Marxism, poststructuralism, and postmodernism.[12] Postcolonial *theory* depended much on the poststructuralist critique of Western epistemology and theorization of cultural alterity,[13] and postcolonial *politics* found its ground and stimulus

---

10. Of late, calls are heard for a revised anthropology, an "engaged anthropology," aimed at assisting "political agency in the face of local and global oppressions, exploitation, and environmental degradation," as well as focused on "participant observation, ethnographic realism, and accessible prose" (McGuckin 2005, 68).

11. During this time, Fanon, Césaire, and Memmi published their works, which would soon become essential texts in the study of colonialist discourse.

12. Poststructuralism can be described as a "diverse array of theoretical strategies that deconstruct 'modernist' universalisms and foundationalist epistemologies, highlighting 'difference' and the slippage of signifiers," and postmodernism as "a cultural condition of instability and hybridity under a regime of globalized capitalism characterized by 'flexible accumulation'" (McGuckin 2005, 68). The post-ist trend can be ascribed to the always-present nudging of those on the periphery, the marginalized and the minorities, toward the center; it characterizes poststructuralism, postmodernism, post-Marxism, postfeminism, and post-Apartheid studies (see Gugelberger 1994, 583).

13. As propounded in the classic ideals of the Enlightenment: "all knowledge as science; the scientific method as applicable to all areas of inquiry; nature or facts as neutral and knowable; research as a search for truth involving value-free observation

in materialist philosophies, such as Marxism (Gandhi 1998, ix).[14] However, postcolonial work is, besides other criticisms, periodically faulted for its political ineffectiveness (see Punt 2009), while Marxist work struggles against accusations of modernist bias and restrictions.

Postcolonial Work as Self-Absorbed Textual Politics?

On the one hand, postcolonialists stand accused of succumbing to late capitalism ("capitalist modernity"), addressing the "superstructure of imperialism" while ignoring its material base (Ahmad 1992). Social formation, then, is neglected and unaffected, and cultural production remains implicated with and in capitalism. A textual focus can recast history as the grand narrative of totalizing Eurocentrism but can also foster a discourse that conveniently neglects to account for failures, inadequacies, and the refusal of dominance and resistance on both sides.[15] The history of Western imperialism, then, is often characterized as a civilizing and pedagogical mission, aimed at the "undeveloped" nations of the world, and subscribing to the "teleological promise of linear time" (Gandhi 1998, 174).[16] Postcolonial work that focuses on history as a heuristic category may even

---

and recovery of facts; and the researcher as a champion of reason who surveys the facts with disinterested eyes" (Segovia 2000, 38).

14. In his recent study on intertextuality, Niall McKay concludes that while the plurality of intertextuality and *différance may* lead to relativism and apoliticism, its politically engaged nature should not be overlooked (McKay 2011). He refers to Julia Kristeva's *The Incredible Need to Believe*, Barthes's emphasis on prophetic truth-telling in *Mythologies*, and Derrida's close reading of Marx in *Specters of Marx* as instances of political engagement, even if agreement on their political conclusions may stay out.

15. Goss argues that "the theoretical vagaries of much postcolonial analysis require a thorough reworking before postcolonialism can be utilised for radical and progressive projects" (Goss 1996, 240). However, it is contentious to postulate postcolonialism as a "critique of history" (Young 2001); it is the subject of debate between Marxists and postmodernists/poststructuralists, recalling the Hegelian notion of equating history with civilization and progress.

16. That is, "its belief in the benign purposiveness of history and nature … [carrying] within it the double charge of Progress and Perfectibility" (Gandhi 1998, 174). All that is eventually gained is an unfortunate illusion of "enlightened supersession of colonial trouble" and an ongoing reparation of the "historical break" between North and South, developed and underdeveloped, and so on, without accounting for growing divisions between contemporary societies and the prevailing presence and/or the legacy of colonialism in the world (Gandhi 1998, 174). The role of

reimpose a European, imperial notion of erasing the diversity and alterity of colonized nations by posing colonialism as a single and valid historicizing category (171–74; see also Jolly 1995, 17–29). In this way, "history" turns into an academic category, evoked and structured in elitist institutions, limiting postcolonial willingness and ability to accept the "opaque and contradictory processes which characterise the politics of the people" (Gandhi 1998, 172), as various historical accounts tend to marginalize the already marginalized.[17]

In fact, the postcolonial emphasis on "textual politics" includes the danger that textuality may subsume or replace politics. The emphasis may derive in part from its theoretical ancestry in poststructuralism,[18] which can be conceived as originally a critique and contestation of bourgeois structures and of humanism that moves even beyond Derridean deconstruction.[19] Deconstruction found its inception in the criticism

---

transnational companies in neocolonialism is of particular concern and not always accounted for adequately.

17. For example, the coercion/retaliation binary not only imposes a monolithic conception but also fails to account, among others, for the "consent of the colonised to colonialism," and therefore tends to erase the "non-players" by an incapacitating unwillingness to acknowledge "those countless, unrecorded histories of affect, conversation and mediation; histories of … non-violence" (Gandhi 1998, 173, citing During 1992, 95, and Nandy 1983, xiv, respectively). The colonial experience, as well as the internal histories of the precolonial class formations and struggles against local oppressions, are important (see Parry 1993, 239).

18. The roots of such moves should not be forgotten. In new critical thought, the poetic text as hallowed article became immune both to the pollution of rational inquiry and to the material world as the origin of such pollution. In turn, new criticism's understanding of the poetic word was fed by the Romantic notion of literature, which compensates for the shortcomings of the world, a notion that in turn allowed for "imagination" and "creative talent" to be attributed to political energies that are necessary for social transformation.

19. This is evident in the work of Kristeva and Barthes. Humanism is a contentious term, seen in the contradictory variety of configurations graced with this term, including Christianity *and* the critique of Christianity, science *and* antiscience, Marxism, existentialism, personalism, National Socialism, and Stalinism (see Gandhi 1998, 27). Then again, the specific form of poststructuralism's critique of humanism, Western metaphysics, and rationality renders it politically inoperative. It cannot engage in a positive political agenda, since its theoretical position promotes the recognition of endless alternatives despite its emphasis on antihumanism and transformation. While poststructuralism might have initiated its own inability to transform itself, its emphasis on antihumanism is nevertheless important and can be useful in

of traditional Western logocentric metaphysics, which privileges speech to the detriment of writing and subscribes to an envisaged external and authoritative reference point. Writing's revolutionary counterclaims now include the contesting of embedded hierarchies of value and meaning. Deconstruction itself, however, stands accused of political evasion, and the deconstructive text can become an all too convenient substitute for political action.[20] In fact, when rationality is destabilized and truth subverted, political stance may become both indefensible and unreasonable. Claims for the "force of writing" can mutate into textual apologetics, "as a productive matrix which defines the 'social' and makes it available as an objective of and for action" (Gandhi 1998, 156, citing Bhabha 1994, 23). When textuality becomes definitional and all absorbing, the materiality and contingency of the world is deleted and the insistence on political relevance of thoughts develops into indefensible privileging of textual supremacy (Gandhi 1998, 157). In fact, in this way textual politics become doctrinal, and texts are treated as ends in themselves since texts are seen to have absorbed politics.[21] In the end, theory and activism could end up in a stifling dichotomy.

Marxist Work as Modernist, Biased, and Restricted?

On the other hand, the battle cry for freedom or militancy, the revaluation of humanism in general and of African humanism in particular, and the

---

theorizing postcolonialism. See also Ahmad 1992 on poststructuralism's pessimism and antihumanism.

20. On the one hand, deconstruction issued in a period when "texts alone would puncture Western knowledge's narcissism" (Gandhi 1998, 159). On the other hand, deconstructive practices also have the potential to erase the anticolonial, native voice and limit the potential of native resistance (see Tiffin 1991, xv), and their unmitigated deconstruction of representation effectively preempts the possibility of constructing a postcolonial identity (Brett 1996, 222). Although it is a safe option ("Unable to break the structures of state power, post-structuralism found it possible instead to subvert the structures of language. Nobody, at least, was likely to beat you over the head for doing so" [Eagleton 1983, 142]), poststructuralism need not generate moral relativism and apoliticism whether naive of or complicit with hegemonic powers—a tendency Terry Eagleton ascribes to some practitioners rather than to a poststructuralist trend itself!

21. However, see Eagleton 2003 for an emphasis on the political implications of poststructuralism and cultural theory in general.

location of Marxist discourse (see Carusi 1991, 97) are also up for evaluation in African biblical studies. The value of materialist or Marxist criticism in reading the Bible receives renewed attention, if not to its classical Marxist-materialist paradigm then at least to the concerns raised therein.[22] Not surprisingly, in South Africa (and also in other African countries), the vast majority of citizens are from the working class, whose most distinguishing trait is its overwhelming black racial composition and hence their victimization during the period of Apartheid—an aspect that, of course, also establishes the link with postcolonial discourse (to which we will return).

Yet Marxist critics at times have been charged by their postcolonial and other counterparts for failing to direct a comprehensive critique against colonial history and ideology and for neglecting to consider the historical, cultural, and political alterity of the colonized world.[23] Another charge leveled is that Marxist scholars are too easily blinded by socioeconomic class, to the extent that they fail to perceive any other social difference, and hence they run the risk of ultimately succumbing to the ideology of racism embedded in Western life and thought (see Gandhi 1998, 24; Segovia 2000, 136–37).[24] Edward Said's recollection of Karl Marx's argument that the benefits of British colonialism more than counteracted its violence and injustices serves as a poignant reminder in this regard (see Gandhi 1998, 33)!

A Marxist paradigm has not always been perceived as helpful in South Africa, or maybe it just has not been used to its full potential. Racial

---

22. Marxist scholars have argued that emphasis on the study of epistemological disruption or discursive negotiations should not obstruct the study of resistance and conflict as political and historical reality. More than antecedents to the present, decolonization and the theories it produced are in opposition to much of contemporary debate and suggestive of missed opportunities in postcolonial theory (see Parry 2004; Robinette 2006, 208).

23. Neville Spencer writes, "Marxists have often found themselves alone defending the idea that there do exist laws of the social world which can be discovered and understood in a manner similar to that by which the natural sciences render the natural world comprehensible" (Spencer 1995).

24. Scholars question the "objective, eventual, final determination of productive and political processes" (Parry 1993, 122), as in Ahmad's contention that "racism is certainly a considerable component in the ideologies and cultures of imperialist countries, but the logic which determines the exercise of power is a capitalist logic" (Ahmad 1992, 311).

oppression, of course, can be read with reference to the proletariat. But it is not exhausted by such reading, since it is prevalent also in the social arena, precisely where the battle for cultural dominance and the formation of (a) national identity is being played out. Furthermore, the benefit of Marxism's notion of consciousness (with its accompanying emphasis on conscientization and mobilization) is at stake when, because of its dependence on humanism, it may reintroduce an imperialist subject. Such subservience to positivist essentialism amounts to the introduction of a new ideology to replace an older one (Carusi 1991, 99).

In the end, Marxism's relationship with poststructuralism is strained because the latter engages in a (Western) critique of Western civilization that proceeds beyond Marxism's economic paradigms. Poststructuralism is already suspicious of universalism (Eurocentrism), which is an important characteristic of Marxist theory. For postcolonial work, poststructuralist theory is vital for understanding Western domination as the manifestation of an injurious association between power and knowledge. It sees colonialism's material effects and implications as an epistemological malaise on which Western rationality depends (Gandhi 1998, 25–26). In fact, postcolonialism not only shares poststructuralism's notion of temporal contingency but probably also gained its institutional ascendancy through these associations with poststructuralism. Given such dissonance, can links or bridges between postcolonial and Marxist work be contemplated?

Developments and Disfavor? Links and Bridges?

My answer is a qualified yes! Postcolonialism already finds itself between the politics of structure and totality and the politics of the fragment—in the fissures between Marxism, on the one hand, and poststructuralism and postmodernism, on the other hand (Gandhi 1998, 167).[25] But the

---

25. The early social location of Derrida and Kristeva in a French Marxist sphere—Kristeva's association with *Tel Quel* and Derrida's later engagements with Marxism—indicates an enduring fascination and regular displeasure with Marxist iterations in history. For poststructuralism's indebtedness to Marxism and the political location of poststructuralism and cultural theory generally, see Eagleton 2003 (cf. Derrida 1994). The *Tel Quel* group in Paris held to the idea of history as a text for interpretation and its writing as an act of politicized production, rather than as attempting objective reproduction of past events. It has also been argued that postmodernism and postcolonialism are two sides of the same coin, with the former as both cultural phenomenon and socioeconomic development (or late capitalism), "an

situation is complicated when postmodernism, for instance, portrays a crisis of legitimation and of rationality, when poststructuralism evinces a celebration of difference,[26] and when deconstructive *différance* can get stuck in its respect for alternatives.[27] Politically, however, this situation is potentially both paralyzing *and* destabilizing, since poststructuralist diversity allows for a distinction between its "ludic" and "resistance" versions. While the ludic version is engaged in the mechanics of signification, poststructuralism's resistance version engages the politics of production and maintenance of subjectivities (McGuckin 2005, 76–77). It is within a framework of destabilizing *and* resistance-focused poststructuralism that links between postcolonial and Marxist work can be sought.

Postcolonial Textual Politics and Cultural-Material Enterprise: Initial Cross-Flows

Culture is an important site of domination *and* resistance, given its dynamic value in both engendering consciousness *and* facilitating hegemony in critical activity. When culture is only accorded value as far as it is aimed toward the social transformation of a world seen as structured hierarchically under the coercion of global capital (Ahmad 1992), it makes enemies of kindred but otherwise modulated work (see Parry 2003, 122).[28]

---

intense dialectical opposition between globalization and disintegration" (Boer 1998, 25). The intense dialectical opposition of globalization and disintegration shows up sharply in postcolonialism, but more than exhibiting the same dialectical opposition, is postcolonialism "constitutive of the postmodern moment in the first place" (Boer 1998, 25–26; see also Milz 2006, 2)? Is it more useful to compensate for postmodernism's emphasis on the global by reading and situating postmodernism in relation to the perspective of historical and geographical specificities rather than the other way around (Tiffin 1991, xi)?

26. Lacan offers a fragmented and split subject, shifting the emphasis from fullness to lack; Kristeva focuses on significance, which "overflows and subverts the limits of the Logos"; Derrida proposes *différance*, where meaning is reduced to a trace of absence/presence; and Deleuze launches an attack on the underpinnings of rational action through desiring mechanisms (Carusi 1991, 100–101).

27. Deconstruction is an immediate and obvious precursor for the postcolonial turn toward textuality. Habermas consigns both poststructuralism and postmodernism to a neoconservative domain (Carusi 1991, 101). But with poststructuralist alternatives as open textual traces that allow and in fact invite other, different readings, other—material—opportunities also beckon.

28. Classical Marxism in turn can benefit from contact with the various forms

However, it is not the time to give up on postcolonial textual politics. Of course, it is a problem when authors appear to romanticize their vision for postcolonial societies on the margins yet at the same time cling to the metropolitan center as the privileged addressee of postcolonial work. Accessibility and responsiveness of postcolonial texts are determined then by aesthetic and political predilections of liberal metropolitan readers.[29] This leads the discourse of literary hybridity into a regrettable political rationalization of readerly preference. At the same time, however, the notions of center and margins are increasingly disturbed by reading texts of colonizer and colonized as mutual, if unequal, narratives of exchanges. This puts nationhood, much berated in liberal discourse, back on the agenda—and not only as abstract and imaginary force. Nationhood often accommodates numerous histories of struggle, which continue to inform the lives and consciences of many people (see Hutcheon 1991, 183). On the other hand, considering nationhood even as fictional construct and at times replaced also by other fictions (such as exile and migrancy[30]) does not displace hybridity altogether.

The notion of hybridity formulates the colonial presence as ambivalent, as divided between "its appearance as original and authoritative and its articulation as repetition and difference" (Wan 2000, 110, citing Bhabha 1994, 107). Hybridity allows room for common ground and the ability to foster a general discourse in the postcolonial setting. Cultural hybridity disavows quests for *true* origins, since it is never merely the aggregation of given identities or essences but identities that are, rather, strategically

---

of resistance with which the working class at present is carrying on its struggle (see Callinicos 1996, 9–17).

29. The eminence of textual politics in postcolonial theory testifies to the process "whereby metropolitan culture obtains a specifically 'romantic' investment in postcolonial literature and its migrant writers. These texts/writings are often seen to embody energies and values allegedly lacking or under threat in the postcolonial world. And these values ... are animated by a single concept, namely, 'hybridity'" (Gandhi 1998, 159–60).

30. Postcoloniality is also about class: "Among the migrants themselves, only the privileged can live a life of constant mobility and surplus pleasure.... Most migrants are poor and experience displacement not as cultural plenitude but as torment" (Gandhi 1998, 16, quoting Ahmad 1995, 161). Elsewhere Ahmad (1992, 8) aligns cultural nationalism with "parochialism, inverse racism, and indigenist obscurantism" but is criticized by Benita Parry since other, diverse articulations of it are also possible (Parry 1993, 128).

claimed and exerted performatively.[31] No particular culture is privileged, and reinstatement of prejudices such as those embodied in the unconditional affirmation of European culture is avoided.[32] Allowing the voices of the marginalized to be heard and stimulating hybrid interpretations at the same time can guard against falling prey to the unfortunate consequence of readings that, through their counterdiscourse, preserve binary opposition and reestablish a privileged reading even when seeking to subvert the basis of discriminatory polarity (Berquist 1996, 33; see also Anthias 2001, 619). Working against prejudiced preferences is not the same as political ineptitude or unwillingness to take sides.

But does postcolonial work not also need more, a proper romantic modality or a reinvestment in emotion and imagination, bucking social rules and conventions, namely, "a willingness to critique, ameliorate and build upon the compositions of the colonial aftermath" (Gandhi 1998, 166)? Does Marxist thinking not provide excellent intersection points for generating critique, enhancement, and advancement?[33] A political reading with an emphasis on national consciousness in preparation for the emergence of an ethically and politically enlightened global community may just strike a chord with Marxism's universalist emphases. Contemplating possible intersections if not synergy between postcolonial and Marxist work is not so implausible, since postcoloniality can hardly be divorced from matters of class (see Gandhi 1998, 16). In fact, postcolonial work in the past has assisted in demonstrating the material impulses of colonialism, such as exploitation of physical resources, abuse of human labor, and institutional control. The reason is that theoretical work reconnects remembrance of the material past with a critique of the contemporary condition, neither resigned to the past nor reassured by the present (see Parry 2004).

---

31. Cultural hybridity emphasizes the diverse and even contradictory but never hierarchically arranged identities of the postcolonial subject; it goes beyond the simple colonizer/colonized contrast (Gallagher 1996, 235; see also Brett 1996, 226).

32. As with many other aspects in postcolonial work, this amounts to a compromise between the therapeutic value of colonial histories and lamenting their loss and the creation of dialogue based on equality and confident participation by all (Wan 2000, 111).

33. Urging the need to move past both "pre-Marx" and "classical Marx" thinking, Aditya Nigam argues that the major resources for providing starting points for a new emancipatory theory nevertheless lies within the tradition of a reinvented Marx (Nigam 1999, 33–43).

Flowing from such considerations, the attempt to relate the textual dimension of postcolonial literary theory to cultural materialism can be framed in terms of intersections and connections between postcolonial and Marxist work where psychoanalytic efforts provide the fulcrum for such deliberation.[34]

A Psychoanalytic Bridge for Materialist Postcolonialism?

Both poststructuralist and Marxist work have from early times reflected interest in psychoanalysis, with earlier (French) poststructuralist work showing particular interest in Jacques Lacan.[35] Poststructuralist interest

---

34. This is, of course, not without contention. For example, some studies, according to one critic, "offer sharp insight on the methods by which postcolonial studies adopted Frantz Fanon's psychoanalytic approaches but neglected his materialist concerns" (Murray 2002, 312–13). Others suggest that postcolonial cultural studies may be offended by notions of "Grand Theory" (Jameson 1993, 27–29). Regardless of possible reasons for a psychoanalytic (over)emphasis in poststructuralist work, they will not be addressed here. McKay suggests that it may be part of an endeavor to "get outside" the text, reacting against a structuralist textual monopoly and attempting to position texts intertextually and in terms of social location (McKay 2011); he is nevertheless critical of a psychoanalytical overemphasis in poststructuralist work. I am less convinced that a division between deconstructionist or postmodern and Marxist or materialist practitioners of postcolonial thought and work (Chrisman 2005) is a consistently useful understanding of a situation where categories are tenuous, boundaries porous, and practitioners transgressive. For example, "deconstructionists" may see colonialism as more than "a cultural, epistemological, or psychological condition," with the political dimension amounting to more than "'will to power' that operates autonomously of the production and regulation of colonial identities through modes of government, sexuality and gender, and educational systems" (Chrisman 2005, 1857). It is probably not only materialist scholars who perceive of colonialism as "a territorial expression of political-economic expansion," entailing "domination, appropriation, and exploitation [that] place the colonizer and colonized populations in a fundamentally antagonistic relationship that Fanon famously described as 'Manichean'" (Chrisman 2005, 1857). Of course, the paths do split, on matters such as nationalism and identity, but can a general, converging trend or drift between these two broad categorizations be excluded?

35. Not surprisingly, since Lacan sought to reinterpret Freud also in light of poststructuralist theories of discourse (Rashkow 2000, 151). Psychoanalysis is used here to refer to observing in indirect and oblique ways the unconscious as that which, as such, remains unknown by the conscious mind, but which is nevertheless real and active in both the individual and the collective psyche (Hyman 2008, 6). The intention

in Sigmund Freud is probably comparable to the role Marx plays in Marxism, but the focus on the achievement of individual and corporate liberation through concepts like "phallic," "ego," or "Oedipal complex" is an unfortunate truncation of extensive psychoanalytic work and insights. In Gavin Hyman's words, "Freud is a religious demythologizer, a liberator, or enemy, depending on one's religious standpoint" (2008, 5). The psychoanalytic presence in French poststructuralist thought has been of a strong Lacanian bent, as theorists like Julia Kristeva and Jacques Derrida appear to drift further from Freud, maybe also due to Freud's association with Marx and Friedrich Nietzsche as important figures of European modernity.[36] Given the psychoanalytic presence, even if criticized, in postcolonial work,[37] as well as evidence of its attraction for Marxist critics,[38] further reflection, by means of a few brief exploratory probes, on psychoanalysis as one potential bridge between the two is appropriate here.

---

here is not to promote psychoanalytic criticism in itself, which would typically attend to a writer's psyche, a study of the creative process, a study of psychological types and principles present within works of literature, or the psychological effects of literature on its readers.

36. The anomaly of Freud's work is that amid the doubts he casted on rationality and intellect, his attempts to ground psychoanalysis as science led him down the road of the very rationalism and positivism his work challenged. Hyman writes, "So what Freud discovers with the one hand—an irreducible heteronomy—he takes back with the other—by bringing this heteronomy back under rational mastery (even if it is accepted that this mastery is partial or incomplete)" (2008, 7).

37. Although she insists that a focus on the colonial remains important, Sara Mills challenges the psychical bent of postcolonial work and theory: "I would argue that post-colonial theory needs to move away from its psychoanalytical focus and move towards an approach which is able to deal with the material facts of colonialism. Because of the critique of post-colonial theory, its overly textual approach, and its focus on psychical processes, it is necessary for a more politicised approach to be developed. It may be that the shift of focus in contemporary theoretical circles will be towards other forms of theory and the interest in colonialism and the post-colonial will wane, simply because the theoretical framework is inadequate" (2005, 171).

38. Even if, for example, Slavoj Žižek is at pains to deny Lacan as "the highest, unsurpassable, point of theoretical truth" for him, mentioning his uncovering of the "final deadlock" in Lacan's ideas and Lacan's use by "leading Derrideans" today (Žižek 2003, 486), the influence of Lacan in his work is instantly recognizable.

Texts and Contexts, Contexts and Texts

The unavoidable psychoanalytic element of "processing" or "constructing" contexts, as well as groups and selves in such contexts, resonates in both postcolonial and Marxist work and recalls the emphasis Lacan put on one's place in society (Rashkow 2000, 151).[39] Nonvalorizing yet serious attention is given to the originating, historical contexts and to texts in both postcolonial and Marxist approaches, intent on accounting for disparate political forces and accompanying ideological formation.[40] Textual politics notwithstanding, postcolonial work is set to engage the spatiality as well as temporality of precolonial, colonial, and postcolonial contexts in its full spectrum of bewildering facets, as do materialist readings, of course. Postcolonial literature that is not only rebellious and subversive but also informed by poststructuralism shows that the anarchic and nihilistic, even in textual form, are also forms of protest (Parry 1993, 131).

As important as resistance against the homogenizing and totalizing implications of a term such as globalization is, the risk of excluding the material realities of globalization abides. Of course, a postcolonial approach in postmodernist dress can become oblivious to changes in the rationalities and structures of contemporary global power, much of which can hardly be understood or challenged without reference to the legacies of European colonialism and the workings of American neo-imperialism (Hardt and Negri 2000). As Lacan emphasizes, as much as adult people are always inscribed by language, language does not constitute the ultimate reality (Rashkow 2000, 151). But Freud's arguments against any totalization of subjectivity, and thus against the postulation of the human

---

39. This emphasis on place is outranked probably only by the emphasis Lacan put on a person's relationship to language (see Rashkow 2000, 151).

40. The ambivalent influence of postmodernism on postcolonial biblical criticism is reflected in the latter's insistence that all models of interpretation, all attempts and situations of retrieving meaning from the texts, and historical reconstructions amount to no more than constructions (see Segovia 2000, 32–33). This insistence is not mourned as the ultimate betrayal of the classic pattern or mode of biblical criticism as objective, value-free, and scientific endeavor, but rather is celebrated for its implicit acknowledgment of the inevitable political nature of biblical studies, its decentering of Eurocentric hegemony in biblical studies, and its embracing of previously excluded or marginalized voices in biblical studies. In the words of Segovia (2000, 40, see also 34), "If the result is a situation of anomie, and I believe that it is, I find that neither regrettable nor deplorable but rather something to be welcomed and embraced."

subject as the confident basis for truth and reality (Hyman 2008, 5–6), have already set the scene for a broader understanding of text and context. When texts are understood as more than lifeless, inscribed documents but as discourse in the sense used by Foucault and others, it signifies a broader spectrum of engagement between animate and inanimate entities, the accompanying dynamic of such engagements, as well as underlying urges, desires, and ideologies.

Ideology

In fact, the construction of contexts in and for theoretical deliberations is not unrelated to a shared concern for ideology in interpretative and constructive work of postcolonial and Marxist interpreters.[41] It is difficult to overestimate the importance or force of ideology in postcolonial and Marxist work. However, as was noted above, the threat of reintroducing an imperialist subject based on an assumption of humanism may restrict the notion of consciousness in Marxist readings. Rather than countering ideology, a new ideology of positivist essentialism lurks! Freud's earlier insight that all people are driven by contradictory and destructive drives, his consideration of the conflicts of the human mind from which it cannot escape, and his conclusion that rational processes are only one part of human physicality (see Hyman 2008, 3) can, however, feed into postcolonial and Marxist concern with ideology.

Interestingly, dualist logic in Marxist theory of ideology, according to which social reality may be very different from its empirically observable surface appearance, has been likened by some to critical realism (see Bhaskar and Callinicos 2003). So, does psychoanalytic insistence that humans are driven by contradictory and self-destructive drives link up with Marxist and postcolonial concern with ideology? The recognition of a deeper level of engagement, of consciousness(es) often buried away in or obliterated by discourse, and the ideology and historiography of the powerful

---

41. The claim that Marxist scholars rely on ideology to situate the relation between imperialist ideologies and material practices, while deconstructionists rely on spatial terms, using space to claim homogeneous political, social, ideological, and cultural identity for groups (so Chrisman 2005), is an unsustainable description in each case, as well as a false contrast. Ideology is at least as important for poststructuralist-inclined theorists as space is for materialist-focused theorists.

provide another important moment of reciprocal recognition and avenue for constructive dialogue between postcolonial and Marxist work.

Power and Agency

It is also in matters related to power and agency—two aspects that can hardly be divorced from contexts, texts, or ideology—that materialist and postcolonial work intersect, even if at times confrontationally. Different perspectives rather than stark opposites appear to inform the ostensible contrast, both in considering different sets of agents and in entertaining a different understanding of power with which the agents engage.[42] While most Marxist thinkers tend to stress the oppressive aspect of power, Michel Foucault's focus on the resistance of those on whom the power is exerted is perhaps typical of the postcolonial impulse. In postcolonial work, the ambivalence flowing from mimicry need not necessarily be limited to a surface effect (Bhabha 1992); from a psychoanalytic perspective, it may even be symptomatic of repression, at least in the Freudian sense (Rieger 2007, 20 n. 37).

Such options, of course, are not necessarily mutually exclusive. The increasing complexity of agency is exemplified in the difficulties of engaging flesh-and-blood human beings, and Fredric Jameson warned some years ago: "We must be very suspicious of the reference to the body as an appeal to immediacy ... structuralism and psychoanalysis both work energetically at the demystification of the illusions of bodily intimacy most strongly suggested by 'desire'" (1993, 43). Scholars argue that post-Marxists in the 1980s identified Marxism's ultimate shortcoming as its theory of the subject and that they found a ready if contested ("bourgeois practice") and provisional remedy in psychoanalysis, as the eminent theory of the subject.[43] Ideology was the theoretical renovation that gave impetus both

---

42. The agency of the scholar or intellectual is also in focus, with a new model of the intellectual as fan. As Fredric Jameson puts it, "That would, to be sure, lead us on to a more psychoanalytic view of groups and ethnic conflict (perhaps along the lines proposed by Slavoj Žižek); but it would also considerably dampen the enthusiasm of populist intellectuals for a collective condition not much better than their own" (1993, 43).

43. The Frankfurt school became the location initially forging "the unlikely alliance of the theory of praxis and the talking cure," which later through Althusser's work on Lacan offered "the crucial missing link" in the form of "a theretofore unwritten theory of ideology" (Kipnis 1989, 149).

to a new wave of Marxist culturalists and to other groups who dropped class and took on the political implications of hitherto unexplored territory "of sexuality, language, and other signifying practices" (Kipnis 1989, 149). Psychoanalytic theory, which appears to offer access to configurations such as culture, sexuality, and language in addition to class, has increasingly become vital for Marxist and postcolonial agency in relation to power.

Alienation and Identity

Contemporary politics of identity—regarding the categories and institutions, as well as the knowledge(s) and the power play(s) by means of which social dynamics and people are structured and regulated—has been placed in the past in a need-versus-desire framework. Aligned with Marxist theory and poststructuralism respectively, *need* then refers to social change as a historical and material rather than a textual, representational, or semiotic process,[44] while *desire* locates the instrument of social change in the coincidental and nonteleological effects of the ongoing liberation of (unconscious) desire and play of signifiers.[45] But what if the efficacy of this framework for explaining social change is questioned, if "desire" is no longer believed to effectively encapsulate "unnameable yearnings" of the unconscious and "need" is not seen as exhausted by its correspondence to food, clothing, shelter, health care, education? Taking a cue from Lacan, for whom the unconscious is connected to a sense of need, absence, and, concomitantly, desire (Rashkow 2000, 151),[46] as well as from Freud,

---

44. Social change is related to the binary of base (economics) and superstructure (politics, religion, etc.), existing as determinate causality. History is neither coincidental and playful (à la Derrida) nor a series of disparate discourses and institutions (à la Foucault), but "the history of changing modes of production and of modifications within the prevailing mode of production" (Morton 1996, 473). Need theory can explain social injustice in global context without eliding geographic localities and local social problems.

45. "Desire" avoids totalities and causalities because it is based on "a libidinal economy of culture" and therefore "produces a politics of isolated localities in undecidable relation to each other ... a politics of incommensurate language games" (à la Lyotard; Morton 1996, 473).

46. Unlike Freud (for whom the mechanisms of the unconscious are generated by the libido), for Lacan, "the less intense awareness of need can take the form of mere lack (*menque*) or of need (*besoin*). Both of these forms of absence force the psyche to

who grappled with the relationship between otherness or heteronomy and domestication (Hyman 2008, 8), is the relation between these two modes of thought necessarily and merely confrontational?[47]

A tendency toward an overstated focus on postmodernist paradigms and strategies of fragmentation and hybridity in postcolonial work (Milz 2006, 2) is often challenged in Marxist work. Even so, it has been proposed that the politicized language of "alienation," which characterized much Marxist work in the past, should be revived, as it "refers to political and economic processes as clearly as cultural and psychological ones" (McGuckin 2005, 77).[48] Psychoanalysis can assist in uncovering the desires we invest in the Other (Kapoor 2005, 1203) and our constructions of the Other—not only the all-important unknown Other for Freud, namely, the unconscious (Hyman 2008, 6).[49] Understanding hybridity or the hybridized as more than mere result or the mixture of cultural elements (which is probably beyond contention) allows for hybridity to be seen as process, an enduring space for constructing discontinuities.[50] To its credit, postcolonialism consistently emphasizes how discursive constructions of the Two-Thirds World point toward not only the inquiries but also (and often more so!) the inquirer. Psychoanalysis illuminates the political assumptions, influences, and effects, as well as the ambiguous character of identity constructed in and influenced by the postcolonial position, not allowing these to be reduced to a matter of "need(s)." This can challenge the reigning identity politics often held in place by the powerful, and by creating or sustaining such "need(s)."

---

make demands. A deeper feeling of absence takes the higher form of desire (*desir*)" (Rashkow 2000, 151).

47. The confrontational is typified by asking: "What kind [of] subject can afford to explain politics and the social world strictly in terms of 'desire' except those whose 'needs' are already met?" (Morton 1996, 473).

48. Žižek's exasperation is telling: "Do I not spend many pages in most of my books explaining how alienation is not the ultimate horizon of the human existence, how it is followed by what Lacan called separation?" (2003, 488).

49. Freud and Lacan treat negativity and otherness differently: "Neither Hegel nor Freud fully recognizes the radical heterogeneity that Lacan labels 'the real'.... Unlike the Hegelian negative, which, through the magical power of self-consciousness, is transformed into something positive, Lacanian negativity resists assimilation and incorporation" (Hyman 2008, 11, quoting Taylor 1987, 93).

50. Floya Anthias (2001, 619–41) proposes the term "translocational positionality" to better express hybridizing as process.

Finally, is there, amid all the criticism against the use of psychoanalytic analysis, still some life left in this approach, when even its purveyors admit to its redundancy? Slavoj Žižek's criticism of psychoanalysis as "outdated" is countered by this claim:[51] "Perhaps we should instead insist that the time of psychoanalysis has only just arrived" (Hyman 2008, 3). However, consenting to psychoanalysis as *the* paradigm for the social sciences is evidently asking too much, even if accusations that psychoanalysis resorts to "fairly arbitrary and speculative reasoning" also smacks of overstatement (Spencer 1995). Not oblivious to the criticism that for all the interest that psychoanalytical readings generate among biblical scholars, such readings remain sources of unbelief and irritation (see Verheyden 2011, 1), psychoanalysis may provide a significant bridge for tracing and promoting much-needed intersections between the perception of postcolonial work as politically impoverished and materialist work as unnuanced and universalizing.

Conclusion: Postcolonial, Marxist Biblical Hermeneutics?

How does one go about ensuring that the benefit of a politics of difference, fluidity, and hybridity, which contests the binaries and essentialism of modern sovereignty,[52] is not outmaneuvered by the strategies of powers (see Hawley 2001, 9)? One possible way in the discipline of biblical studies is by joining forces, such as among postcolonialism, psychoanalysis, and Marxism. Simplistic configurations and links between postcolonial and materialist perspectives and work should be avoided as much as idiosyncratic postulations and turf wars. Accusations that postcolonialism is too culturalist and bypasses the consideration of materialist conditions

---

51. "Outdated scientifically, in that the cognitivist-neurobiologist model of the human mind has superseded the Freudian model; it is outdated in the psychiatric clinic, where psychoanalytic treatment is losing ground to drug treatment and behavioural therapy; and it is outdated in society more broadly, where the notion of social norms which repress the individual's sexual drives doesn't hold up in the face of today's hedonism" (Hyman 2008, 3).

52. Others question the simplification and rejection of the "colonizer/colonized binary" as part of the espousal of models of power that in the end diffuse the historical conflict of colonization. As idealist theories, they miss the political necessities of decolonization and the theory that was produced for and through struggle, when "master" and "slave" had not merely archival but strategic significance (see Robinette 2006).

cannot be ignored; however, neither can cultural readings automatically be disqualified as excluding material readings (the same is true vice versa).[53] Psychoanalytical intersections may be useful not only as a bridge between Marxist and postcolonial work but also in allowing each to find common ground or at least shared interests in the other. Imperialism's multiple and fractured discourses call on various categories, both those of political economy and those of culture. Postcolonial and Marxist biblical hermeneutics will do well to remember that the diverse and complex nature of hegemony precludes the removal of culture and ideology from a differential and mediated relationship with forces of production within a social formation.

Works Cited

Ahmad, Aijaz. 1992. *In Theory: Classes, Nations, Literatures.* London: Verso.

———. 1995. "The Politics of Literary Postcoloniality." *Race and Class* 36.3:1–20.

Anthias, Floya. 2001. "New Hybridities, Old Concepts: The Limits of 'Culture.'" *Ethnic and Racial Studies* 24:619–41.

Berquist, Jon L. 1996. "Postcolonialism and the Imperial Motives for Canonization." *Semeia* 75:15–35.

Bhabha, Homi K. 1992. "Postcolonial Criticism." Pages 437–65 in *Redrawing the Boundaries: The Transformation of English and American Literary Studies.* Edited by Stephen J. Greenblatt and Giles B. Gunn. New York: Modern Language Association of America.

———. 1994. *The Location of Culture.* London: Routledge.

Bhaskar, Roy, and Alex Callinicos. 2003. "Marxism and Critical Realism: A Debate." *Journal of Critical Realism* 1.2:89–114.

Boer, Roland. 1998. "Remembering Babylon: Postcolonialism and Australian Biblical Studies." Pages 24–48 in *The Postcolonial Bible.* Edited by R. S. Sugirtharajah. Sheffield: Sheffield Academic.

———. 2007. "The Perpetual Allure of the Bible for Marxism." *Historical Materialism* 15:53–77.

---

53. Fanon is often cited as an example of someone who connected cultural reading, psychoanalytic approaches, and materialist analyses.

Brett, Mark G. 1996. "The Ethics of Postcolonial Criticism." *Semeia* 75:219–28.
Callinicos, Alex. 1996. "Whither Marxism?" *Economic and Political Weekly* 31.4:9–17.
Carusi, Annamaria. 1991. "Post, Post and Post: Or, Where Is South African Literature in All This?" Pages 95–108 in *Past the Last Post: Theorizing Post-colonialism and Post-modernism*. Edited by Ian Adam and Helen Tiffin. New York: Harvester Wheatsheaf.
Chrisman, Laura. 2003. *Postcolonial Contraventions: Cultural Readings or Race, Imperialism and Transnationalism*. Manchester: Manchester University Press.
———. 2005. "Postcolonial Studies." Pages 1857–59 of vol. 5 in *New Dictionary of the History of Ideas*. Edited by Maryanne Cline Horowitz. http://tinyurl.com/SBL0684b.
Derrida, Jacques. 1994. *Specters of Marx*. Translated by Peggy Kamuf. London: Routledge.
During, Simon. 1992. "Post-colonialism." Pages 88–100 in *Beyond the Disciplines: The New Humanities*. Edited by K. K. Ruthven. Papers from the Australian Academy of the Humanities Symposium 13. Canberra, ACT, Australia: Australian Academy of the Humanities.
Eagleton, Terry. 1983. *Literary Theory: An Introduction*. Oxford: Blackwell.
———. 2003. *After Theory*. New York: Basic Books.
Gandhi, Leela. 1998. *Postcolonial Theory: A Critical Introduction*. New York: Columbia University Press.
Gallagher, Susan VanZanten. 1996. "Mapping the Hybrid World: Three Postcolonial Motifs." *Semeia* 75:229–40.
Goss, Jasper. 1996. "Postcolonialism: Subverting Whose Empire?" *Third World Quarterly* 17:239–50.
Gugelberger, Georg M. 1994. "Postcolonial Cultural Studies." Pages 581–85 in *The Johns Hopkins Guide to Literary Theory and Criticism*. Edited by Michael Groden and Martin Kreiswirth. Baltimore: Johns Hopkins University Press.
Hardt, Michael, and Antonio Negri. 2000. *Empire*. Cambridge: Harvard University Press.
Hawley, John C. 2001. "Introduction." Pages 1–18 in *Postcolonial, Queer: Theoretical Intersections*. Explorations in Postcolonial Studies. Albany: State University of New York Press.
Hutcheon, L. 1991. "Circling the Downspout of Empire." Pages 167–89 in *Past the Last Post: Theorizing Post-colonialism and Post-modernism*.

Edited by Ian Adam and Helen Tiffin. New York: Harvester Wheatsheaf.

Hyman, Gavin. 2008. "Religion and Psychoanalytic Thought: A Contemporary Re-evaluation." *Theology* 111.3:3–11.

Jameson, Fredric. 1993. "Cultural Studies." *Social Text* 34:17–52.

Jolly, Rosemary. 1995. "Rehearsals of Liberation: Contemporary Postcolonial Discourse and the New South Africa." *PMLA* 110:17–29.

Kapoor, Ilan. 2005. "Participatory Development, Complicity and Desire." *Third World Quarterly* 26:1203–20.

Kipnis, Laura. 1989. "Feminism: The Political Conscience of Postmodernism?" *Social Text* 21:149–66.

Marchal, Joseph A. 2008. *The Politics of Heaven: Women, Gender, and Empire in the Study of Paul*. Paul in Critical Contexts. Minneapolis: Fortress.

McGuckin, Eric. 2005. "Travelling Paradigms: Marxism, Poststructuralism and the Uses of Theory." *Anthropologica* 47:67–79.

McKay, Niall. 2011. "Luke and Yoder: an Intertextual Reading of the Third Gospel in the Name of Christian Politics." MTh thesis, Stellenbosch University.

Mills, Sara. 2005. *Gender and Colonial Space*. Manchester: Manchester University Press.

Milz, Sabine. 2006. "Global Literary Study, Postcolonial Study, and Their (Missing) Interrelations: A Materialist Literary Critique." *Postcolonial Text* 2.1:1–5. http://tinyurl.com/SBL0684d.

Mokoena, Michael. 2011. "ANCYL: We Will Replace Zuma." *IOL News*. http://tinyurl.com/SBL0684e.

Morton, Donald. 1996. "Review: The Class Politics of Queer Theory." *College English* 58:471–82.

Mosala, Itumeleng Jerry. 1989. *Biblical Hermeneutics and Black Theology in South Africa*. Grand Rapids: Eerdmans.

Murray, Stuart. 2002. Review of *Postcolonial Theory and Criticism*, by Laura Chrisman and Benita Parry. *Yearbook of English Studies* 32:312–13.

Nandy, Ashis. 1983. *The Intimate Enemy: Loss and Recovery of Self under Colonialism*. Delhi: Oxford University Press,.

Nigam, Aditya. 1999. "Marxism and the Postcolonial World: Footnotes to a Long March." *Economic and Political Weekly* 34.1–2:33–43.

O'Brien, Suzie, and Imre Szeman. 2001. The Globalization of Fiction/the Fiction of Globalization." *South Atlantic Quarterly* 100:603–26.

Parry, Benita. 1993. "A Critique Mishandled." *Social Text* 35:121–33.

———. 2004. *Postcolonial Studies: A Materialist Critique*. London: Routledge.

Punt, Jeremy. 2003. "Postcolonial Biblical Criticism in South Africa: Some Mind and Road Mapping." *Neot* 37:59–85.

———. 2004. "Current Debates on Biblical Hermeneutics in South Africa and the *Postcolonial* Matrix." *R&T* 11.2:139–60.

———. 2006. "Why Not Postcolonial Biblical Criticism in Southern Africa: Stating the Obvious or Looking for the Impossible?" *Scriptura* 91:63–82.

———. 2009. "Postcolonial Theory as Academic Double Agent? Power, Ideology and Postcolonial Biblical Hermeneutics." Pages 274–95 in *Postcolonial Interventions: Essays in Honor of R. S. Sugirtharajah*. Edited by Tat-siong B. Liew. The Bible in the Modern World 23. Sheffield: Sheffield Phoenix.

Rashkow, Ilona. 2000. "Lacan." Pages 151–53 in *Handbook of Postmodern Biblical Interpretation*. Edited by A. K. M. Adam. St. Louis: Chalice.

Rieger, Joerg. 2007. *Christ and Empire: From Paul to Postcolonial Times*. Minneapolis: Fortress.

Robinette, Nick. 2006. Review of *Postcolonial Studies: A Materialist Critique*, by Benita Parry. *Cultural Critique* 62:207–9.

Segovia, Fernando F. 2000. *Decolonizing Biblical Studies: A View from the Margins*. Maryknoll, NY: Orbis.

———. 2005. "Mapping the Postcolonial Optic in Biblical Criticism: Meaning and Scope." Pages 23–78 in *Postcolonial Biblical Criticism: Interdisciplinary Intersections*. Edited by Stephen D. Moore and Fernando F. Segovia. The Bible and Postcolonialism. London: T&T Clark.

Spencer, Neville. 1995. "The Rediscovery of Reality." *Greenleft Weekly*. June 7. http://tinyurl.com/SBL0684f.

Sugirtharajah, R. S. 1999. "Vernacular Resurrections: An introduction." Pages 11–17 in *Vernacular Hermeneutics*. Edited by R. S. Sugirtharajah. The Bible and Postcolonialism 2. Sheffield: Sheffield Academic.

Taylor, Mark C. 1987. *Altarity*. Chicago: University of Chicago Press.

Tiffin, Helen. 1991. "Introduction." Pages vii–xvi in *Past the Last Post: Theorizing Post-colonialism and Post-modernism*. Edited by Ian Adam and Helen Tiffin. New York: Harvester Wheatsheaf.

Verheyden, Joseph. 2011. "A Son in Heaven, But No Father on Earth: A Note in the Margin of a 'Tale of Two Kings.'" *HvTSt* 67:1–6. http://tinyurl.com/SBL0684g.

Wan, Sze-kar. 2000. "Does Diaspora Identity Imply Some Sort of Universality? An Asian-American Reading of Galatians." Pages 107–31 in *Interpreting beyond Borders*. Edited by Fernando F. Segovia. Sheffield: Sheffield Academic.

West, Gerald O. 1995. *Biblical Hermeneutics of Liberation: Modes of Reading the Bible in the South African Context*. 2nd ed. Pietermaritzburg: Cluster.

———. 1998. *The Academy of the Poor: Towards a Dialogical Reading of the Bible*. Sheffield: Sheffield Academic.

Young, Robert J. C. 2001. *Postcolonialism: An Historical Introduction*. London: Blackwell.

Žižek, Slavoj. 2003. "Critical Response/A Symptom—of What?" *Critical Inquiry* 29:486–503.

Imperial Fetish:
On Anti-imperial Readings of the Bible

Roland Boer

My argument is that the current spate of "anti-imperial" studies of the Bible manifests a fetishism of empire. I understand fetish here in two senses, one in line with Freudian psychoanalysis, in which the fetish marks both the disavowal of castration and the affirmation that the penis is still there, albeit displaced onto another object, the other following a Marxist trajectory in which the fetish becomes an element of the socioeconomic context, indicating a transfer of powers between human beings and object fetishized. However, unlike a trend—which really began with Theodor Adorno and the Frankfurt school and runs through to Slavoj Žižek (2002, 286–88; 2006, 108)—in studies of the fetish, which all too quickly assume an overlap between Freudian and Marxist senses, I take a different line: I argue that the two senses need to be pushed to their extremes before they blur out the truth of the fetish of empire. In other words, I take up a mode of dialectical analysis inspired by Adorno, in which one takes each side of the dialectic, drags it as far as it will go, and then, panting and sweating, a little further. Only then, when they are beyond exhaustion, may they be connected. The argument is structured as follows: It begins with a representative survey of recent positions on empire. From there, I pursue a Freudian reading of this anti-imperial trend, before turning to a Marxist analysis.

Anti-empire: A Brief Survey

Of all the new critical approaches to the Bible tried and tested during the last two or three decades, postcolonial criticism has arguably taken off in a way that poststructuralist, ideological, psychoanalytic, and new historicist (to name but a few) approaches can only envy. The exception is feminist analysis, which compares with the strength and breadth of postcolonial criticism. However, particularly in New Testament criticism, postcolonial criticism has mutated, coming into contact with both die-hard historians and liberation exegetes, who have assisted in both the popularity of postcolonial criticism, and its transformation into what may be called "anti-imperial" studies. In publication after publication, we find variations on the argument that the Bible offers in its disparate texts anti-imperial protest, polemic, and propaganda (e.g., Horsley 2000, 2002, 2003; Carter 2001, 2006; Elliott 1997, 2000, 2008; Brett 2008).

As a representative survey of this burgeoning study, I take the collection edited by Richard Horsley (2008) called *In the Shadow of Empire: Reclaiming the Bible as a History of Faithful Resistance*. I do so for a couple of reasons. To begin with, it offers distillations of earlier arguments by some of the major voices in anti-imperial readings of the Bible. Further, it comes from the belly of the imperial beast, for all the authors are from or based in the United States—Richard Horsley, Norman Gottwald, Walter Brueggemann, Jon Berquist, John Crossan, Neil Elliott, Warren Carter, Brigitte Kahl, and Greg Carey. However, to the authors' great credit, it is not a collection that seeks to universalize from the particular history and context of the United States. Unlike many books that one peruses on the Bible and Christianity, which take the United States situation and assume it applies to the whole world, the authors of this book are extremely conscious of that context. In fact, they often point out that the "empire studies" phase of biblical criticism in the United States arose in response to American imperial aggression. Here we find a number of salient insights, such as Norman Gottwald's point that early Israel is most like present-day Cuba, Nicaragua, Venezuela, or Iraq (see Gottwald 1999, 2001); or Jon Berquist's observation that the Persian Empire was the cradle of the literature and religion of Israel in terms of law, temple, and covenant, and yet it also nurtured the cries of resistance that emerged from the cradle (see Berquist 2003); or Horsley's argument that one may use medical anthropology to understand exorcisms (illness is always social and political), as well as his suggestion that readings of the sayings and the Lord's Prayer—with their simple statements concerning daily food, poverty, and hunger—be done in the context of hunger, debt bondage, and death-dealing poverty (see Horsley 1993, 1995, 1996, 2002).

The other contributions are also mostly salient, but I would like to focus on some underlying issues in relation to the anti-imperial turn. First, there is an obvious confessional tone, with such works targeted at "faithful citizens and members of religious communities" (Horsley 2008, 182), although those interested would come from the more liberal wings of the churches and synagogues, especially those with a distinct social-justice agenda. In that light, such work becomes "political homiletics" with an outward agenda to bring about a change of mind and action. Perhaps the clearest signal of this political homiletics is the way ancient empires, especially that of Rome in relation to the New Testament, become analogous with the American empire, the new Rome. The tendency to use "empire," following Michael Hardt and Antonio Negri's famous book (Hardt and Negri 2000),[1] enhances the connection. In that way, lessons may be learned and the application to life may be made.

Second, an explicit awareness shows forth concerning the context of many of these studies within the United States empire. Not for nothing have anti-imperial readings burst forth with the end of the Soviet Union and the attendant threats of the Cold War, for now we have but one empire. These readings evince a profound disquiet about the role of that empire and its use of bowdlerized biblical language to justify its aggressive global agenda. But they also mark at a deeper and unacknowledged level a growing sense that the last empire left standing is stumbling, facing expensive and unwinnable wars and the vast shift of economic activity to China and the Asian region.[2]

Third, the growing awareness of the material context of the Bible, particularly of early Christianity, may also be listed as a contributing factor to anti-imperial readings. As archaeological work slowly makes more and more information available, it becomes clearer that the material reality of the early Christian communities played a determining role in the way their thought developed. Hence the shifts from the introspective readings of—for example—Paul, in which theology somehow floated freely in the air, being relevant only to the individual lives of believers, to the "new perspective" (Stendahl 1976; Sanders 1977), with a focus on the Jewish context, and what might be called the "new new perspective," with its concern for the Roman Empire.

---

1. Despite these tendencies, I have yet to find an extended awareness of the main point of Hardt and Negri's studies (2000, 2004), namely, that the new form of empire is acephalous, not to be identified with any nation-state, for it has transcended such obsolete forms and has become a new stage of capitalism.

2. I return to this point in my Marxist reading below.

But is it possible to go a step further and argue that fetishism plays a role in these anti-imperial studies? I would like to see whether it does, conscious of the fact that I for one am very sympathetic to such studies, for they challenge the comfortable sleeping arrangement of the church and power that has bedeviled the history of Christianity.

On the African Coast: Origins of the Fetish

Since it is customary to begin discussions of fetishism with either Freud or Marx, I would like to backtrack a little and set the scene for their appropriations of what even by the 1830s (when Marx first encountered the idea) was an old tradition of thought. On this matter nothing quite surpasses the three studies by William Pietz (1985, 1987, 1988) from three decades ago. It begins with the Portuguese colonial encounter, as they maintained their presence on the crucial route to the Indies, with African coastal societies in the sixteenth and seventeenth centuries. The term *fetish*—a pidgin word created in a mercantile interspace—came to be used by the Portuguese as a way of describing the material religious practices encountered there, especially the amulets worn on the body or perhaps consumed. The category of the fetish emerged in the intersection of Christian feudal, African lineage, and merchant capitalist social relations; it was the result of the intersection of two cultures that were incomprehensible to one another; it was elaborated by Enlightenment intellectuals in Europe from the late eighteenth century into a general theory of religion;[3] it was even used by Dutch, French, and English Protestants to describe Roman Catholic sacramental objects.

The very need for a new term arose out of the inadequacy of the traditional theological category of "idol." Pietz goes to great lengths to trace the way "idolatry" developed as a category in medieval theology; how it designated a false god with identifiable rituals, beliefs, and objects of worship; and how its initial application to the Africans did not seem to work. So we find that *fetish* was coined in order to take account of the direct material effects of the fetish in terms of physical and psychological well-being.[4] It

---

3. For August Comte, it becomes the first stage (followed by polytheism and monotheism) of his first great period of human history. Comte (1851–1854) used the term in his *Système de politique positive*. After the theological age, of which fetishism is the first stage, we have the metaphysical and scientific stages.

4. The word has had to fend off a series of efforts to describe its etymology. It is an English translation of the pidgin *Fetisso*, connected to the Portuguese *feitiço*, which in

also was seen to play a central role in social ordering, irrational as that order may have seemed to be. Traders would go as far as to swear an oath on a fetish in order to ensure a deal, much to the chagrin of the church. It was this material and social feature of the fetish that was unique.

Most significantly, for my purposes at least, the Portuguese first began to use the term in an attempt to indicate that the Africans "misunderstood" the nature of material objects and to explain their "irrational" resistance to mercantile activity. In short, it was an effort to make "sense" of the incomprehensible. Further—and this will become important for both Freud and Marx—the fetish was a marker of displacement for the uncomprehending and colonial Portuguese: instead of realizing the proper nature of social and mercantile relation, the Africans seemed to displace those relations onto fetishes. Freud and Marx will give this sense of displacement their own twists, one into the tension between disavowal and affirmation and the other into the transfer of powers between fetish and human beings, but it has a common root.

Pietz goes on to trace the various uses of the fetish in ethnography and the history of religion, Marxism and positivist sociology, psychoanalysis and the clinical psychiatry of sexual deviance, modernist aesthetics and Continental philosophy, eventually working his way to develop a theory of the fetish that envelopes its material, historical, social, and bodily terms. However, what interests me here is the way both Marx and Freud took up the idea, each drawing it from a reasonably common tradition and giving it his own characteristic reworking that would, for all their apparent similarities, make their theories of fetishism quite distinct. I begin with Freud, thereby exercising a reversal of the linear historical narrative of the "long nineteenth century," which would begin with Marx.

Freud's Double-Bind

By Freud's time, the fetish as a central category of religion[5] had not only been established (that had happened by 1800) but also been properly

---

the late Middle Ages designated "magical practices" or "witchcraft." However, efforts have been made to derive the word from Latin *fatum*, signifying both fate and charm (de Brosses); *factitius*, linking the magic arts and the work of art (Edward Tylor); or *facere*, designating the false representation of things sacred, beautiful, or enchanting. See Pietz 1985, 5; and Pietz and Apter 1993, 3–4.

5. Taken with his own theories, Freud generally makes little reference to this ear-

worked over by European thinkers, especially in the new disciplines of sociology, anthropology, and psychology. Freud was, of course, fascinated by the figurines, statues, and objects that he had gathered from antiquities dealers around the world. In those famous photographs from his study in Bergstraße 19, scores of them are arrayed literally before him as he writes late into the night. Surrounded by what the historians of religion, psychologists, and sociologists called fetishes, he had an idea ready to hand. But he gave it an extraordinary twist.

In his characteristically concrete fashion, Freud describes the fetish as "a substitute for the penis" (Freud 2001a, 152).[6] In contrast to his earlier and simplistic observation—to be found within the history of religions before him—that the fetish was merely a displacement of the sexual object (Freud 2001a, 153–55), Freud argues in this relatively late piece that the fetish plays a double role, at once standing in for "the woman's (the mother's) penis that the little boy once believed in and—for reasons familiar to us—does not want to give up" (Freud 2001a, 152–53) and at the same time manifesting the fear of castration, for if a woman can be castrated, then his own penis is in danger. In response, the boy activates a complex process of denial, rebelling against the threat of potential castration by asserting that his mother still has a penis, albeit displaced onto another object. The outcome is that in the physical world the woman still has a penis in spite of all, "but this penis is no longer the same as it was before" (154), for something has taken its place. Even more, the fetish becomes a "token of triumph over the threat of castration and a protection against it" (154). However, once the fetish has gained a life of its own, it may no longer obviously indicate the penis, becoming more generally both a displacement of desire and a focus of it: feet, boots, hair, fur, underwear, hands, bicycles, books, and what have you.

The key for my analysis is the double-bind of the fetish, its substitution for the penis and its blocking of the fear of castration.[7] Freud pushes

---

lier history, although there are enough hints to suggest he was fully aware of it (Freud 2001a, 153).

6. The full-fledged theory of fetishism came late in life, in a paper as brief as it was to be influential, delivered to the Vienna Psychoanalytical Society in 1927. See also the comments in "An Outline of Psycho-Analysis" (Freud 2001b, 202–4).

7. Almost in line with Freud's brief comments on the fetish, Lacan makes relatively little of it, and Žižek's passing comments are content to stay within Freud's framework of the fetishistic disavowal: "I know, but nevertheless …" (Žižek 1991, 245;

this tension in his last pages, writing that in "very subtle instances both the disavowal and the affirmation of the castration have found their way into the construction of the fetish itself" (Freud 2001a, 156). He gives the example of a man whose fetish was an athletic support belt, which doubled up as swimming trunks; this item signified both castration and its lack, for when worn it covered up the genitals completely and thereby concealed any distinction. But he goes further, suggesting that the double-bind of disavowal and acknowledgment of castration may manifest itself as a tension between affection and hostility, simultaneously present whenever the fetish is encountered. Two examples: the fetish of cutting hair, which is at the same time an act of hostility and desire; Chinese foot-binding, where the mutilation of the woman's foot is at once an attack on the fetish and a process of worshiping it. Unfortunately, Freud does not develop these examples beyond a mere mention, although he later suggests that fetishism first brought him to the fundamental defensive process of the splitting of the ego and its manifestations in a whole series of psychological states (2001b, 202–4; 2001c, 277). But for my purposes, this combination of contradictory approaches to the fetish moves in two directions. One is backward to the origins of the term *fetish*. As Pietz has argued, the word itself is the result of a long interstitial moment: between Portuguese traders and West African peoples, between two cultures that could barely understand one another, producing a word that is itself a concoction, a pidgin term that bears the traces of this tension within it.

The other moves forward to the role of "empire" within biblical studies. Is it too a disavowal and affirmation of castration at the same moment, a hostility to the American empire that is at the same time an expression of affection, all of which is voiced through reading the Bible in terms of its challenge to the Roman Empire? Of course, biblical critics following this trajectory attack both Roman and American empires as unjust, exploitative, and aggressive. The penis must be castrated in whatever way possible—in this case through the interpretation of biblical texts that are so vital for so many in the United States. Yet it may seem a stretch to argue that this act of criticism is at the same time a disavowal, a denial that seeks to maintain that penis, albeit now through a fetish. So let me

---

2001, 14–15, 126; 2008, 15–16, 296–98, 309–10), although he does ensure that it is distinguished from the phallic signifier (Žižek 1993, 161).

suggest four overlapping reasons why this may well be what is happening behind the scenes.

The first is a historical one, particularly in the way an earlier, liberating moment of American history is invoked. The United States was once a paradise for workers, a place for revolutionaries to flee to safety from the turmoil of European revolutions in the nineteenth century. Etienne Cabet came there with his "Icarian" communities; Wilhelm Weitling, a founder of German communism and at one time close collaborator with Marx and Engels, also ended up in the United States, founding communities and continuing his agitation. Marx famously wrote a letter to Abraham Lincoln, praising the way the United States was a beacon of hope for workers of the world (Marx 1985). The examples go on, but the point is that it marks an earlier moment that has, in the opinion of some, been betrayed. These early ideals are at times invoked as worth restoring—a distinct moment of affirmation of a kinder, gentler imperialism.

However, this move is actually consistent with the internal logic of empires in the Bible, especially the Hebrew Bible. In those texts, what often looks like an anti-imperial voice actually plays the same imperial game. In the political and economic situation of the ancient Near East and Mediterranean, each state would try to overwhelm and control its neighbors. Those that were successful began the path to empire and some achieved it, such as the Assyrians, Babylonians, Persians, Greeks, and then the Romans. Naturally, the smaller states would oppose this larger empire, which had to suppress one revolt after another. But the only reason the smaller states did so was because they too wished to dominate and establish their own empires. Many simply could not but that did not stop them wishing and trying to do so; resistance to the empire of the day actually followed the same imperial logic.

Second, a hermeneutical move is consistently deployed in many of the anti-imperial readings of the Bible: the equation of the various empires of the Bible with empires today. Differences are duly noted, but then the comparisons are made: exploitation, enslavement, plunder, grinding the poor into the dust. But once the hermeneutical elision has been made, the critique of empire within the biblical text becomes a critique of empire today. Hermeneutics slips easily into homiletics, in which the work in question becomes an urging to act, to take a biblical stand against empire.

Once we have this hermeneutical coupling, a third move becomes possible: namely, to voice the opposition to empire in terms of the "kingdom of God," a term I leave in its explicitly imperial translation. Both ancient and modern empires become subject to such critique, since they have already been shown to be allies. Against them is the alternative kingdom, the other empire against which Rome and now the United States must stand judged. Is this not a classic moment of disavowal and affirmation, of cutting off one empire for the sake of another that replaces it? Now, it may not show up in exactly this form, for one may invoke notions of justice, the poor, ethics, faithfulness, and so on, but these become all too quickly an alternative code that has its source with the divine empire.

All of which brings me to the fourth role of the imperial fetish, which builds on the explicitly theological nature of the previous one. Many of the anti-imperial works have as their audience the churches and synagogues in which struggles over the Bible rage (as one would expect with such an ideological state apparatus, to gloss Louis Althusser). Within such a theological framework, the ultimate resistance to empire is framed in terms of allegiance to God, to a totally other who brooks no compromise or betrayal with any state. Quite simply, empire (of whatever variety) seeks to usurp the place of God, and so it must be resisted. Of course, there are more than enough who feel—since Constantine at least—that one form of empire or another is actually God's empire, but those who resist empire point out that such an identity is actually compromise and betrayal. Here too we find the pattern of disavowal and affirmation, where the awareness of castration is met with an assertion that we still have our empire in another place.

So it seems that empire may well function as a fetish in Freudian terms, or at least it provides one angle for assessing the current wave of anti-imperial readings of the Bible in a slightly different way. If this is the case—that empire functions like a fetish, disavowing and affirming, hostile and affectionate—then what is the appropriate response to this fetish? It is certainly not to fall into the logic of fetishism, for that merely reasserts a displaced empire. Instead, I suggest that anti-imperial critics need to embrace castration itself. But in order to see how that works, let us turn to Marx.

Marx's Fetish Transfer

Bringing Marx into the picture takes us back some fifty years to an earlier moment in the complex history of the fetish.[8] Marx remained fascinated

---

8. What follows is a summary of a much longer argument I have developed elsewhere; see Boer 2012.

with the fetish, drawing it initially from a study by Charles de Brosses (1760) when he was researching his lost treatise *On Christian Art* in the early 1840s, adapting and remolding it for his analysis of religion, politics, money, labor, alienation, commodities, and then capital as a whole. But he never lost the distinctly religious sense of the term, as his late notes on John Lubbock from *The Ethnological Notebooks* (Marx 1972) from the early 1880s show.

For Marx, the extraordinarily useful feature of the fetish is that it signals a transfer: as the fetish is invested with ever more powers, those responsible for making the fetish surrender themselves to it. However, in order to make such an argument, Marx had to bring about a basic shift in the focus of the fetish. When he first appropriated the term, it was firmly ensconced in the history of religions. He sought to bring it to earth, to reshape the idea so that it applied to social and economic realities rather than the mystifying realms of religion. In other words, Marx took what was still an argument focused on the relation between human beings and their gods and applied it to the relations between human beings and the products of their labor, a move from the criticism of heaven to the criticism of earth. Or, as he put it in the fourth thesis on Feuerbach:

> Feuerbach starts out from the fact of religious self-estrangement (*der religiösen Selbstentfremdung*), of the duplication of the world into a religious world and a secular one. His work consists in resolving the religious world into its secular basis. But that the secular basis lifts off from itself and establishes itself as an independent realm in the clouds can only be explained by the inner strife and intrinsic contradictoriness of this secular basis. The latter must, therefore, itself be both understood in its contradiction and revolutionised in practice. Thus, for instance, once the earthly family is discovered to be the secret of the holy family, the former must then itself be destroyed in theory and in practice. (Marx 1973b, 6; cf. Marx 1976, 4)

In order to make sense of this shift, I distinguish between the signifying link between an object and a deity and the transferring relation between an object and the human beings who produced it—in short, the "fetish link" and the "fetish transfer." By fetish link, I mean the signifying relation between an object and a deity or superhuman power to which it refers. It may apply to the religious sense of fetishism or indeed to the theological idea of idolatry that it replaced in the early colonial encounters. The key to the critiques of religious fetishism is not mere mockery at the stupidity of worshiping a mere object of stone, wood, or metal, but the breaking of the link between the object and the deity that the worshiper assumes. Once you assert that the superhuman entity to which the object points no longer exists, then the worshiper is left with a fetish and nothing to which it points. The worshiper attributes extraordinary powers to this mere object and thereby belittles his or her own existence. Marx took this argument of the fetish link and applied it to social and economic relations, to what I call the "fetish transfer." This relation is comparable in form but different in content, for it takes place between human beings and the products of their labor. In Marx's hands, the term *fetish* tends to deal with the transferring relation, for he wished to find out why there seemed to be a transfer of powers between a range of elements within capitalism—commodity, money, value, capitalist, profit, wealth, and so on—and the human beings who produced those elements. The theory of fetishism provided him with an answer—a mutual transfer of powers between human beings (who lost out) and products of their labor—that would later gain philosophical rigor with Georg Lukács's elaboration of reification: the tendency in capitalism for living relations to become thing-like while things themselves seemed to have life breathed into them. In sum, as he adapted the idea of fetishism, Marx brought about a fundamental shift of his own: instead of the signifying link between fetish and god characteristic of the religious theory of fetishism, Marx focused on the transferring relation between object produced and human being who produced it. The basic form of the relation may be the same—a transfer of powers and attributes from human beings to an object—but the way the argument is deployed is quite different. (However, even this shift is implicit within the religious theory of fetishism, for the Portuguese used it not merely to indicate that the Africans they encountered were mistaken in their belief about the superhuman powers of the fetish, but also that they displaced the material and mercantile relations between things onto the fetish.)

Let me give one example of Marx's shift in focus—one that has repercussions for the anti-imperial readings of biblical texts. Apart from the well-known argument concerning "the fetishism of commodities and the secret thereof" in the famous section of *Capital* by that name—in which commodification is a process of abstraction of the products of labor at the expense of those who produce them—I focus on Marx's wider observations where the fetish transfer is extended to the whole of capitalism. Toward the close of the exceptional *Economic Manuscript of 1861–63*, Marx deploys the same logic of transfer, but now we find a full list of the abstractions from the social process of labor: the capitalist as a personification of capital; the productive powers of capital; use, exchange, and surplus value; the application of forces of nature and science; the products of labor in form of machinery, wealth, the conversion of production relations into entities, interest, rent, wages, and profit. All of them face the laborer as objective, alien realities that rule his or her life. In other words, capital as a whole has become a fetish, a power to which the worker is subject. All its components "stand on their hind legs vis-à-vis the worker and confront him [sic] as capital" (Marx 1994, 457–58).[9] Capital itself "becomes a very mysterious being" (Marx 1994, 459), if not the "religion of everyday life (*diese Religion des Alltagslebens*)" (Marx 1998, 817; 1973a, 838).[10]

There are three distinct implications of Marx's approach for the fetish of empire, one theological, one material, and one that brings us in touch with the Freudian analysis I undertook a little earlier. As far as theology is concerned, the anti-imperial critics would be able to say, yes, that is precisely what we attack, the brutal effect of this economic system, championed by the United States, on the people of the world. We are one with Marx in criticizing its deleterious effects, except that we want to add a biblical and theological dimension. In other words, at this point the liberationist theological dimension of anti-imperial criticism comes to the fore: the fetishism of capital is really another form of idolatry, the erecting of false gods over the one true God.

However, the liberation-theological reading of Marx on fetishism, along with those involved in the Marxist-Christian dialogue of the 1960s and 1970s, made a direct, albeit slightly superficial, connection between Marx's use of fetishism and the traditional critique of idolatry (Sobrino 2004a, 57, 146, 165–67; 2004b, 59, 99; Dussell 1993; 2001, 298–99; Sung 2007; Hinkelammert 1986; Assmann and Hinkelammert 1989; Scott 1994: 75–109; Löwy 1996, 56–57; Evans 1984, 146–48; Lischer 1973, 554–55; Suda 1978; Thiemann 1985). They read Marx's critique of fetishism as an extension of the polemic against idolatry, which they now appropriated within a theological framework. So idolatry is not restricted to the false gods of other religions or to the materialism of modern life, but it also applies to the elements of capitalism: its many parts, such as the foreign

---

9. See also the description of wealth as a fetish in Marx 1987, 387.

10. Apart from Walter Benjamin's oft-noted fragment "Capitalism as Religion" (Benjamin 1996, 288–91), the theme has been developed in a very different direction from liberation theology or Marxism by a group of what may be called "economic theologians" such as Cobb 1999, Meeks 1989, and Loy 1996.

debt, gross domestic product, current account balance, and growth, are all parts of a destructive cult that worships these idols as gods. Moreover, the economic theories that explain, justify, and support these idols are false theologies that demand endless sacrifices. In short, they are false gods that demand blood and destroy their worshipers.

I cannot deny that this revitalization of theology via Marx's idea of fetishism constitutes a significant step forward in developing a theological critique of capitalism. Yet it falls short of the mark in one important respect. Proponents of this critique read fetishism as an extension of idolatry into new areas of analysis—capitalism and its attendant theories and justifications—without noticing the shift that had already been effected before Marx even got hold of the idea of fetishism: the subsuming of idolatry as a subset within fetishism. The key moment in that shift was the work by Charles de Brosses (1760) that Marx read in the early 1840s. In a stunning case of theoretical inversion, de Brosses absorbed idolatry into the new term of fetishism. De Brosses drew on studies of fetishism in western Africa and applied them—in a process that would become standard among ancient historians—to the ancient Egyptians. Here, too, are primitives, went the argument, encountering us in our own day and time; surely their religious practices would be similar to those of other primitives, even if they lived millennia before our far more civilized society. The crucial moment in de Brosses's work is when he begins searching for evidence of ancient Egyptian religious practice. There was, of course, some scattered material available in the mid-eighteenth century—a pyramid or two, a tomb opened, perhaps an inscription. But the primary source for de Brosses is the Bible, which he took as a reliable historical source. (The full skeptical brunt of biblical criticism had not had an impact as yet.) So all of the various stories concerning Egyptians and their gods, magicians, and beliefs, especially those clustered around the accounts of Joseph, Israelite slavery, and escape under Moses, became evidence for ancient fetishism. Where there were accounts of Canaanite practices, in which the Israelites engaged with alarming and frequent ease when they had settled in the land, these too provided data regarding fetishism. Marx assumed this theoretical inversion, making fetishism the prime category and subsuming idolatry within it. From there, he modified the theory to develop his critique of capitalism. In other words, the liberation theologians fail to see this basic move and thereby engage in a regressive critique in which idolatry is primary.

Second, I want to ask a materialist question: why is this anti-imperial approach to the Bible happening now, especially in the United States? That development involves a characteristic Marxist move, an analysis of the "earthly"—that is, socioeconomic and geopolitical—dimensions of this anti-imperial turn, for this latest development did not arise in a vacuum, nor was it due simply to a confluence of indignation at the behavior of the United States on the global scene. I would suggest that these anti-imperial readings have taken off at a curious moment when the last superpower standing began to stumble in a way obvious to all. These readings—a confluence, as I pointed out earlier, of liberation theology, postcolonial criticism, and imperial studies—noticeably appeared only after 1989, after the rolling back of actually existing communism in Eastern Europe, after the claim that "we won" and the "end of history" had been attained. Capitalism was finally free to conquer what was left of the world. But this is only half the story, for the march has been anything but triumphant. Not only did the United States and its "allies" stumble in Iraq and Afghanistan, but also the tectonic shift of financial power from the United States to China that was first revealed in 2008–2009 is by far the more important feature of the current situation. It continues in the second decade of the new millennium, as China's growth continues to be the envy of all—even with a reduction of growth to about 7 percent per annum. The empire's feet seem to be made of clay.

In the period of imperial stumbling, anti-imperial arguments continue to appear with a vengeance. But what is the function of those arguments? Do they offer a much-needed corrective to the desire to restore the United States to its former glory, as election campaigns in the United States do on a regular basis? On the surface they do, of course, but I would suggest another function: the provision of an ideological ground on which to make sense of the empire's problems and potential fall. Imperial aggression, exploitation, the willingness to shoot first and ask questions later—in short, sinfulness—provide the crucial framework for understanding the current stumbles and systemic problems facing the empire, if not the fall itself.

Finally, at the end run of a Marxist analysis, we loop back to connect with the Freudian argument I made above. In this case, I am interested in the fetish transfer itself, in the attribution of power to an object—commodity, money, labor power, and indeed empire—that comes at the expense of human relations. Alongside the very critique of the exploitative economics of empire, especially as they are outlined by a Marxist analysis, do not the anti-imperial critics also partake of the fetish transfer? By focusing so much on the empire (of whatever ilk), by attempting to provide an alternative to it, the danger is that one enhances the very object under criticism by giving it so much attention. No matter how evil the fetish may be, like a spongy monster it absorbs the criticisms and gains at the expense of those who level the criticism at it. In this respect, the fetish transfer of Marx comes closest to the simultaneous disavowal and affirmation of the fetish in Freud. The mechanism is not quite the same; the outcome is: the affirmation of empire through a negative critique.

Conclusion

So what is to be done? I suggest both an embracing of castration itself and the blocking of the fetish transfer. Here Freudian and Marxist critiques do indeed come together. As far as psychoanalysis is concerned, the way to overcome the fetish is not to say, "I know I am castrated, but nevertheless I am not," but to say "I am castrated, and that is exactly what I want." As for Marx, he set out to develop a way to block the fetish transfer, to negate the attribution of powers to the fetish at the expense of human relations. In this respect, he did take an element from the critique of idolatry: not the deriding of another who stupidly worships a block of wood (for there is no god), but the ban on images that Theodor Adorno would develop so well.[11] That ban operates on the basic assumption that one must not have an image in the first place, for that would establish a signifying link that could then be broken. So you simply block the possibility of such a link. So also does the critique of fetishism in Marx take an ax to the transferring relation between fetish and human beings. Marx may have sought to describe this fetish transfer, but that is merely the first step, for he wants to destroy the transfer itself and thereby free human beings from their enslavement to the fetish. The best thing to do is prevent that transfer from taking place in the first place. On this matter of what may best be described as political iconoclasm, I finally come around to agreeing in a rather different way with anti-imperial readings of the Bible.

---

11. By applying the ban on images—a central feature of the critique of idolatry from the second commandment—to the transferring relation of fetishism, Adorno develops a comprehensive strategy for blocking the reifying effects of fetishism in philosophy, utopian thought, music and art, theology, and even student politics. I develop this further on page 72 of my next essay.

Works Cited

Assmann, Hugo, and Franz J. Hinkelammert. 1989. *A idolatria do Mercado*. Petrópolis: Vozes.
Benjamin, Walter. 1996. *Selected Writings*. Vol. 1, *1913–1926*. Edited by Marcus Bullock and Michael W. Jennings. Cambridge: Belknap Press of Harvard University Press.
Berquist, Jon L. 2003. *Judaism in Persia's Shadow: A Social and Historical Approach*. Eugene, OR: Wipf & Stock.
Boer, Roland 2012. *Criticism of Earth: On Marx, Engels and Theology*. Leiden: Brill.
Brett, Mark. 2008. *Decolonizing God: The Bible in the Tides of Empire*. Sheffield: Sheffield Phoenix.
Brosses, Charles de. 1760. *Du culte des dieux fétiches ou Parallèle de l'ancienne religion de l'Égypte*. Paris: n.p.
Carter, Warren. 2001. *Matthew and Empire: Initial Explorations*. Harrisburg, PA: Trinity Press International.
———. 2006. *The Roman Empire and the New Testament: An Essential Guide*. Nashville: Abingdon.
Cobb, John. 1999. *The Earthist Challenge to Economism: A Theological Critique of the World Bank*. New York: Macmillan.
Comte, Auguste. 1851–1854. *Système de politique positive*. Paris: Carilian-Goeury et Vor Dalmont.
Dussell, Enrique. 1993. *Las metáforas teológicas de Marx*. Estella [Navarra]: Editorial Verbo Divino.
———. 2001. "From Ethics and Community." Pages 296–318 in *The Postmodern Bible Reader*. Edited by David Jobling, Tina Pippin, and Ronald Schleifer. Oxford: Blackwell.
Elliott, Neil. 1997. "Romans 13:1–7 in the Context of Imperial Propaganda." Pages 184–214 in *Paul and Empire: Religion and Power in Roman Imperial Society*. Edited by Richard A. Horsley. Harrisburg, PA: Trinity Press International.
———. 2000. "Paul and the Politics of Empire: Problems and Prospects." in *Paul and Politics: Ekklesia, Israel, Imperium, Interpretation. Essays in Honor of Krister Stendahl*. Edited by Richard A. Horsley. Harrisburg, PA: Trinity Press International.
———. 2008. *The Arrogance of Nations: Reading Romans in the Shadow of Empire*. Minneapolis: Fortress.

Evans, C. Stephen. 1984. "Redeemed Man: The Vision Which Gave Rise to Marxism." *Christian Scholar's Review* 13.2:141–50.
Freud, Sigmund. 2001a. "Fetishism." Pages 152–57 in vol. 21 of *The Standard Edition of the Complete Psychological Works of Sigmund Freud*. Edited by James Strachey. London: Hogarth.
———. 2001b. "An Outline of Psycho-analysis." Pages 144–207 in vol. 21 of *The Standard Edition of the Complete Psychological Works of Sigmund Freud*. Edited by James Strachey. London: Hogarth.
———. 2001c. "Splitting of the Ego in a Process of Defence." Pages 275–78 in vol. 23 of *The Standard Edition of the Complete Psychological Works of Sigmund Freud*. Edited by James Strachey. London: Hogarth.
Gottwald, Norman K. 1999. *The Tribes of Yahweh: A Sociology of Liberated Israel 1250–1050 BC*. Reprint with new preface. Sheffield: Sheffield Academic.
———. 2001. *The Politics of Ancient Israel*. Louisville: Westminster John Knox.
Hardt, Michael, and Antonio Negri. 2000. *Empire*. Cambridge: Harvard University Press.
———. 2004. *Multitude: War and Democracy in the Age of Empire*. New York: Penguin.
Hinkelammert, Franz J. 1986. *The Ideological Weapons of Death: A Theological Critique of Capitalism*. Maryknoll, NY: Orbis.
Horsley, Richard A. 1993. *Jesus and the Spiral of Violence: Popular Jewish Resistance in Roman Palestine*. Minneapolis: Fortress.
———. 1995. *Galilee: History, Politics, People*. Philadelphia: Trinity Press International.
———. 1996. *Archaeology, History and Society in Galilee*. Philadelphia: Trinity Press International.
———. 2000. "Rhetoric and Empire—and 1 Corinthians." Pages 72–102 in *Paul and Politics: Ekklesia, Israel, Imperium, Interpretation. Essays in Honor of Krister Stendahl*. Edited by Richard A. Horsley. Harrisburg, PA: Trinity Press International.
———. 2002. *Jesus and Empire: The Kingdom of God and the New World Order*. Minneapolis: Fortress.
———. 2003. *Religion and Empire: People, Power, and the Life of the Spirit*. Minneapolis: Fortress.
———, ed. 2008. *In the Shadow of Empire: Reclaiming the Bible as a History of Faithful Resistance*. Louisville: Westminster John Knox.

Lischer, Richard. 1973. "The Lutheran Shape of Marxian Evil." *Religion in Life* 42:549–58.

Löwy, Michael. 1996. *The War of Gods: Religion and Politics in Latin America*. London: Verso.

Loy, David. 1996. "The Religion of the Market." *JAAR* 65:275–90.

Marx, Karl 1972. *The Ethnological Notebooks of Karl Marx*. Edited by Lawrence Krader. Assen: Van Gorcum.

———. 1973a. *Das Kapital: Kritik der politischen Ökonomie; 3.3. Der Gesamtprozeß der kapitalistischen Produktion*. Vol. 25 of *Marx Engels Werke*. Berlin: Dietz.

———. 1973b. "Thesen über Feuerbach." Pages 5–7 in vol. 3 of *Marx Engels Werke*. Berlin: Dietz.

———. 1976. "Theses on Feuerbach (Original Version)." Pages 3–5 in vol. 5 of *Marx and Engels Collected Works*. Moscow: Progress.

———. 1985. "To Abraham Lincoln, President of the United States of America." Pages 19–21 in vol. 20 of *Marx and Engels Collected Works*. Moscow: Progress.

———. 1987. "A Contribution to the Critique of Political Economy." Pages 257–417 in vol. 29 of *Marx and Engels Collected Works*. Moscow: Progress.

———. 1994. *Economic Manuscripts of 1861–1863 (Conclusion): A Contribution to the Critique of Political Economy*. Vol. 34 of *Marx and Engels Collected Works*. Moscow: Progress.

———. 1998. *Capital III*. Vol. 37 of *Marx and Engels Collected Works*. Moscow: Progress.

Meeks, M. Douglas. 1989. *God the Economist: The Doctrine of God and Political Economy*. Minneapolis: Fortress.

Pietz, William. 1985. "The Problem of the Fetish, I." *Res* 9:5–17.

———. 1987. "The Problem of the Fetish, II." *Res* 13:23–45.

———. 1988. "The Problem of the Fetish, III." *Res* 16:105–123.

Pietz, William, and Emily Apter. 1993. *Fetishism as Cultural Discourse*. Ithaca, NY: Cornell University Press.

Sanders, E. P. 1977. *Paul and Palestinian Judaism: A Comparison of Patterns of Religion*. Philadelphia: Fortress.

Scott, Peter. 1994. *Theology, Ideology and Liberation*. Cambridge: Cambridge University Press.

Sobrino, Jon. 2004a. *Jesus in Latin America*. Eugene, OR: Wipf & Stock.

———. 2004b. *The True Church and the Poor*. Eugene, OR: Wipf & Stock.

Stendahl, Krister. 1976. *Paul among Jews and Gentiles*. Philadelphia: Fortress.

Suda, Max Josef. 1978. "The Critique of Religion in Karl Marx's Capital." *JES* 15:15–28.

Sung, Jung Mo. 2007. *Desire, Market, and Religion*. London: SCM.

Thiemann, Ronald F. 1985. "Praxis: The Practical Atheism of Karl Marx." *JES* 22:544–49.

Žižek, Slavoj. 1991. *For They Know Not What They Do: Enjoyment as a Political Factor*. London: Verso.

———. 1993. *Tarrying with the Negative: Kant, Hegel and the Critique of Ideology*. Durham: Duke University Press.

———. 2001. *On Belief*. London: Routledge.

———. 2002. *Revolution at the Gates: Žižek on Lenin, The 1917 Writings*. London: Verso.

———. 2006. *The Parallax View*. Cambridge: MIT Press.

———. 2008. *In Defence of Lost Causes*. London: Verso.

Freud, Adorno, and the Ban on Images

Roland Boer

It is less recognized than it should be that Theodor Adorno's key noncategory of the *Bilderverbot*, or ban on images, owes as much to overturning Sigmund Freud's argument concerning idolatry as it does to the biblical ban on images. Of course, both bounce their thoughts off the second commandment of Exod 20 (and Deut 5). Yet Freud's interpretation runs the risk of replicating precisely what the ban seeks to overcome, for the abstraction he espies in the ban is precisely the move that reinstalls idolatry. For this reason, Adorno seeks to deploy the ban on images in a way that blocks the possibility of any form of idolatry. Not only am I interested in the way the arguments of Freud and Adorno unfold, but also I am vitally concerned with the political implications of Adorno's development of what may be called political iconoclasm. What does it mean to engage in a process that cuts down any possibility of reification in a system—capitalism—for which reification is its very lifeblood?

The following argument has two stages, beginning with Freud's arresting argument concerning the ban on images in *Moses and Monotheism*. This enables me to step back and ask what is going on with the ban on images in the biblical text itself, and so I argue that it constitutes a defense mechanism to block the critique of idolatry. Second, I pick up a line that has been taken less commonly, namely, from Freud to Adorno. The latter famously sought common ground between Marxism, Nietzsche, and psychoanalysis, although his psychoanalytic forays have not stood well the test of time—except for one item: the ban on images, the *Bilderverbot* that became a leitmotif of his philosophy. However, these are not merely arcane concerns of philosophy, for they have significant ramifications for any viable politics in our day and age. So I focus on what may be called the "political iconoclasm" of Adorno's deployment of the ban on images.

On (Not) Cutting the Idol Link

I begin with Freud's argument in *Moses and Monotheism* concerning the ban on images and idolatry. Freud (2001, 112) writes that the religion of Moses brought a "far grander conception of God, or, as we might put it more modestly, the conception of a grander God." Moses achieved this breakthrough by banning any images of God. The ban on seeing, hearing, or touching this God is crucial for Freud, for "it meant that a sensory perception was given second place to what may be called an abstract idea—a triumph of intellectuality over sensuality or, strictly speaking, an instinctual renunciation, with all its necessary psychological consequences" (113). In other words, the ban on images is a mark of intellectual superiority, abstraction, and renunciation. In the first part of this lopsided work, Freud contrasts this imagined Hebrew religion with the Egyptians: while the one was monotheistic, the other was confusedly polytheistic; one simply refused to contemplate an afterlife, the other obsessed about it; and one was intellectually superior, the other inferior. The religion of the ancient Hebrews had, in short, soared to the "heights of sublime abstraction" (22).

Rather than dwell on the obvious problems with such an argument—the mythical status of Freud's narrative, the dangerous territory of Hebrew exceptionalism, the assumption that the origins of Western thought may be found in the Hebrew Bible—I would like to step back and ask a prior question that goes to the heart of Freud's concerns: what does the ban on images seek to forestall? An initial answer would be idolatry, one that Freud accepts. On that level, the ban belongs to the genre of the critique of idolatry: we should not worship animals, stars, found objects, or things made with our hands in the sweat of our brows. Or as the biblical text of Isaiah puts it, in one of the best polemics against idolatry still to be found:

> All who make idols are nothing, and the things they delight in do not profit; their witnesses neither see nor know. And so they will be put to shame. Who would fashion a god or cast an image that can do no good? Look, all its devotees shall be put to shame; the artisans too are merely human. Let them all assemble, let them stand up; they shall be terrified, they shall all be put to shame.
>
> The ironsmith fashions it and works it over the coals, shaping it with hammers, and forging it with his strong arm; he becomes hungry and his strength fails, he drinks no water and is faint. The carpenter stretches a line, marks it out with a stylus, fashions it with planes, and marks it with

a compass; he makes it in human form, with human beauty, to be set up in a shrine. He cuts down cedars or chooses a holm tree or an oak and lets it grow strong among the trees of the forest. He plants a cedar and the rain nourishes it. Then it can be used as fuel. Part of it he takes and warms himself; he kindles a fire and bakes bread. Then he makes a god and worships it, makes it a carved image and bows down before it. Half of it he burns in the fire; over this half he roasts meat, eats it and is satisfied. He also warms himself and says, "Ah, I am warm, I can feel the fire!" The rest of it he makes into a god, his idol, bows down to it and worships it; he prays to it and says, "Save me, for you are my god!"

They do not know, nor do they comprehend; for their eyes are shut, so that they cannot see, and their minds as well, so that they cannot understand. No one considers, nor is there knowledge or discernment to say, "Half of it I burned in the fire; I also baked bread on its coals, I roasted meat and have eaten. Now shall I make the rest of it an abomination? Shall I fall down before a block of wood?" He feeds on ashes; a deluded mind has led him astray, and he cannot save himself or say, "Is not this thing in my right hand a fraud?" (Isa 44:9–20 NRSV)[1]

This biblical critique gives the initial impression that idol worshipers are intellectually inferior, as Freud might put it, for they worship an oddly shaped block of wood, a chiseled piece of stone or perhaps a polished metal icon that can never be more than the material out of which it is made. The passage from Isaiah plays up the sheer ordinariness of the idol with a good dose of satire, seeking to puncture the exorbitant claims made for it. But this text also points to the need for an analysis of the material object in question and not the vapid claims made on its behalf.

A deeper analysis needs to go behind the text a little in order to uncover its workings. To begin with, I would like to shift perspective from the polemicist to the so-called worshiper of the idol. Now the idol becomes a mere symbol or pointer to the deity, a tangible, earthly marker of the god's connection to this world. The idol worshiper does not think of statue or icon as the god itself; instead, it is a finger pointing to the deity. Here it is worth considering the first and second of the Ten Commandments together, for they reveal this precondition of the critique of idolatry (Exod

---

1. See also the explicitly political polemic in Isa 40:19–20; 41:6–7; 42:17; 45:16–17; and 46:1–2, 5–7. Not to be outdone, Paul in the New Testament puts the same point in his own way. Thus Paul argues that due to darkened minds (Rom 1:21) the dead, created thing comes to life and gains the power to rule and dominate human lives instead of God (Rom 1:23, 25).

20:3–6; Deut 5:7–10). The second commandment forbids the making of any graven images, while the first commands one not to have any other god before Yahweh. These two commandments are not discrete items, for they flow into one another (as Freud implicitly recognized): one should have neither other gods nor idols, for they are intimately connected. In other words, there is a signifying link between god and idol, deity and representation, and the one who shows reverence for the idol does so in order to honor his or her god to whom the idol directs one's attention.

The polemicist steps in and breaks the signifying link between object and god. He or she is not so much a conqueror of the neighboring tribe, scoffing at the god of the vanquished who was of little use in the battlefield or of little success in seduction, but is more likely to be a monotheist or an atheist. (They share more common ground than they care to admit.)[2] Both may say: "That piece of wood points to nothing, for there is no god to whom it refers. Therefore all you are worshiping is that block of wood, which comes from a tree, half of which you used to make a shelf and half a ridiculous object that you worship. Can you not see how stupid it is to worship a clump of wood or stone? It does nothing, says nothing, thinks nothing. It sits there dumbly while you worship it." In other words, the critic of idolatry snaps the signifying link between representative object and deity. If the deity no longer exists, then there is no link, and so one worships what now becomes an idol.

Both monotheist and atheist come after the fact, responding to an existing polytheism that must—they feel—be negated. Atheism, in the way we understand it, is of course the latest religious position, but even monotheism is a late development, a perspective that is imposed on the earlier texts of the Bible.[3] The critique of—indeed, the very identification of—idolatry as the worship of an animate or inanimate object can happen only after the belated arrival of monotheism, which then generates its own critique of the earlier gods who make a rapid exit from the cosmos. What

---

2. It is quite possible for a polytheist to make this argument as well, selecting one or two gods out of a larger collection for the argument that follows. Indeed, the polytheist could also take up the ban on images for all the gods. But it is a more difficult position to hold, for the polytheist by definition recognizes a multiplicity of gods.

3. There is more than enough evidence to suggest that an earlier polytheism was gradually overlaid in the texts of the Hebrew Bible by monotheism. Thus the various references to the veneration and worship of multiple gods become, in light of this late overlay, myriad examples of waywardness and apostasy. See, for example, Day 2002.

happens to all the interstellar detritus, the symbols and signs that they have left behind in their hasty departure? They become idols.

But the monotheist and atheist do differ on one point, for the monotheist argues that all gods apart from one's own are unreal delusions, while the atheist points out that the monotheist's claim falls under the same logic. So the atheist observes that the monotheist must be consistent: if you are going to break the signifying link of all others, then you must carry that logic through to your own religion. Those images in your church, the crucifix on the altar, the Bible you read, or indeed Jesus Christ himself, are all forms of idolatry. You set up a signifying line between them and your God, whether Bible or Christ as revelation, icon or crucifix as symbols of your God, or even the word "God" or "Yahweh" itself. But your God does not exist, cannot be experienced or verified, heard or encountered in any real sense, so you too are an idolater, worshiping a text, human being, or nicely polished object. You are, the atheist continues, no better than the teenager who lovingly polishes his first car, or the fetishist who drools over spiked heels, or those who hope for a messiah to lead them to the promised land.

The fallback position for the monotheist, especially in Judaism, Christianity, or Islam, is iconoclasm—or rather, since iconoclasm assumes an existing image to be smashed, a ban on images in the first place: aniconism. For this reason, the second commandment is so powerful: one is not permitted to make any image whatsoever, not of anything on the earth, in the seas, or in the heavens. Now I would like to part with Freud's argument, especially his point that the ban on images manifests greater intellect since it is the first moment of abstraction. Instead, at its heart, the ban on images is the manifestation of a fear that the process of idol criticism will continue inexorably. Once you have denied the existence of all the other gods bar one, then it is but one step further to deny the existence of the last one standing.[4] So, one seeks to close down the mechanism by which this might happen: without such a representation, there is no fixing point for the signifying chain, no possibility to set up a connection between earthly object and superhuman being. Instead, one must direct one's attention to God alone. Without a signifying link, it becomes impossible to break such a link. One can hardly pull out the chain-cutters to sever a chain that does

---

4. Hence the perpetual assertion, such as: "Thus says the Lord, the King of Israel, and his Redeemer, the Lord of hosts: 'I am the first and I am the last; besides me there is no god. Who is like me? Let him proclaim it, let him declare and set it forth before me'" (Isa 44:6–7a NRSV).

not exist. So, responds the monotheist, your argument has no bite; I am not an idolater.

Of course, the monotheist would have to admit that there have been more than a few slip-ups in the ban of images. Witness the synagogue with its symbols—menorah or star of David—or the church with its crucifixes, stained-glass windows, and iconography. Moreover, one cannot escape the reliance on "Holy Scriptures" that is felt to varying degrees to be the revelation of God or—at a minimal level—the written experiences of those human beings who have experienced God. The histories of Judaism, Christianity, and Islam are overflowing with moments when people became enamored of an earthly representation of God. Yet the monotheist might respond in a way that is consistent with the critique of idolatry: These are examples of disobeying the command against graven images, which is an exceedingly difficult command to follow consistently.

Adorno, or, Toward Political Iconoclasm

> It is the fact that the prohibition on graven images [*das Bilderverbot*] that occupies a position of central importance in the religions that believe in salvation, that this prohibition extends into the ideas and the most sublime ramifications of thought. (Adorno 2008, 26; see also Adorno 2003b, 46)

I have, of course, wound my argument in the direction of Adorno's critique, which is suspicious of any effort to allow space for the signifying link of idolatry. Not even the monotheist's last stand is to be tolerated, for it allows a small window through which the dynamic of idolatry may once again invade the scene. Adorno develops a political iconoclasm, a resolute resistance to any form of commoditization, reification, and thereby idolatry. Why? These are constitutive of capitalism and its attendant ideologies, so he seeks to find a way to deny them any space whatsoever. Adorno's strategy is to return to the biblical text and develop in his own way the ban on images, or *Bilderverbot*.[5] This philosophical motif appears throughout his work: in the effort to produce a nonconceptual philosophy or rather to

---

5. Surprisingly, relatively few critics recognize the importance and pervasiveness of the *Bilderverbot* in Adorno's thought. Christopher Brittain at least does so, and one may usefully read his observations by way of introduction, although he neglects the rich heritage of this motif in Freudian and Marxist thought (especially by way of the

unlock the nonconceptual through the conceptual; in his central category of the nonidentical; in his refusal to speculate or represent utopia; in his (appropriately) incomplete attempt at an aesthetic theory; in his thoughts on the personality cult and secularized theology. In brief, his achievement was to extend the blockage of the signifying connection between idol and god, which was embodied in the ban on images, to the relations between human beings and the various elements of capitalism.

However, Adorno's return to the biblical texts is done in a way that undermines the very heart of Freud's argument for the abstraction implicit in the ban—recall that the ban on sensuous representations of the deity is the foundation of abstract thought, at least for Freud. In order to see how that happens, let me introduce a crucial distinction between what may be called the idol link and the reifying relation. If we use a spatial metaphor, the former is vertical, designating the relation between the object produced here on earth and the god to whom that object is supposed to point; the reifying relation, by contrast, is horizontal, dealing with the relations between human beings and things here in earth. In fact, all of the preceding section was an elaboration of the vertical relation, or what I am calling the idol link. The critiques of idolatry sought to break that link, arguing that no god exists and that the worshiper—stupidly—serves a mere object of wood, stone, metal, or perhaps animal or human. In order to block the same logic being applied to one's own god, we find the ban on images in the Hebrew Bible.

If the previous section's concern was the idol link, then this section has as its focus the reifying relation. Briefly put, Adorno's innovation was to take this idol link and apply it to the relations between human beings; that is, to transfer the idol link to the reifying relation. How so? The command to block all possible connections between the deity and representations here on earth is now applied to the reifications that take place between human beings and the products of our labor. In the same way that second commandment seeks to sever the signifying chain between deity and worshiper, so also does Adorno wish to snap the link between human being and object made.

Let me say a little more about the reifying relation that Adorno seeks to block. This relation takes place between human beings and the prod-

---

fetish); see Brittain 2010, 88–98. Other works worthy of note include Pritchard 2002 and Buchholz 1991.

ucts of their labor. It is an argument drawn originally from Marx but profoundly transformed: Marx sought to understand why there seems to be a transfer of powers between a range of elements within capitalism—commodity, money, value, capitalist, profit, wealth, and so on—and the human beings who produced those elements. For Marx, the theory of fetishism (see my essay on imperial fetish in this volume) provided him with an answer—a mutual transfer of powers between human beings (who lost out) and products of their labor—that later gained philosophical rigor with Georg Lukács's (1988, 83–110) elaboration of the theory of reification (cf. Jameson 1991, 95–96): the process by which living beings, thoughts, activities, relations, and so on become abstracted and thing-like, especially when the "thing" in question is the commodity; conversely, that "thing" acquires the properties that have so quickly been divested from those beings, thoughts, activities, and relations.

So let us see how Adorno goes about his task of applying the ban on images to the transfer of powers characteristic of commodities and workers within capitalism. Adorno's move is to pick up the biblical injunction against images from Exod 20/Deut 5 and boldly slide it from the initial signifying link of the idol to the transferring connection between human beings and objects produced. In a way analogous to the barring of the passage from image to god, so also one blows up the bridge that connects the object produced and the human being who has produced it. In the same way that the ban on images removes any anchor for the signifying line between god and idol, so also does its application to the transferal of powers between product and human being chop off any foothold that such a transferal might gain. In Adorno's skillful hands, the ban on images becomes a way of preventing the reifying transfer from taking place in the first place. One difference between the targets of the two strategies does remain. The ban on images in the Bible is twofold, while its application to capitalist reification is singular: the former is designed to negate the possibility that the signifying link may be broken by preventing that link from being established in the first place, but the application to the reifying transfer of powers is more direct, for it simply seeks to prevent the transferring connection from taking place at all. Yet even here the two strategies are analogous: one seeks to quarantine God from idolatry, while the other desperately wishes to protect human beings from the baleful effects of capitalist reification.

Adorno seeks a way to resist the pervasiveness of capitalism in the capillaries of everyday life. Its irrepressible ability to commodify every aspect of tangible and—increasingly—intangible reality and the seemingly inescapable reification that attends every act, thought, and product means that any resistance has to be trenchant and radical. Adorno resolves not to allow even the smallest fingerhold for the reifying processes of capitalism. For as soon as one produces a concept, offers an image of a better world, or puts one's trust in a leader, it (or he or she) becomes reified and even commercialized. Witness the way in our day how "Ideology" or "Politix" have become clothing labels, or the way Bob Dylan ended up doing car advertisements, or how Che Guevara's image made its way onto ice-cream labels and T-shirts for bourgeois teenagers. In other words, the ban on images becomes in Adorno's hands a grimly defended barricade against the persistent and permeating waves of capitalist commodification.

In order to understand this wielding of the ban on images as a mode of resistance, we need to be aware of the context in which Adorno (and Horkheimer) worked. They voiced their opposition in terms of a profound dismay at the technological leaps of capitalism (if only they could have seen the cyber-technologies of today), the repressive state apparatuses of the police and the military, and the lock-down of the Cold War, all of which produced a sense that capitalism had dug itself in and would not be dislodged. But at a deeper level they were caught in a double-bind. The first was the melancholic ambivalence over what Germany meant: Adorno hated the United States and his exile there during the Second World War, longing to return to Germany and to be able to express himself in German. Yet that return brought on a melancholy that came from the awareness of what had been perpetrated there in the very recent past. It would have been like the children of migrants, who inherit from their parents a profound ambivalence about home: the old country is far better than this primitive place to which we have emigrated, but then the old country is dreadful, since otherwise we would not have left in the first place. The second double-bind was the cost of defeating fascism: it brought with it an unprecedented penetration (and I use the word deliberately) of American money and commercial practices into a now-bankrupt and war-torn Europe. Was the cost worth it? Adorno was not so sure, since he espied the techniques of fascism within United States-style commerce and propaganda. It did not help matters that Adorno saw Stalin's ascendency in the East as a dissipation of hope for an alternative. In the face of these onslaughts, Adorno resolved not to give the patterns of commodification and reification any purchase within his philosophy.

I have sought to fill out the logic and background to Adorno's appropriation of the ban on images, but now let me review briefly a few of the instances when Adorno deploys the ban. One of the most controversial is his effort to produce a nonconceptual philosophy, the most significant manifestation of his effort to refuse philosophical systematizing.[6] Over against the central role of concepts—ontology, immanence, transcendence, univocality, analogy, *Dasein*, truth, event, and on and on—Adorno attempts in his search for a negative dialectic to block the production of such concepts in the first place. He does not simply refuse to use concepts as such but seeks to show how those concepts undermine themselves, turning them through an immanent method into a nonconceptual framework in which one never pins one's colors to any concept at all. An almost impossible process that produced a formidable mode of philosophizing (in which each sentence is a discrete argument in itself so that one dos not succumb to the pattern of logical argumentation[7]), its underlying drive is to prevent the possibility of any concept becoming reified and hijacking philosophy as it does so.

Another is its application to utopia. One must not, argues Adorno, spend months and years perfecting a blueprint of utopia, since that becomes an image, an idol at the feet of which one lays one's hopes and expectations. It comes to replace utopia itself, standing in as an idol for what cannot yet be achieved. Or in the case of the personality cult, Adorno (with Horkheimer) argues that as soon as we recognize someone with charisma, who convinces us with stunning oratory or perhaps simple sayings of deep wisdom, who promises much if only we will trust him or her, we are lost. They do not merely mean that such leaders will disappoint, leading us to a mosquito-infested marsh or treacherous jungle to eke out a slave-like existence, or that they end up seducing the young boys and girls while owning a fleet of Rolls-Royces, or that the Swiss bank account will swell while we become penniless. Rather, they mean that the process of deification has already taken place, that the human being has become like

---

6. Apart from the extraordinary effort at working through such a nonconceptual approach in Adorno 1973 and Adorno 2003a, see also his much more accessible comments in the lectures given at the time he was working through this approach: Adorno 2008, 57, 62, 68–75, 94–95, 185–86; 2003b, 87, 95, 102–13, 139–40, 229–31. For reflection on philosophical systems, see Adorno 2008, 22–43; 2003b, 40–54.

7. Adorno's preference for microanalysis (he notes his debts to Benjamin here) also plays a role in such sentences.

god, an idol in whom we have invested our own powers and resources. That process, they suggest, has been enabled in a way not seen before by Christology: as Christ has become man and then returns to the heavens, human beings may now join him on the return journey, becoming deified in the process—or at least they become so in the eyes of their adorers. Being a God-human (according to traditional Christology) opens the door for others to reverse the equation and become a human-God (Horkheimer and Adorno 1987, 206–9; 2002, 145–47; see also Boer 2007, 433–35).

Finally, and to his posthumous shame, Adorno also applied this logic to the waves of student revolts that began to wash over German campuses in the 1960s (Adorno 1998, 259–78; 2003b, 73–84; 2008, 47–54). Apart from questioning action for the sake of action, organizing for the sake of organizing, and apart from pointing to the futility of protests in light of the all-pervasive nature of capitalism and the strength of the forces of repression, Adorno also applied the ban on images. He did so in relation to the separation between theory and practice. The students argued that radical philosophical theory was fine, but what about practice, especially if you keep Marx's eleventh thesis of Feuerbach in mind? In response, Adorno pointed out that the separation of theory and practice was itself a result of the reification of life under capitalism. Instead of separating them and succumbing to the reifying effects of capitalism, Adorno argued for a resistance in which thought and practice could be kept together: "Thinking itself is a kind of behaviour; it is, whether one likes it or not, a kind of practice, even in its purest logical operations" (Adorno 2008, 53; see also 2003b, 83).[8] It would be more radical, according to Adorno, to see theory and practice as one whole rather than follow the dictates of a reified separation. In other words, do not make an idol of political action, especially if it is done in the name of something better, of a utopian possibility that you can espy in the near future. That would be to slip from one idol (practice) to another (utopia), both of which will disappoint you. We might want to disagree with Adorno and take Antonio Negri's line that resistance emerges from the midst of capitalism rather than through an effort to block its path, but even here Adorno shows an extraordinarily

---

8. Adorno also writes, "Thinking is a doing, theory a form of praxis; already the ideology of the purity of thinking deceives about this. Thinking has a double character: it is immanently determined and rigorous, and yet an inalienable real mode of behaviour in the midst of reality" (1998, 261).

rigorous adherence to the ban on images, to keeping the barricade in place to thwart the reifying transfer.

Conclusion

A little earlier, I suggested that Adorno's analysis turns the tables on Freud's argument that the ban on images marks the moment of abstraction, of the break from sensuous representations of the deity. The trap for Freud is that his argument falls into the very logic he seeks to overcome, but I can make that argument only after having passed through Adorno. Simply put, a central feature of the process of reification is precisely abstraction: in drawing powers from human beings and granting them to objects produced, one abstracts them, creating entities that take on a life of their own. For example, commodities are abstracts in this sense, as is the dollar or yuan and its slide up and down the league table of currencies, as is the "economy," and so on. That argument relies on the connection made by Adorno between the ban on images and the reifying relation, but once the connection is made, we cannot avoid the conclusion that Freud is producing yet another version of idolatry—of abstraction and abstract thought.

As for the political implications, they are as stark as Adorno suggests. His proscriptions are far from any "lifestyle" choice, where one refuses certain types of obvious commercialism. Wearing only secondhand clothes, growing one's own food or perhaps visiting the farmer's market occasionally, avoiding television and the Internet, even dispensing with smartphones and the like will hardly make a significant impact on the structures of commoditization and their attendant cultural forms. Adorno has in mind a political project so resolutely far-sighted that it becomes almost impossible to imagine. This can lead to a counsel of despair (an affliction of Western Marxists), leaving any alternative for a barely discernible future. In light of this situation, I would like to close with a slight twist. Let me begin by asking whether reification is restricted to capitalism and its workings, or whether one also finds processes of reification under socialism. We have plenty of experience with socialism by now, almost a century since the Russian Revolution. What we find there is that reification, the process of iconography, even of idolatry, took a very different path (think of the veneration of revolutionary leaders, for instance). Is it possible, then, that the future Adorno imagines is one not necessarily free from any form of image production, but rather a very different form for which the language all too easily falls into known modes of expression?

Works Cited

Adorno, Theodor W. 1973. *Negative Dialectics*. Translated by E. B. Ashton. New York: Seabury.
——. 1998. *Critical Models: Interventions and Catchwords*. Translated by Henry W. Pickford. New York: Columbia University Press.
——. 2003a. *Gesammelte Schriften*. Vol. 6, *Negative Dialektik*. Edited by Rolf Tiedemann et al. Frankfurt am Main: Suhrkamp.
——. 2003b. *Vorlesung über Negative Dialektik: Fragmente zur Vorlesung 1965/66*. Edited by Rolf Tiedemann. Frankfurt am Main: Suhrkamp.
——. 2008. *Lectures on Negative Dialectics: Fragments of a Lecture Course 1965/1966*. Translated by Rodney Livingstone. Cambridge: Polity.
Boer, Roland. 2007. *Criticism of Heaven: On Marxism and Theology*. Leiden: Brill.
Brittain, Christopher Craig. 2010. *Adorno and Theology*. London: Continuum.
Buchholz, René. 1991. *Zwischen Mythos und Bilderverbot*. New York: Peter Lang.
Day, John. 2002. *Yahweh and the Gods and Goddesses of Canaan*. London: T&T Clark.
Freud, Sigmund. 2001. *Moses and Monotheism*. Pages 7–137 in vol. 23 of *The Standard Edition of the Complete Psychological Works of Sigmund Freud*. Edited by James Strachey. London: Hogarth.
Horkheimer, Max, and Theodor W. Adorno. 1987. *Dialektik der Aufklärung und Schriften 1940–1950*. Vol. 5 of Max Horkheimer, *Gesammelte Schriften*. Edited by Alfred Schmidt and Gunzelin Schmid Noerr. Frankfurt am Main: Fischer Taschenbuch.
——. 2002. *Dialectic of Enlightenment: Philosophical Fragments*. Translated by Edmund Jephcott. Stanford, CA: Stanford University Press.
Jameson, Fredric. 1991. *Postmodernism, or, the Cultural Logic of Late Capitalism*. Durham, NC: Duke University Press.
Lukács, Georg. 1988. *History and Class Consciousness: Studies in Marxist Dialectics*. Translated by Rodney Livingstone. Cambridge: MIT Press.
Pritchard, Elizabeth A. 2002. "*Bilderverbot* Meets Body in Theodor W. Adorno's Inverse Theology." *HTR* 95:291–318.

Part 2
Textual Engagements

The End-or Medium

Jione Havea

Stories, like darkness, ripple and irrupt, bounce and interrupt
    the material, the immanent
    the hidden, the repressed
    the illusive, the economic
    the political, the transgressive
Ways of hearing, reading, and telling stories
    like Saul seeking the wise woman at Endor,
    move toward, approach, each other
    ebbing, nudging, flowing, as if to never settle
The touching of stories with ears, eyes, and tongues
    as well as noses
    are openings for *talanoa*
    at once process, product, event, medium, end

Talanoa Roots

Talanoa, among the natives of Oceania, is story, telling, and conversation, together (Havea 2010a). It is not one or the other of those, or one in the place of the others, but one in relation to the other two. *Talanoa* is the three—story, telling, conversation—weaving, multiplying. The three come together as one; they are one. If one receives more attention, that one serves as a reminder for the other two. The one that is at the foreground calls attention to the ones that are not as present or that have been neglected or repressed.

    Talanoa—story, telling, conversation—is medium and end, event and process, channel for remembering and for forgetting, opportunity for reconsidering and for remixing. It digs around for the neglected and the repressed, but it can also cover for the oppressor. It reveals and conceals. Like desire and memory, *talanoa* can be wild and lame; like production and faith, it works best in company; like sex and control, it can be bad and good; like the repressed and the waves in the sea, it can rise, irrupt, and break. *Talanoa* rolls and breaches and ripples (Havea 2010b). I do not know if *talanoa* was at the beginning, but *talanoa* is around us all, and i expect it to stay to the end.[1]

Talanoa is less about origins and more about belonging (Moala 2011, 3–6), returning memories to the tip of tongues, to the flow of orality, of mediation and mediums. This essay is accordingly the working of *talanoa*, which is like a river: "*It tickles from the source until it flows flows flows. Down the mountains of the mountains. Branching onto the land the land the land. Flowing. Spiralling. Flowing towards the sea. Spiralling towards the sky. Where it grows wings and flies towards the universe of the unknown*" (Figiel 1999, 3–4 [emphasis original]).

My attention in this *talanoa*, uneasily squeezed into writing, is on three subjects at the edges of the worlds of the living and of the dead in 1 Sam 28: (1) Saul scrambles in the world of the living, seeking attention and affirmation, while (2) Samuel lies from the world of the dead, the proverbial other side, and (3) the unnamed woman medium at Endor has the ability to open the two worlds, and the two subjects, toward one another. This woman is at the edge, a medium at the end. She is the End-or (hear: "and/or" also) medium.

Fear Drives

The Philistines, dreaded neighbors of Israel since the days of Samson (Judg 13–16), muster their forces to Shunem—also identified as the home of Abishag (1 Kgs 1:1–4) and of the older woman who hosted Elisha (2 Kgs 4:8–10)—for war against Israel, who were gathering at Gilboa under Saul's command. The narrator sets readers up to easily see the Philistines as the aggressive party.

Separated by the Harod Valley, the opposing camps would have eyed each other in clear view. "When Saul saw the Philistine force, his heart trembled with fear" (1 Sam 28:5 NJPS).[2] The narrator does not explain why. Saul's fear could be due to the appearance of the Philistine force, in

---

1. I prefer the lowercase "i" because i use the lowercase with "you," "she," "they," and "others" also. I do not see the point in capitalizing the first person when she or he is because of everyone else.

2. All translations of the Bible are my own, unless indicated otherwise.

units of hundreds and thousands (1 Sam 29:2), because size matters when it comes to war. Size matters, and war is men's business. But i suspect also that the narrator wants readers to discredit Saul as the leader with no guts, the man who is not manly enough. As king, he too is a man of war, and he should not be easily intimidated. When the narrator announces, "His heart trembled with fear," one sees Saul as a loser. That is one effect of the narrator's *talanoa*.

The narrator does not indicate whether Saul knows that David, whom Samuel has anointed to be king in the place of Saul, has become the "bodyguard for life" for King Achish of Philistia (1 Sam 28:2). Two of Saul's rivals, David and Achish, gather as one. The rival king of Israel joins with the king of the rival neighbor. This rivalry would have added to Saul's fear. But David, at this point, is only part of Saul's problem. Saul is also under pressure from YHWH and Samuel, who made him king and then ignored him as if he were a floating island. Detached. Unwanted.

Saul was made Israel's first king, but not by his choice or design. He was the tall, handsome son of Kish, a wealthy Benjaminite. Saul went to look for his father's missing asses (1 Sam 9:1–3), and Samuel kissed and oiled him to be ruler over YHWH's people (1 Sam 10:1). Saul's mission to find the lost asses coincided with Israel asking for a king to rule over them like the other nations (1 Sam 8). Israel sought change because Samuel's sons were devious, so the request meant the rejection of the house of Samuel. YHWH selected Saul to begin a different form of governing (1 Sam 9:17). Saul was the chosen one, who became king in response to the people's fear of Samuel's sons. Ironically, it was Samuel who pushed Saul into the political and public eye. In the eyes of the biblical narrator, Saul's ascension was not an accident. It was his fate (Gunn 1980).

Samuel's support for Saul did not last (1 Sam 15:26). He soon anointed David (1 Sam 15:35–16:13) to replace Saul as king. But no one removed Saul, so Israel ended up with rival kings, Saul and David, each leading a circle of men. With David oiled to be messiah, Samuel stopped seeing Saul, up to the day Samuel died. Israel lamented for Samuel and buried him at his hometown, Ramah, then Saul forbade "[recourse to] ghosts and familiar spirits in the land" (1 Sam 28:3 NJPS). The connection between the burial of Samuel with Saul's decree is so strong that it seems to me that Saul did not want the spirit of Samuel to return (Havea 2011). Samuel was dead and buried, and Saul prohibited any access to him. Let the dead man rest in peace, undisturbed, like a sinking island, in the other world, far away from here.

YHWH becomes more distant and unresponsive (1 Sam 28:6) as if Samuel's death cuts YHWH off from Saul. It becomes apparent that it is up to Saul, as we say in the islands, to swim or drown. In Oceania, however, as my I-Kiribati friends reminded me when they problematized the claim that their islands will drown because of climate change with the observation that more people die in Kiribati due to suicide than to drowning, drowning is a reality but not an option. In the face of the Philistine force, Saul has to swim in a sea of fear. Fear drives him against his own will and judgment, against his own decree, which was a *tapu* (prohibition, sanctification) he set for the whole of Israel.

Fear is at the depths of this *talanoa*. Fear drives Israel to break from the house of Samuel; fear of the Philistines drives Saul to demand, "Find me a woman who consults ghosts, so that I can go to her and inquire through her" (1 Sam 28:7 NJPS). Fear rules Saul and drives this *talanoa*.

In circles where having and exercising power is favored, fear is a weakness. Fear hinders creativity, clouds judgment, and deflates resistance, which is necessary in the war for control. Fear is the mark of sissies, and it is not acceptable, especially in the case of a king.

But in settings where freedom is limited, as in the case of prisons, fear keeps one alive. Resistance is not welcomed in prisons, where one survives not by confronting the authorities but by *dealing* with the situation. In prisons, dealing is not about submitting to another or compromising one's integrity but negotiating so that "one stays on top" of how and "what goes on" to and around oneself. Dealing is what people who have no control over themselves and their surroundings do, and fear is a key ingredient in their dealings. In their circles, fear is not a weakness but a necessary condition for survival and sanity. Among persons in prison with whom i read this story, Saul's fear is a step toward dealing, toward staying on top of things. Going against his own decree is part of his dealing. Reversing opinions and breaking taboos are common in the realms of dealing and of *talanoa*. Seen in these lights, i sympathize with Saul's fear and his demand for a woman to give him counsel. Fear drives Saul and his *talanoa*, and there is nothing wrong with that.

I admire the fear that inspires dealing, especially when this has to do with people who have limited or no power. That is not to say that all forms of fear are healthy. Fear might be a symptom of powerlessness and psychological disillusion, but it is a means of survival in incarceration. Fear on the part of authorities, who do not like when something penetrates the coverings of their powers, often leads to acts of repression and injustice.

This is where the case of Saul is interesting because, as king, he is a person of power. He is top among the national bourgeoisies. Since Saul's struggle is with YHWH and Samuel, who holds more authority in the story world, i—controlled by the *talanoa* of the narrator—opt to see Saul as one who is dealing, swimming in order to survive. He, of course, is not completely powerless, for he has men under his control, to whom he commands, "Find me a woman."

There is a woman at Endor, the courtiers tell Saul, who consults "familiar spirits" (1 Sam 28:7). The courtiers do not say if she was an Israelite, but David Jobling (1998, 186) is certain: "To be a medium (or a wizard, etc.) is therefore to be a foreigner and to be rightly expelled. The mediums cannot be Israelites for they have made themselves not Israelites by what they do."

The exact location of Endor is not known, but Endor is the name for one of the towns that the Manassites could not dispossess (Josh 17:1–12), so it is "beyond the border" even if it is geographically close to Gilboa (Pigott 1998, 437). Endor is a reminder of Israel's incomplete occupation of the land of Canaan, and a reminder also of the ability of the people of the land to resist the onslaught of YHWH's people.

This story sets readers up to expect the crossing of multiple borders: from Gilboa to Endor, to and from the spirit world and the world of the living, and from Ramah (where Samuel is buried) to Endor (where the woman medium lives). Endor is one point of transit.

Night Encounter

Night falls. Time of transition. Disguise comes on. Bodies cross over. Movement. Transit. Saul and his men come to Endor, one of the towns that reminds readers of colonial Israel's failure, looking for a woman whose practice Saul prohibited among Israelites. Failure. Forbidden. They come looking for a woman to do a prohibited act, and they come at night. Since she is at Endor, outside the lines of Israel's occupation, she lives and operates outside of Israel's jurisdiction. But the narrator presents her as if she speaks the same language as Saul and his men and as if she shares the same rules and values as the Israelites.[3]

---

3. This narrator is not on top of the consequences of border crossing. He or she overlooks that in crossing borders one crosses cultures and languages. Assuming sameness across borders is one of the marks of colonialists, which this narrator bears.

That night at Endor, faces meet but do not greet each other. It is not a meeting between friends. There is no "Welcome!" or "You got me at hello!" Fear. Rush. The disguised man has a desire, and he wastes no time. He asks the unnamed woman to bring up a familiar spirit whom he does not name. In her response, not knowing that she is addressing Saul himself, she speaks as if she is under Saul's spell: "You know what Saul has done, how he has banned [the use of] ghosts and familiar spirits in the land. So why are you laying a trap for me, to get me killed?" (1 Sam 28:9 NJPS). She too knows that dealing is necessary. Her life is important.

If the night encounter between Saul and the woman medium took place in Tuvalu, it would be called *mea te pouliga*, "thing of the darkness." In this Tuvaluan phrase is the assumption that certain actions are appropriate only for the night, in the darkness. There are two ways to understand this. First is the understanding that certain actions are bad and should be hidden (in the darkness) from the eyes of others. Those actions (e.g., having sex, telling stories about the ancestors, explaining customs and practices, etc.) are not appropriate for the daytime.

When Europeans came to Oceania, they saw the natives as people of the darkness, as compared to the fair-skinned white people of the light, and the ways of the native people were judged to be *mea te pouliga*. Dark-skinned people do things of the darkness, which showed how they are uncivilized and unchristian. According to this understanding, the *mea te pouliga* should not be done at all. The Samoan novelist Sia Figiel (1996, 236) challenges the racialized favoring of fair skins and discrimination against darkness and darkened peoples: "Lightness died that first day in 1830 when the breakers of the sky [fair-skinned Europeans who came as traders, colonizers, and missionaries] entered these shores, forcing us all to forget … to forget … to bury our gods … to kill our gods … to re-define everything, recording history in reverse." Darkness, *mea te pouliga*, came to Oceania with the landing of light/fair people.

There is a second explanation: *mea te pouliga* are necessary to be done, but because they involve breaking some taboo (hence they will bring a curse), they are performed in the dark so that the curse does not spread to people who might accidentally see what is done. *Mea te pouliga* take place in the dark so that innocent people are saved from the curse that will follow. The *mea te pouliga* may be as simple as sharing a *talanoa* about an ancestor with someone from outside that particular ancestor's circle of relations or as revolting as offering a gift or sacrifice to another (rival, enemy) deity. In both cases, one intentionally violates a taboo and expects a curse. But in violating the taboo in the darkness, one aims to contain the curse. This is a different kind of civilization: where one knows the social limits and taboos, as well as the costs for violating those, and is willing to bear the burden without spreading it to others. It is because of this that *mea te pouliga* continue in Tuvalu and in other islands of Oceania.

It helps my *talanoa* to see Saul's mission as *mea te pouliga*. He comes to break a taboo, and he is willing to keep the burden on himself, so he assures the woman medium, "As the Lord lives, you won't get into trouble over this" (1 Sam 28:11). He comes to a medium and promises an end.

The promising, disguised Saul then demands, "Bring up Samuel for me." A dead man is to be recalled, to be troubled, so that he no longer rests in peace. Anxiety. Saul's request invites a question that many Pacific Islanders ask when someone dies: "Were they ready to go?" If they were *not* ready to die, they might return even if they are not wanted back.

The peace one receives at death does not matter as much as the peace one reaches before dying, and this has to do with whether the dead person met all expectations and responsibilities. The Islanders' question reveals the belief that if one was not ready to die, her or his soul will linger in the world of the living. This is a problem for the dead soul, who becomes restless, and for her or his relations, who share the blame for mishaps that befall the community. The worlds of the living and of the dead always connect. One lives in both worlds, the material and the spiritual, at all times.

If there are unfulfilled expectations and responsibilities from the dead person, those who are still living would call for her or him, and this reason lurks behind Saul's demand. He demands the return of Samuel, his reawakening, his arousal, because there is some unfinished business. Saul has dealing to do with Samuel. Restlessness. It is not time for rest.

Night remains.

Talanoa ripples.

Torment Me

A rejected king seeks a rejected medium to bring up a dead (i.e., ejected from life) prophet who had rejected the king earlier. Why does a rejected person seek for his tormentor, all the way to the other side? For revenge? Resolution? More torment?

Torment is intoxicating for the tormentor, who (i am told) enjoys some sort of release in the rush of exercising power and in the illusion of control. There is something addictive for the tormented as well, at least in the way Scriptures present them as having the ability to convert the pressure of terror into the pleasure of submission. For instance, stories of torment present natives as if they want to be colonized (e.g., Rahab betrays her people to help Israel crush Jericho in Josh 2–6), and the oppressed appear to be afraid of being released (e.g., Israel resubmits to YHWH in Josh 24). They find pleasure in terror, they want to be ruled, and they hunger for more (Havea 2007). The oppressed come to depend on their masters. This is what Frantz Fanon (2008, 64–88) calls the dependency complex. In refusing release, the oppressed remains a "thing" rather than becoming a human, which comes with the process of liberation (Fanon 2004, 2).

Stories of torment are addictive also for the tellers and the listeners. It is more difficult to put down a story in which a hero spills guts and blood than one about the righteous and upright winning glory through nonviolence. Texts of terror, as Phyllis Trible (1984) calls them, are captivating. They feed people's hunger for pain and thirst for cruelty. Torment and terror attract and win practitioners and converts, and there are many in the scriptural texts (Havea 2007).

In the Bible, prophets have a *neck* for tormenting kings. Moses tormented Pharaoh (Exod 4–14), Balaam did Balak (Num 22–24), and in 1 Samuel, Samuel has a go at Saul. Samuel oiled Saul for the throne, then turned around and despised him, similar to how some rapists hate their victims (see 2 Sam 13:1–22). Yet Saul seeks Samuel. Is the allure of torment too strong for Saul, enticing him to come because death will not part him from Samuel? Is Saul too naive to realize that he will only get more torment from Samuel?

I want to believe that Saul expects Samuel to rise and return as a different person, transformed by the peace of death. The biblical narrator appears to be open to my expectation, but the rising Samuel is not. Death seems to have had no effect on him. Samuel has reached his end: once a tormentor always a tormentor. Though he was a prophet, Samuel was no medium. Death has lost its sting. In the case of Samuel, death is terminal rather than transitional; it signifies the point of arrival rather than of departure. By seeking Samuel's return, Saul challenges the termination that comes with death. With the help of the medium, Samuel's secret in dying, as suggested in Alice Walker's "Dying," begins to unravel:

> Dying is yours
> alone,
> precious

human being
whatever
you have done.

Dying is
your secret. (Walker 2010, 138)

This reading would have a more comforting feel if Saul were searching for the remedy that is in venom, as we find in the deadly sea urchin we call *alamea* in Tonga. It is a delicacy for Islanders, but, as the case is with most valued things, it will be fatal if one steps on its back. To reverse the toxin, one needs to simply turn the *alamea* over and stand on its underside. The healing is in *alamea* itself. If Saul is seeking Samuel for the same reason, in order to turn Samuel over so that he might give Saul some relief, Saul would come across as a wise character. Freud and Derrida, i imagine, would have sung Saul's praises: "David won Samuel's heart, and thousands more, but Saul turned him over." The biblical narrator does not allow Saul that privilege, for he portrays Saul as a spoiled child who looks for and demands something he should know that he will not get. For the narrator, Saul just cannot learn his lesson. He comes to Endor to ask for more torment.

Face Recognition

Saul comes to Endor even though Samuel is buried at Ramah. How the medium is able to manifest Samuel in Endor is the stuff of legends. If she were a native of Oceania, she would have known of the passages in the underworld, even deeper than the caves where natives used to store and live, and 1 Sam 28 is her *talanoa* also.

> The woman knows her job and goes about it initially (v. 11) without any of the ballyhoo we associate with spiritualism. She has the efficiency of a telephone operator: "What name?" And she gets the connection right the first time! (Jobling 1998, 187)[4]

---

4. Jobling suggests an alternative reading that showcases the woman's *dealing* spirit. She knows who Saul is from the start, and she manipulates the event so that Saul thinks that he is in charge (Jobling 1998, 188). She is wise.

She sees a divine being coming up from the earth. She recognizes him as Samuel. She screams. Excitement. She recognizes Saul as well. The appearance of the dead prophet, an old man wrapped in a robe, exposes the disguised king. Recognition. Seeing Samuel and recognizing Saul makes the medium a figure for Hannah: "He is šā'ûl" (1 Sam 2:28), Hannah said; "You are šā'ûl" (1 Sam 28:12), the medium says (Green 2003, 108). The appearance of one becomes the recognition of the other. They are not strangers to one another. Greeting. The *talanoa* of two, Saul and the medium, becomes *talanoa* of a threesome, with the rising of Samuel.

The woman is a medium. She breaks through limits and brings a body across to the other side. She crosses borders. She breaks taboos. She performs *mea te pouliga*, and i imagine she knows that that comes with a burden. Is this another reason why she screams when she recognizes Saul? Delight. He is the one who can pardon her for doing a forbidden task, for being a medium. He is the one who can remove the curse. If she were an I-Kiribati, a native of Kiribati, Saul would have had to announce *tekeroi* (ban is lifted) over her.[5] Along this line, she comes across as a *dealing* woman also. She is, as they say in Tuvalu, a *fefine manuia*, a blessed woman, a woman of blessings, of fortunes. It is also in the nature of mediums to be, as Abram was expected to be (see Gen 12:1–4a), windows of blessings for others. She opens a window for Saul to gain a blessing through her, but Samuel does not cooperate.

Samuel does not even acknowledge her presence, as his attention is burning for Saul, and in my first reading, i could not excuse his lack of respect for her (Havea 2011). A typical patriarch he is. But ignoring her, on second thought, proves that she is not a problem in Samuel's eyes. She is only a medium, so she is not to be condemned, even though she is the one who makes things happen. It is she, not Saul, who disturbs Samuel's rest. In this regard, Samuel's burning fury against Saul lets her off the hook. In contrast to Saul's fear, which led him to the woman, Samuel's anger blinds him from her. To an extent, then, it is good for her that Samuel is so angry with Saul.

Like a grumpy old man, Samuel is not happy about being disturbed (1 Sam 28:15). But he has to be disturbed because Saul is in great trouble on account of the Philistine forces and God's absence. Saul is in distress, and he needs Samuel's direction. Samuel's response is expected: God has

---

5. Most I-Kiribati people pronounce *tekeroi* over food, even after offering a prayer, before eating a meal.

rejected Saul and replaced him with David. Nothing is new here. Then Samuel announces the death of Saul: "Tomorrow your sons and you will be with me" (1 Sam 28:19). Irony. To be with Samuel is to be dead, to expire. Death is not what Saul is seeking, but death will enable the removal and replacement that has been lacking in the story of Israel's monarchy. Death is necessary if replacement (by David) is to take place. Of course, replacement is necessary because there can only be one monarch, and this is one of the problems that monotheistic religions and colonialist nations keep up. This is most devastating when control is over land, economy, literature, customs, minds, and/or means of expression (Nicole 2001). Radical decolonization is thus required (Smith 2008).

This *talanoa* aims to do something along that line on Samuel, who accelerates the story from recognition to condemnation and to the death sentence. He wastes no time. He draws Saul's story to closure and takes over the story of the medium. Time's up. Night has not lifted. Samuel knows not how freeing *tekeroi* is.

The medium brings Samuel up from the earth, and he takes over her place in the narrator's account. When she returns to the narrator's view, Samuel sinks into the night. She and Samuel switch places, and this is expected of a medium. A medium substitutes for someone else; she can embody the process of mediation.

Substitution in 1 Sam 28 is not limited to that between the woman and Samuel. Samuel also substitutes for God, insofar as he speaks on behalf of God, and Saul substitutes for Israel, who shares his fate. David is an interesting case, for he lurks behind 1 Sam 28 as the substitute for Saul. In due course, David will substitute for Israel and for God.

Nationalization of Death

Whether death exists and in what form, or does not exist at all, remains a riddle: "They say before you die, you do not die; while you are alive, death does not exist; and after you die, death does not exist either. Before death, there is no death; and after death there is no death" (Hanh and Berrigan 2009, 7). Death is a koan. But there is general agreement that death sets persons adrift, into the domains of the buried and the realms of the forgotten. Death fractures.

Death also draws people together. The ones who pass on join the ancestors at a mythical place Polynesians call *Pulotu*: Their bodies sink into and therefore become one with Earth; the survivors gather to mourn and remember and to dedicate their dead relative to the collective memory. This connecting sentiment is present in the African poet Mazisi Kunene's "Cycle" (Soyinka 1975, 48–49). Kunene explains that ancestors and people who have died are "asleep under the ground" (like *Pulotu* for Polynesians) on which people dance during festivals. Where people dance, there the ancestors once stood and danced with and for their dreams. "They dreamed until they were tired / And handed us the tail with which we shall dance." When dancers stomp and kick up the dust in the ground, they reawaken the dreams of the ancestors. In time, dancers will join the ancestors under the ground, leaving their dreams and dust for their children and grandchildren to reawaken when they come in the future to dance. When one dies, one approaches those who are "asleep under the ground." When one dies, one leaves a point of contact for those who are to come. Dancing enables generations to connect—the dead, the living, and the coming. Death is about approaching, and it mends (weaves) across "the grounds" of memory, dreams, festivals, dusts, and bodies.

Samuel returns from death to confirm that the impending death of Saul will fulfill YHWH's rejection of Saul. Saul's death will commit Saul to Samuel. *Me voici!* There is no mention in this story of whether YHWH too meets death, but as far as Saul is concerned, the silent YHWH is as good as dead. Samuel does not hold that position, for he sticks to YHWH, even beyond death.

"Tomorrow your sons and you will be *with me*," announces Samuel. Returned from death, Samuel represents death, and it is toward him (qua death) that Saul is now moving. YHWH has broken up with Saul, but Saul is moving toward Samuel. He came to Endor seeking Samuel, and the next day he will be with Samuel. Saul will not come alone. His sons will die with him on the same day, and "YHWH will also deliver the Israelite forces into the hands of the Philistines" (1 Sam 28:19). It is not clear if this means that the Philistines will enslave or kill the Israelites, but Saul's death will indeed affect the nation.

Saul will die because he failed to execute the wrath of YHWH against the Amalekites (1 Sam 28:18), and the Philistines will overpower the Israelites because they were backing Saul. The king's death is entangled with the nation's life. "The king whom the Israelites had demanded to lead them in battle (1 Sam. 8:20) would drag them instead to their defeat. Samuel did not tell Saul what to do because there was nothing he *could* do—the message from the grave was grave indeed!" (Pigott 1998, 439). The king's wrongdoing will be costly to the Israelites.

In life and in death, Saul's fate entwines with the life of the nation. The wrongdoing that resulted in his rejection by God and Samuel was prompted by his concern for the harmony of the people: "I did wrong to transgress the LORD's command and your instructions; but I was afraid of the troops and I yielded to them" (1 Sam 15:24 NJPS). Afraid that the people might disperse, Saul favored the people over YHWH and Samuel.

Does Saul, in the end, put his personal agenda ahead of the interest of the people? Paul Borgman (2008, 62) thinks so: "Saul is surely doomed because of his handling of fear.... Saul's quest for certainty through the medium stems from fear regarding his own status rather than care for Israel: *am I not the king, am I not to be sustained as king and admired above all others?*" (emphasis original). Even if Borgman is correct that Saul was self-centered and that he was seeking to break away from Israel, Samuel will not allow it. Samuel ties Saul's death to the submission of the Israelites to the Philistines. They rise and fall together.

YHWH turned from Saul, but Saul will not let YHWH go. He does not leave Samuel alone either. Saul does not want to let YHWH or Samuel break away. Along similar lines, Samuel will not let Saul break away from Israel. The lives of these characters interweave so tightly that the death of one affects the others, and the people around them. The impending death of Saul is nationalized; his life and death intersect with the nation. Nationhood-ing. Transference.

Nationhood Assault

The strife in 1 Sam 28, at one level, is an international one: Philistia against Israel. The king of each represents his nation, but the two nations do not come to blows in 1 Sam 28. Rather, 1 Sam 28 tells of the struggles of Saul, from whom the throne of his nation has been torn. He is not the true king of Israel; according to Samuel, David is the real king. This is the internal site of the strife.

But there is no confrontation between Saul and David in 1 Sam 28 either. David, on the other hand—and this ties Israel's internal affair to its international one—is backing the Philistine king. David is the king of Israel; David sleeps with the enemy; David is enemy also. The personal, the public, the national, and the transnational whirl together.

Samuel returns from death to seal the rejection of Saul and thereby adds another level to the strife. Saul is also rejected *by* the other side, the side of death. The rejection of Saul is complete. He is opposed by a neighboring nation, rejected by his God, and rejected by the dead also. Saul is nationalized and at once denationalized. Who then holds and feeds Israel's interests? In other words, appealing to Judith Butler and Gayatri Spivak (2010), who sings this nation's song?

Nationhood is problematized in 1 Sam 28. The nation is under pressure from a foreign power and the leaders are in disarray, across several (positional and ideological) borders. The angry song that Samuel rises to sing is for death and disempowerment, toward ending Saul's era. The quandary herein is whether the nation ends with the demise of Saul. The narrator does not entertain this possibility, for even though the king is nationalized, the nation is not personalized. A king may die and be forgotten, and even deserted as Moses was in the wilderness, but the nation does not die with him. In other words, the product (king) may represent the process that produces it (nation), but the process cannot be reduced to the product. What then makes Israel a nation? What is the tone and rhythm of its nationhood?

The fervor of nationalism that cradles 1 Sam 28 is problematized by the ambiguity of Israel's nationhood. As such, i agree with Spivak (2010, 13, 21) "that there is no nation before nationalism" and "that imagination feeds nationalism." The problem with 1 Sam 28, then, true also with the Hebrew Bible in general, is that it presents nationalism (imagination, ideology) as if that is nationhood (state, nation). There is nationalism in 1 Sam 28, but this does not presuppose that a nation was there also. Nationalism can be free of reality.

There are border crossings in 1 Sam 28, which are significant for my reading not because those open the story up to the possibility of transnationalism but because those put this *talanoa* in the polylingual paths of traders and traitors. Crossing borders requires one to swim in the tides of tongues and risk being lost in translation, which are the realms in which mediums operate. Mediation. Translation. Negotiation.

The fact that the biblical narrator ignores how border crossings push one into a different language world (Philistia, Endor) is evidence that this narrator is deafened by the fervor of nationalism. First Samuel 28 would definitely have been different if it were told by the medium of Endor. Her *talanoa* would be less nationalist and more transitional and migrational. Voyage. Home song. Longing.

Unleashing Acceptance

It is easy to read between the lines that Saul is imprisoned by the need for acceptance, so he goes to great lengths to gain approval. Belonging. He comes looking for Samuel's approval, similar to how blacks seek the approval of whites. "As painful as it is for us to have to say this: there is but one destiny for the black man [sic]. And it is white" (Fanon 2008, xiv). The myth of whiteness is driven by the inferiority complex, which Fanon exposes and challenges at several levels. "There should be no attempt to fixate man [sic], since it is his [sic] destiny to be unleashed.... The misfortune of the man [sic] of color is having been enslaved" (205). Such is the burden of the black person, made worse by the persisting feeling that God does not care. The Zimbabwean poet Mashingaidze Gomo (2010, 46) hits the mark full on: "I think there are two gods in heaven: a god for white people who blesses them even when they are being evil to us and then there must also be a god for African people and he [sic] doesn't care what happens to us."

At one level, Saul craves acceptance. Acceptance is at no time unnecessary or unwelcome, and it is most desired during times of loneliness and struggle. But there is more for Saul in 1 Sam 28 than acceptance. He comes to Endor to demand a response from Samuel because he is not satisfied with YHWH's silence. He comes because he does not want his voice to be taken away (see Anyidoho 2011, 67). In not answering Saul, YHWH treats him as a nonsubject, as if he is among the wretched of the earth and the subalterns who cannot speak. In my reading of Saul's coming to Endor, i am led to agree that "there is not one colonized subject who at least once a day does not dream of taking the place of the colonist" (Fanon 2004, 5). So i imagine that Saul comes for a hearing, to push for an answer. Saul does not come to lie down so that Samuel would walk over him but in order to do some dealing.

Saul is a reminder of Job, who debates his traditionalist friends and demands that YHWH appear and answer his charges. Saul explains that he calls Samuel so that Samuel can tell him what he is to do (1 Sam 28:15b). Explanations like that, showing that the speaker needs the one addressed, usually draw people into *talanoa*, if they are on the same standing and if they share respect for one another. This does not work in Saul's favor because Samuel, who used to be among Israel's national bourgeoisie, is not very accepting. Samuel blasts Saul with words that are so terrifying that they floor him (1 Sam 28:20). Saul drops also because there is no strength in him, for he has not eaten all day and all night.

Samuel seems to take Saul's mission as an act of aggression, and Samuel's response is aggressive. Aggression is at the seams of this *talanoa*, even if the aggression is expressed only with words. No one raises an arm to strike another in the opposite camp. What we have is the verbal war before the physical one, and in this round, Samuel drops Saul to the ground. Samuel withholds acceptance. He is like God, who, as the Samoan poet and writer Albert Wendt (2009, 63, 116) puts it, "can be frigid (or impotent)" and "can also suffer breakdowns." Unlike Samuel, the Medium is more accepting, even if she is leading Saul on (Jobling 1998, 188).

The Medium Hosts

Darkness remains. Saul lies on the ground, and the woman comes toward him. In the beginning, she was the one whom Saul was seeking. At the end, she approaches her seeker. She moves to Saul because she sees that he is disturbed. She did not see him being disturbed when he first came. He became disturbed after Samuel had words with him.

The woman medium addresses Saul out of care. She suggests that he eat what she will prepare. She wants Saul to put his life in her hands, as she has put hers in his hands. She offers hospitality and the opportunity to gain strength. Become strong. Be upstanding. He refuses. His men join in, and he gives in to them. He rises. Sits on the couch. She butchers a fatted calf, kneads flour, bakes bread, and places those before Saul and his men. She is not wicked as people imagine a witch to be (so Pigott 1998, 435, 440). "At the level of plot this simple act of hospitality of a proscribed woman to her authoritative king is arguably the kindest gesture we have seen extended to Saul" (Green 2003, 112).

Having partaken of the woman's generosity, Saul and his men again, silently, melt into the darkness.

Works Cited

Anyidoho, Kofi. 2011. *The Place We Call Home and Other Poems*. Banbury: Ayebia Clarke.

Borgman, Paul. 2008. *David, Saul, and God: Rediscovering an Ancient Story*. New York: Oxford University Press.

Butler, Judith, and Gayatri Chakravorty Spivak. 2010. *Who Sings the Nation-State? Language, Politics, Belonging*. Calcutta: Seagull.

Fanon, Frantz. 2004. *The Wretched of the Earth*. Translated by Richard Philcox. New York: Grove.
———. 2008. *Black Skin, White Masks*. Translated by Richard Philcox. New York: Grove.
Figiel, Sia. 1996. *Where We Once Belonged*. Auckland: Pasifika.
———. 1999. *They Who Do Not Grieve*. Auckland: Vintage.
Gomo, Mashingaidze. 2010. *A Fine Madness*. Banbury: Ayebia Clarke.
Green, Barbara. 2003. *King Saul's Asking*. Collegeville, MN: Liturgical Press.
Gunn, David M. 1980. *The Fate of King Saul: An Interpretation of a Biblical Story*. Sheffield: JSOT Press.
Hanh, Thich Nhat, and Daniel Berrigan. 2009. *The Raft Is Not the Shore: Towards a World Where Spirituality and Politics Meet*. Mumbai: Jaico.
Havea, Jione. 2007. "Pleasure and Grief, in Violence." Pages 71–84 in *Religion and Violence*. Edited by Jonathan Inkpin. Adelaide: ATF.
———. 2010a. "The Politics of Climate Change, a Talanoa from Oceania." *International Journal of Public Theology* 4:345–55.
———, ed. 2010b. *Talanoa Ripples: Across Borders, Cultures, Disciplines*. Albany, NZ: Massey University; Auckland: Masilamea Press.
———. 2011. "Return, Medium of Endor." Pages 255–66 in *Out of Place: Doing Theology in Crosscultural Brinks*. Edited by Jione Havea and Clive Pearson. London: Equinox.
Jobling, David. 1998. *1 Samuel*. Berit Olam. Collegeville, MN: Liturgical Press.
Moala, Kalafi. 2011. *Tonga: Tale of Two Kingdoms*. Nuku'alofa: Taimi.
Nicole, Robert. 2001. *The Word, the Pen, and the Pistol: Literature and Power in Tahiti*. Albany: State University of New York Press.
Pigott, Susan M. 1998. "1 Samuel 28: Saul and the *Not* So Wicked Witch of Endor." *RevExp* 95:435–44.
Smith, Linda Tuhiwai. 2008. *Decolonizing Methodologies: Research and Indigenous Peoples*. Dunedin: University of Otago Press.
Soyinka, Wole, ed. 1975 *Poems of Black Africa*. Ibadan: Heinemann.
Spivak, Gayatri Chakravorty. 2010. *Nationalism and the Imagination*. Calcutta: Seagull.
Trible, Phyllis. 1984. *Texts of Terror: Literary-Feminist Readings of Biblical Narratives*. Philadelphia: Fortress.
Walker, Alice. 2010. *Hard Times Require Furious Dancing*. Novato: New World Library.

Wendt, Albert. 2009. *The Adventures of Vela*. Honolulu: University of Hawai'i Press.

Haunting Silence:
Trauma, Failed Orality,
and Mark's Messianic Secret

Tat-siong Benny Liew

The ending of Mark's story of Jesus is "one of the most widely-known problems in New Testament studies, involving both text-critical and exegetical issues" (Hurtado 2009, 427). My teacher in graduate studies, Mary Ann Tolbert, has argued that the seemingly disappointing and tragic ending— with the women disciples leaving the empty tomb in fear and in silence after they were told to tell Jesus's male disciples the good news of Jesus's resurrection and a future reunion with them in Galilee in 16:7–8[1]—is Mark's rhetorical ploy to put the ball on the court of Markan listeners and readers, since they are the only ones who have heard Mark's story of Jesus, including the news of Jesus's resurrection, but have not yet failed, as the disciples, both male and female, have all seemed to have done within Mark's story world because of their fear of persecution, suffering, and death (Tolbert 1989, 288–99). The hope—and the burden—is now on us as readers or listeners. We have to decide if we will tell the story of Jesus with courage or tremble and flee in fear and in silence. Greco-Roman rhetoric when Mark was written, Tolbert argues, was meant to persuade listeners and readers into action, and Mark's ending, according to Tolbert, is an effective use and illustration of this.

According to Joel F. Williams (1999, 26–35), there were basically five main scholarly positions regarding Mark's ending by the end of the twentieth century: (1) "a positive response to the miraculous"; (2) "a disaster for

---

[1]. Like most scholars, I assume here that Mark should end at 16:8. For a helpful discussion of the issues and debates about where Mark ends, see Lincoln 1989 and Williams 1999, 22–26.

the disciples"; (3) "an irony to provoke reflection"; (4) "an unstated apostolic commission"; and (5) "a balance between promise and failure." Obviously, an interpretation of a particular scholar may involve a combination of these positions, as Tolbert's does. Scholars are still trying to come up with alternatives to make sense of Mark's ending in the twenty-first century.

More recently, for example, Larry Hurtado has attempted to rehabilitate these women disciples in Mark, though his suggestion is in many ways a resurrection of an argument made by the China-born Anglican priest and scholar Charles Moule (1955–1956) over half a century ago. The argument is that Mark's final verse should not be read as the women not speaking to anyone but should be read instead as the women not speaking to anyone *else*. That is, not anyone besides those whom they were told to tell in Mark 16:7 by the mysterious figure at the empty tomb, namely, the disciples and Peter. Hurtado supports this by referring to two earlier incidents in Mark, where Jesus seemingly also commands to silence the leper he healed in 1:44 and those who saw him healing a deaf-mute in 7:36 with a phrase similar to that found in 16:8 ("say nothing to anyone" or "tell no one"). But the command turns out to be a *"restriction* on communication" rather than a "total prohibition" (Hurtado 2009, 439), because Jesus makes it clear that the cured leper should go and show himself to the priest right after this so-called command-to-silence, and Hurtado interprets the speaking in 7:36–37 as the witnesses speaking about Jesus *among* themselves and not to people outside their small circle.

In this essay, I would like to point out a questionable assumption that underlies most of the proposals that have previously been made to read Mark's enigmatic ending and then venture to suggest yet another alternative interpretation.

Silence and Agency

What many of these previous readings—whether by Tolbert, Moule, Hurtado, or myself (Liew 1999, 142–43)—agree on, despite their different emphases and nuances, is the assumption that silence equals failure. This explains why the only way for Hurtado to rehabilitate the women at the empty tomb is to dispute their silence and to suggest that they have indeed spoken and spoken up to someone. This assumption that equates silence with failure has been shared by many in the academy, across various disciplines, and for a long time, especially those who find themselves in a marginalized situation. In one of the earliest introductions to Chinese and

Japanese American literature, Frank Chin, Jeffrey Chan, Lawson Inada, and Shawn Wong suggest that a language or a voice of their own, so to speak, would save Asian Americans from their plight of marginalization in the United States. They write:

> Language is the medium of culture and the people's sensibility, including the style of manhood.... Stunt the tongue and you have lopped off the culture and sensibility. On the simplest level, a man in any culture speaks for himself. Without a language of his own, he no longer is a man. (Chin et al. 1991, 37)

The masculinist assumption that goes along with the voice-equals-agency assumption is clear, but the latter assumption is by no means a monopoly of men. This very assumption is at least partly why Gayatri Spivak (1988) titles her famous essay about power differentials in colonial and postcolonial contexts, "Can the Subaltern Speak?" Not speaking is to be mute, without voice, without agency, and without fight. This assumption does not consider, however, that there may be different manners of and causes for silence. Stephen Dedalus, the protagonist in James Joyce's (2007, 218) very first novel, claims, for example, that he has three weapons to protect himself as he leaves Ireland: "silence, exile and cunning." Writing from a different context and culture, King-kok Cheung (1993) has also argued that silence for many Asian American women writers can actually be articulate and full of force. "Rather than being signs of inferiority," Rey Chow (2014, 15) writes more recently about colonial and postcolonial experience, "aphasia [which, for Chow, includes the loss of voice] ... can be conceptualized anew as forms of unveiling, as what expose the untenability of 'proper' (and proprietary) speech as such." After all, as I have mentioned through Hurtado's work, the hero and protagonist of Mark's Gospel, Jesus, has also commanded persons to silence, an observation that was first made and made famous by William Wrede (1971) in the early twentieth century with what Wrede called the "messianic secret." In other words, we as readers may wonder if the women's silence at the end is in some way not only consistent with but also following Jesus's earlier commands to silence in Mark (Kotrosits and Taussig 2013, 15). Whether this is the case or not, it should be clear that silence in Mark's Gospel is not a single occurrence and that it could be strategic.[2] The women's silence at

---

2. For Wrede, these commands to silence by Mark's Jesus are Mark's way of cov-

Mark's ending is particularly intriguing, given the Greco-Roman cultural expectation that women, unlike men who can endure and keep things inside, are prone to emotional outburst in face of deaths—and hence the literary trope of women lamenting at funerals (Foley 2001, 19–56; Alexiou 2002). As Sophocles writes in the play *Antigone*, when a mother departs suddenly and in silence upon hearing of her son's death, "there is a weight of danger ... in [such] silence" (*Ant.* 1256).

Between Terror and Ecstasy

While I have previously read the women's silence as a failure because Mark attributes their silence to fear in 16:8 (Liew 1999, 143 n. 13), I want to emphasize now that Mark actually identifies two elements regarding the women's fear in that same verse. These two elements are *tromos* and *ekstasis* in Greek. While the words are generally translated as "terror and amazement" (NRSV), "trembling and astonishment" (ASV; NASB), "trembling and bewildered" (NIV), "terror and dread" (CEB), one can hear from even the sound of the Greek word *ekstasis* the root for the English word, *ecstasy*. However one may want to read these women's "fear," one should not miss or dismiss that what they experience at the end of Mark's story world contains also an element of joy and excitement. In fact, the Greek word for "fear" in Mark 16:8 is *phobeō*, and Anne-Marie Smith (1998, 29) defines phobia—in a book on the feminist Julia Kristeva that is subtitled "speaking the unspeakable"—as "the polarized [experience] of fusion and separation." In other words, phobia is a kind of conflicted feeling or contradictory impulse; it is a reaction to something that both attracts and alienates. Since *ekstasis* in Greek literally means "out of one's place, one's stance, or one's standing" (such as falling out of one's chair), one may say that the women's ecstatic experience at the empty tomb disturbs, disorients,

---

ering up the "secret" that the historical Jesus really did not understand or proclaim himself as the Messiah during his life on earth. Since Wrede, one particularly popular explanation for these commands to silence by the Markan Jesus is to see it as part of this Jesus's need to correct a pervasive or even perverse attraction to or desire for glory among his potential followers. See, for example, Tolbert 1989, 227–30 and Martin 2012, 81–88.

    I am glad to see that scholars have begun to read silence in a more nuanced way. For an example in the study of classics, see Lardinois and McClure 2001; for an example in New Testament studies, see Dinkler 2013.

or even displaces them with something even akin to an out-of-the-body experience or a sense of self-transcendence. Such an exhilarating experience can be so overpowering that it becomes alienating and terrorizing because it shows them something alien within themselves. Traditionally, this self-transcendence that is both exciting and estranging and hence made unspeakable is often read as nothing less and nothing more than the mysterious and supernatural resurrection from death that the women learn about Jesus and perhaps see as a promise for themselves. After all, the only other time when Mark uses the word *ekstasis* is in his fifth chapter, when Jesus raises the twelve-year-old daughter of Jairus after a diagnosis of death (Mark 5:42). The fear and silence of the women at the tomb, in this reading, is not because they are failing as disciples but rather because they are grasping something significant about Jesus and possibly about themselves.

With the word "corpse" (*ptōma*) in 15:45, Mark is adamant that Jesus is really dead because of his crucifixion (Hurtado 2009, 432). A crucified but raised corpse, as it is being related to the women disciples in 16:6, is akin to a ghost or a zombie in contemporary English. It is what Slavoj Žižek (2006, 47) calls the "undead," a "third domain" that is "neither alive nor dead" and hence undermines the distinction between the two in a "monstrous" manner. Jesus's death and resurrection in Mark means that he is now both beneath and beyond what is generally considered human life and existence. This third domain of being both beneath and beyond might explain the mixture of terror and ecstasy that Mark ascribes to the women at the empty tomb.[3]

The Uncanny and the Unhomely Haunting of Colonial Trauma

However, I would like to venture a reading of this ending that goes beyond this reading about resurrection and amazement. Žižek's "undead" also brings to mind Sigmund Freud's (1953–1974, 17:219–52) famous discussion of the "uncanny," which actually ends with a brief mention of silence

---

3. This is, for example, in many ways the argument Timothy Dwyer (1996) makes, namely, Jesus's life and resurrection in Mark represents the in-breaking of God's kingdom, which understandably leads to both awe and fear—and often also silence—on the part of human beings. See also the explanation and references regarding those who read the women's silence as "a positive response to the miraculous" in Williams 1999, 26–28.

(17:252). Starting from a more general understanding of the uncanny as an affect related to fear because of experiencing something that is simultaneously "foreign" and "familiar" and hence the uncanny as something that defies categorization and brings about a disturbing sense of "intellectual uncertainty," Freud ends by attributing this uncanny experience more specifically to the return of an infantile fear of or primitive desire for a magical, animistic world that was once familiar but has become foreign because of repression. Homi K. Bhabha (1997) provides a more literal translation for the German term Freud uses for "uncanny" (*unheimlich*)—"unhomely"—to propose that seeing something unfamiliar at home or in the family, or realizing something unknown in what you think you know intimately, is actually most unsettling. Juliana Chang (2012, 18) further relates Bhabha's "unhomely" to colonization, as "colonization is a condition in which the familiarity of home is made strange, while the strange is made intimate and domestic," and hence how imperial secrets are often hidden in domestic spaces.

Domestic spaces in the Greco-Roman world from which Mark came were, of course, assumed to be feminine spaces that supposedly belonged to women. If Hurtado (2009, 431–32) is correct that Mark features the women disciples as observers or witnesses of Jesus's death, Jesus's burial place, and Jesus's empty tomb, then is it thinkable that these women are chosen for this role because, as representatives of domesticity, family, and intimacy, what they are observing or witnessing, and what is hidden and unspoken among them, are the dirty secrets of imperialism or the symptoms of colonial ills?[4]

Since the late 1990s, scholarship has begun to take Roman colonization seriously in talking and thinking about the New Testament's first-century context. Bhabha (1994) is arguably best known for challenging and deconstructing the fantasy of coherence, unity, and harmony that empires like to proclaim and promote. Part of this fantasy for the Roman Empire was that of *pax Romana*, on which New Testament scholars are increasingly working and writing (e.g., Wengst 1987; Elliott 1994; Carter 2000; Horsley 2003).[5] With its claim of and on peace, *pax Romana* functioned

---

4. A related emphasis has been made by Ann Laura Stoler, who sees matters of intimacy and sentiment (so people's domestic, familial, sexual, and affective lives) as key to the operation of colonial power. See, for example, Stoler 1995, 2002, 2006a, 2009.

5. It seems like scholars within the camp of what Stephen D. Moore (2006, 17–19)

partly to justify Rome's imperial hegemony and to cover up the violence and discord that it had stirred up or the countless deaths and losses that it had caused. These deaths and losses, however, could not be blocked out so easily. In his discussion of the uncanny as a repression that returns or recurs, Freud (1953–1974: 17:228, 233, 241–42, 245) talks about "a phantom of horror," "a doll which seems to be alive," "return of the dead … and ghosts," "the dead … becom[ing] visible as spirits," a "table that causes ghostly crocodiles to haunt [a] place," and "a haunted house." Jacques Derrida (1994) and Avery Gordon (2008) have done much to popularize the idea of haunting within the academy (e.g., Cho 2008; Parham 2009; Schwab 2010; Blanco and Peeren 2010). Haunting disrupts a linear understanding of time that divides the past, the present, and the future. Haunting, like a ghostly figure, could be understood as a presence that is ironically marked by absence and lack. Haunting has to do with ghostly remains, remainders, and reminders that disrupt the very order that works to destroy and preclude them; it has to do with traumatic experiences or traumatic memories that people do not want to remember, prefer to disavow, yet cannot forget. *Pax Romana*? As Ann Laura Stoler (2006b, 1) writes in her introduction to the edited volume, *Haunted By Empire*, "To be haunted is to be frequented by and possessed by a force that not always bears a proper name."

With the turn to affect in the larger world of humanities, New Testament scholars have also begun to read Mark in terms of trauma, pain, and haunting.[6] Focusing on how the Gospel of Mark deals with (1) Jesus's relationship with his biological family and unfaithful disciples; (2) the First Jewish-Roman War; (3) money through episodes about the rich young

---

calls "empire studies" tend to refer to this term, *pax Romana*, much more often in their work than those who engage postcolonial theory to read the New Testament within the context of Roman colonization. This is, of course, not to say that the latter group never uses this term in their work, but only that they tend to give it a passing reference. Moore himself, for example, mentions the term *pax Romana* only one time in the same book where he makes the differentiation between "empire studies" and "postcolonial readings" within New Testament studies (see Moore 2006, 101).

6. For examples of scholarship on affect in the humanities, see Tomkins 1995; Sedgwick 2003; Ahmed 2004; Brennan 2004; Gregg and Seigworth 2010. For the use of affect theory in biblical studies, see Koosed and Moore 2014. I should acknowledge also an early attempt by Laura E. Donaldson to read the "spirit-possessed" daughter of the Syro-Phoenician woman in Mark 7:24–30 and of the Canaanite woman in Matt 15:21–28 through the medium of Endor in 1 Sam 28:3–25 and the concept of haunting; see Donaldson 2005.

ruler, Jesus's cleansing of the temple, and the widow's offering; and (4) the end of times or the end time, Maia Kotrosits and Hal Taussig suggest that Mark does not romantically resolve trauma. Instead, Mark gives us a "reparative" but realistic picture of how one may live with inevitable loss and with widespread pain by remaining open to life's mystery and "diffuse goodness" with "fear and amazement."[7] For Kotrosits and Taussig, Mark's story or memory of Jesus is less about masculine mastery and more about childlike vulnerability. Mark, for them, is not an "answer" to but a "phenomenology" of loss and trauma, and how these experiences "haun[t] and disorien[t] us ... [and] creat[e] in us a sense of unknowing" (Kotrosits and Taussig 2013, 3, 7, 42). After all, the centurion's pronouncement of Jesus as "truly the son of God" toward the gospel's end (Mark 15:39) contains more ambiguity and irony than certainty, especially since the women at the empty tomb never deliver the message of Jesus's resurrection, and the resurrected Jesus does not appear in Mark (Kotrosits and Taussig 2013, 12–13, 34).[8] Because of their silence, these women are at least fallible if not exactly failed disciples in the eyes of Kotrosits and Taussig, though Kotrosits and Taussig also emphasize in the context of suffering and healing that silence may result from a mixture of fear and wonder (101–3, 150).

Reading from her location as not only a racialized Asian woman but also a nonnative speaker of English, Jin Young Choi (2015) argues that Markan discipleship has less to do with knowledge about Jesus's identity or about a messianic secret and more to do with encountering and perceiving a mystery that cannot be mastered. The mystery, for Choi, is a traumatic and thus haunting cultural memory of colonized subjects—as evidenced by Mark's identification of Jesus as a "ghost" (Mark 6:45–52) and by Mark's depiction of Jesus as present in absence through the empty tomb (Mark 16:1–8)—that demands from its readers not necessarily some kind of head knowledge but a perceptive and ethical response. This emphasis on mystery implies for Choi that incomprehension in Mark should be read as a

---

7. The word "reparative," as Kotrosits and Taussig (2013, 153) explain, is used by Eve Kosofsky Sedgwick to communicate a performance of hope; for Sedgwick (2003, 123–52), the practice of reparation is itself the hope.

8. Kotrosits and Taussig also point to how the story about the woman who anoints Jesus during Mark's passion narrative (Mark 14:3–9) seems to distract readers away from Jesus. This, for them, may work to relativize Jesus and his deeds as not being necessarily more important than those of many nameless and forgotten people in history (Kotrosits and Taussig 2013, 35–36).

feature to underscore the nature of a mystery rather than as a failure, just as silence might signify a different form of agency rather than its absence. Choi (2015, 55) proposes that gendered subalterns and "linguistic others" like herself, though often silenced in public, often do perceive and pass on their understanding through their bodies. This visceral response or relation, embodied improvisation, experiential understanding, or lived truth is for Choi a subversive form of speaking, which Choi also detects as true for certain minor or marginalized characters in Mark's Gospel, especially the Syro-Phoenician woman (Mark 7:24–30) and the deaf and mute person who encounters Jesus (Mark 7:31–37). For Choi, the mystery of social trauma is itself a form of coded language of colonized people.

Between Trauma and Haunting

Let me follow up on these two recent and provocative readings of Mark by theorizing trauma and haunting further and teasing out the implications of that theorization for reading Mark, though I do so not to swear allegiance to a particular theory or theorist.[9] Gordon differentiates her understanding of haunting from not only Derrida's (1994, 10) "hauntology" but also trauma. For Gordon (2011, 2), haunting is an awareness or animation of some violent and abusive system that is or can no longer be invisible or unknown; it points therefore to the incompleteness of obliteration, obscuration, or repression on the part of the system of power. Gordon is adamant that this incomplete "containment and repression" of violence means that "haunting, unlike trauma by contrast, is distinctive for producing a something-to-be-done" (2). Haunting's "something-to-be-done" signifies an "emergent state" that contests the future by recognizing what was repressed in the past or what has become ghostly in the present, while trauma is a "deeply regressive and repressive state" that keeps one stuck in the past and its endless repetitions in the present (3–4). Gordon is also clear that this "something-to-be-done" goes beyond Derrida's epistemological emphasis on "the limits of knowledge" with its focus on the "praxis, decision, action, responsibility" (7) of people who, with what she calls

---

9. Note that Kotrosits and Taussig never mention the work of either Derrida or Gordon; while Choi does have Gordon's work listed on her bibliography, her use of it is limited to three footnote citations, all of which contain no comment or elaboration. Similarly, Choi (2015, 83) has only one brief mention of Derrida's work on hauntology by way of Gayatri Chakravorty Spivak's feminist critique of Derrida.

"complex personhood" (2008, 4–5), live and carry on the urgent but slow work of resistance and emancipation regardless of what is pronounced or prohibited by the system of power.[10]

According to Gordon, then, in contrast to her haunting that points to alternative knowledge or alternative way of living that is always already present but is being subjugated or unacknowledged (often because such alternatives are associated with oppressed groups in a society with unequal or uneven power structures), Derrida's hauntology points to the need to hold knowledge loosely and to remain open to what is yet unknowable to us. Hauntology rejects epistemological and intellectual certainty regarding the other and the past because of what may yet come in the future. Like a ghost or a specter, the other, the past, or an other from the past (including one who has died) may disrupt our present and what we think we know of the future. The difference, therefore, lies in emphasizing what is unknown (Derrida) and what is unacknowledged (Gordon). Despite this difference, both Derrida and Gordon use the figure of the ghost to call us to an ethical response to the other.[11]

While Gordon's haunting tends to emphasize a ghostly visibility,[12] trauma has more to do with inarticulability or failed orality in Freud's exploration. Freud himself struggled to articulate his exploration of trauma through three different but equally enigmatic forays.[13] In *Studies on Hys-*

---

10. Using the phrase "carrying on regardless" from Raymond Williams, Gordon (2011, 7–17) turns to illustrate what she means by haunting and by "something-to-be-done" through how prisoners "enslaved" in the industrial prison complex of the United States "redeem time" while "serving time" by acting as if they are free even or especially when they are not.

11. Reading Taussig and Kotrosits as well as Choi with this theoretical background, one may see that Taussig and Kotrosit's emphasis on mystery is closer to Derrida's unknown or unknowing, while Choi's emphasis on mystery is closer to Gordon's unacknowledged or unrecognized.

12. I say "tends to" because Gordon (2011, 3) does state in her theorization of haunting that "when the repression isn't working anymore the trouble that results creates conditions that demand re-narrativization." In other words, Gordon's haunting as a demand for action is by no means exclusively focused on sight. At the same time, Gordon seems to fall into the trap of equating articulation with action, since her reference to "conditions that demand re-narrativization" is quickly followed by "conditions that also invite action" (3).

13. Note that Freud never appears in the work of Taussig and Kotrosits; neither does he appear in the bibliography of Choi's book. My reading of Freud's work on trauma here is greatly indebted to the work of James Berger (1999, 20–29, esp. 22–23).

teria, Freud (1953–1974, 2:3–305) first suggested that an overwhelming event, though seemingly forgotten, would return in the form of not only repetitive but also compulsive behaviors, only to conclude that such neurotic symptoms were caused by repressed drives and desires rather than a severely distressing and traumatic experience. Next, in *Beyond the Pleasure Principle*, which started with treatment of World War I veterans and their repeated nightmares, Freud (1953–1974, 18:7–64) again shifted his emphasis from trauma to a "biological urge" that he called the "death drive." Finally, in *Moses and Monotheism*, Freud's (1953–1974, 23:7–137) overarching idea of history as a complicated web of traumas in which a catastrophe is repressed but returns and refashions itself and other catastrophes is again layered over by a mythical Oedipus complex. As Carol Delaney (1998, 190) aptly observes regarding what she calls the "last major study" of Freud:

> The book ... is not written in his pellucid style, and it is extremely repetitive. That, in itself, is significant ... for [Freud] felt that repetitions often pointed to an unresolved issue of obsessive concern.

In every turn and return, Freud's attempts to voice memories of historical traumas seem to be reduced to or reconstructed into language of universal drive or biological determination. Memory of trauma is failed orality that refuses to be spoken even or especially when it refuses to be forgotten. Freud's trace of this failed orality would resurface in his comparison of melancholia or unresolved mourning—that is, the inability to accept or overcome a loss—to a "swallowing" that chokes the diner. Traumatic memories as something you will not let go but hold on to, even or especially when those memories are fragmented, will lead to oral failures in more than one sense: your mouth will find it difficult to not only find the words but also feed yourself on food.

Rather than seeing Freud's failed orality (trauma) and Gordon's ghostly visibility (haunting) as polar opposites or fully separable stages, I want to emphasize that the relations between them are best depicted with a Venn diagram that allows for not only overlaps but also a nonlinear dynamic. After all, Gordon (2008, xvi; 2011, 2) admits that trauma may be a part of or a cause for haunting, but I would argue that haunting can also be a part of or a cause for trauma. Gordon's haunting, like Derrida's hauntology and Sigmund Freud's trauma, also sees time not in terms of a steady and straightforward progression from the past to the present and then the future, as her references to Walter Benjamin's "Theses on the Philosophy of History" and George Marcus's "historical alternatives" show (Gordon 2011, 18 n. 10, 5–7). In addition, Gordon herself, in an expression of agreement with Raymond Williams, suggests that "a certain melancholy ... is bound to the work of carrying on regardless" (Gordon 2011, 8) or to her own understanding of haunting. Melancholy, as I have just mentioned, is Freud's symptom for unresolved trauma; it therefore shows, given Gordon's specific mention of it, both what marks and connects trauma and Gordon's haunting. Despite its twists and turns, failed orality in Freud's convoluted struggle to look into trauma is rather articulate, for its repetitious resurfacing represents, as Gordon's haunting suggests, a stubborn demand or even an imperative for reckoning and for justice that will never rest or go away. Trauma, as Freud shows, will only keep coming back in different forms because, as Gordon's (2011, 5–6) "carrying on regardless" suggests, there is no closure or utopian resolution. For both Freud's trauma and Gordon's haunting, the need to keep on trying to say what you experienced or practice what you see is equally persistent if not necessarily perpetual.

Unfortunately, Gordon seems to have mistaken Freud's muffled or muddled message about trauma, or what Anne-Marie Smith calls "speaking the unspeakable" and what Annie Rogers (2006) calls the "hidden language" of "the unsayable," as silence and hence, like so many scholars before her, a lack of action. In contrast, then, to her animating and action-oriented haunting, this "inaction" for Gordon is also related to the invisibility and unknowability of not only an abusive system but also her reading of trauma as an inadequate exposition. However, trauma has been theorized in terms of a "complex relation between knowing and not knowing" (Caruth 1996, 3). Or, in the words of Derrida's (1994, 10) exploration of hauntology, it is about "*comprehend*[ing] ... incomprehensively" (emphasis original), so there is no epistemologically certain and utopian illusion (1999, 246–51). What I am getting at is that in her emphasis on being aware of ongoing but disavowed abuse or past but not forgotten violence, Gordon has herself forgotten that partial knowing is still knowing, just as wordless language (like body language) can still communicate. This is unfortunate, because a ghost, which she uses to concretize her thoughts on haunting, is, as she repeatedly acknowledges, both present and absent (2008, 16–17); in other words, a ghostly presence is neither a full presence nor a complete absence.

Finally, Gordon's (2011, 3, 5, 7) differentiation between trauma as "witness" and haunting as "action" falls into the trap of a binary logic.

Witnessing is not only an action itself but can also be a re-action to incriminate and stop—rather than, as Gordon (2011, 5) claims, to "justify"—one's violent abusers. What Cathy Caruth says of her reading of and book on trauma is really not that different from Gordon's praxis-oriented haunting that produces a "something-to-be-done." Caruth writes:

> It is this plea by an other who is asking to be seen or heard, this call by which the other *commands* us to awaken (to awaken, indeed, to a burning), that resonates in different ways throughout the texts this book attempts to read, and which, in this book's understanding, constitutes the new mode of reading and of listening that *both the language of trauma, and the silence of its mute repetition of suffering, profoundly and imperatively demand*. (1996, 9 [emphasis added])[14]

Although Gordon does not mention this, her critique of Derrida's hauntology as merely epistemological brings to mind Marx's famous declaration: "The philosophers have only *interpreted* the world, in various ways; the point is to *change* it" (Marx and Engels 1968, 30). Her work on haunting also echoes faintly, albeit on a more subversive and affective register, Marx's words that "tradition of all the dead generations weighs like a nightmare on the brain of the living" (Marx and Engels 1968, 97). What Gordon (2011, 1–2) does mention is her background in and continual commitment to Marxism (as shown by her reference to the works of Marcus and Raymond Williams), even though she faults Marx for his turning a blind eye to racism. No one can accuse Gordon of being a straitjacket sociologist or a vulgar Marxist, but I cannot help but wonder if Gordon's dismissal of Freud's work on trauma has something to do with the tendency to reject or at least rebuff Freud and the field of psychoanalysis among not only some of her colleagues in sociology but also some of her fellow Marxists.[15] What I hope to show is that Marxist and psychoana-

---

14. Caruth's (1996, 93–107) "burning" foreshadows her reading of an episode Freud addresses in *The Interpretation of Dreams* as an example of how trauma expresses itself in convoluted ways. In this episode, a grieving father who had just lost his son dreamed that his son came to wake him up because his son was being burnt by fire. When the father woke up, he found that the elderly person who was supposed to watch over his son's corpse in the next room had fallen asleep, and one of the tall candles had fallen on his son's dead body (Freud 1953–1974, 5:509–10).

15. For one reading of how scholars of humanities and those of the social sciences diverge in their openness to and use of psychoanalysis, see Wiegman 2012, 22. For

lytical studies are not mutually exclusive by definition; in fact, they can address similar concerns, inform each other, and, in the case of Mark, work together to help shed new light on reading Mark's ending in Mark's colonial context.

Jouissance and the Empty Tomb

The women at the empty tomb at the end of Mark's Gospel witness something and are told to tell a story that is so traumatic, so haunting—that is, again, so excruciating *and* exhilarating—that they leave in silence. The words that Gordon uses for haunting cannot be more suitable to help describe what is being implied in this closing scene of Mark's Gospel.

> Haunting was precisely the domain of turmoil and trouble, that moment … when things are not in the assigned places, when the cracks and the rigging are exposed, when the people who are meant to be invisible show up without any sign of leaving, when disturbed feelings won't go away. (Gordon 2011, 2)

When the women arrive with spices at Jesus's tomb after the Sabbath to, Mark tells us clearly, anoint Jesus's lifeless body, they find out of their "assigned places" not only the large stone in front of the tomb but also the corpse of Jesus that is supposed to be inside the tomb (Mark 16:1–6). Also out of place in Jesus's tomb is this mysterious youth in a white robe; his presence and words about Jesus dis-close the reality about Jesus: he has left the tomb to go to Galilee (Mark 16:5–7). Jesus, despite the trauma of Roman colonization and crucifixion—or, rather, like trauma—departs only to return unexpectedly to not only a colonized world but also specifically Galilee, where he first came to proclaim God's gospel and galvanize a movement (Mark 1:9, 14, 16, 39; 3:7). Although or perhaps because the resurrected Jesus does not actually appear, what we have in Mark is "the experience of the non-present, of the non-living present in the living present, of that which lives on" (Derrida 1999, 254)—with "present" here taking on both a temporal and a spatial connotation, since Jesus, having passed away, is supposedly of the past and the supposedly risen Jesus

---

an early attempt to combine Marxist politics and Freudian psychoanalysis that also mentions the obstacles that such a combination may present to hard-core Marxists, see Fenichel 1967.

does not show up. In Mark, the resurrected life or the afterlife of Jesus is only conveyed and sustained by the words of the mysterious youth at the empty tomb.

Trauma and memories of trauma defy time, death, and burial; they live on in different forms to animate the past, the present, and the future, since the youth gives the women a promise of what is to come in Galilee ("he [Jesus] is going ahead of you in Galilee," Mark 16:7). The women, to use Gordon's words again, are clearly "trouble[d]" and "disturbed," but Gordon's (2011, 3) point about "what will happen [with haunting] … is not given in advance" may also apply to the women's fear, flight, and silence. What I want to emphasize here is not the failed discipleship of the women; instead, their silence or failed orality serves to underline and underscore not only the traumatic gravity of the Jesus story but also the women's understanding that they cannot really or ever totally understand the level of that gravity or the lingering, open-ended effects and affects of their connection with that trauma. Jesus's story has become their story; that is to say, their (colonial) trauma is bound up with Jesus's. The women's leaving the empty tomb in silence is "not to keep a word in reserve or withdrawn," but because secrets, especially those regarding (colonial) trauma, are "no more in speech than foreign to speech" (Derrida 1995b, 27). The women at the tomb, I will argue, occupy the overlapping space of a Venn diagram; in terms of Gordon's delineation and differentiation, they find themselves in between—or in the middle of both—trauma and haunting.

Following Caruth's (1996, 7) theorization that trauma involves "the oscillation between *a crisis of death* and the correlative *crisis of life*" (emphasis original), Shelly Rambo (2010, 25–26) provocatively describes trauma as not only "a dissolution of the death-life boundary" but also "a crisis in the middle." The resurrection of Jesus means that he is both dead and alive, while the fact that this resurrection is only reported by a youth means that Jesus is also both present and absent. The women at the empty tomb are caught in the middle of this crisis as they are asked to serve *by* and serve *like* the mysterious youth as middle persons to relate a message from the resurrected Jesus to Jesus's disciples, but they also find themselves in the crisis of another kind of middle: they experience, again according to Mark, something between terror and ecstasy (Mark 16:8).

Lacanian psychoanalysis has a term for the mixed or in-between experience of these women: *jouissance*. *Jouissance*, for Lacan, refers to a traumatic enjoyment that involves both pain and pleasure, suffering and satisfaction (Borch-Jacobsen 1991, 93–96; Homer 2005, 89–91). Rather than seeing these experiences (and I would add, fear and ecstasy) as binary or antithetical opposites that are mutually exclusive, *jouissance* signifies a doubleness that infuses energy.[16] Chang's (2012, 63) helpful and nuanced explanation of Lacan's *jouissance* points to two emphases that are most important to my reading of Mark's ending. First, Lacan sees *jouissance* as an experience that is so intense that it causes language to collapse and words to fail. Once again, therefore, *jouissance* as traumatic enjoyment involves silence or failed orality. Second, Lacan's *jouissance* collapses law and meaning, with law and meaning here referring to the sense of coherence that we get from a fantasy that we also call reality. *Jouissance* might be without speech, yet it signifies powerfully for Lacan what lies outside language and law, namely, the contradictions, fragmentations, and incoherence that are often undercover but actually undergird the foundation of a society and the subjects or subjectivities that make up that society.

What the women experience at the end of Mark's Gospel, let me suggest, is the *jouissance*, or the unspeakable traumatic enjoyment in the recognition that a tomb, with or without a corpse, cannot prevent Jesus and Jesus's story from being kept alive in *this* world, and that story's effectual bursting of the *pax Romana* bubble. Instead of peace, prosperity, and life, *pax Romana* only signified for the colonized that they were living at the edge of death. As Tacitus reports, "The Romans rob, butcher, plunder and call it empire; and where they make a desolation, they call it peace" (*Agr.* 30).

As is well known, people in the Greco-Roman world, despite having different customs and practices, were rather concerned with having a proper burial. There were, for instance, burial clubs or associations being formed precisely because of this concern, and people joined in order to ensure for themselves a proper burial. As W. R. Halliday (1925, 60) writes, their primary function "was to provide members at death with a decent

---

16. Recalling my earlier discussion of "ecstasy" as meaning literally in the Greek "out of one's stance or standing," I would like to point to Sara Ahmed's (2004, 27) discussion of pain through the work of Elaine Scarry as a "violation or transgression of the border between inside and outside" of one's body or one's self (see also Kotrosits and Taussig 2013, 53). In other words, the line between pleasure and pain is very fine and thin indeed. Scarry (1985, 5) has also suggested, of course, that pain's "resistance to language is not simply one of its incidental or accidental attributes but is essential to what it is." Given the fine and thin line between pain and pleasure, Scarry's words about "resistance to language" are taking us to the Lacanian understanding of *jouissance*.

funeral, rescuing them from the common pit into which the bodies of the destitute were cast, and at the same time to afford the living members periodic opportunities for social reunion."

Of course, just as a burial club could perform more than one function for its members, people at the time could have had a myriad of reasons for their common concern for a proper burial, including possibly a desire to prevent the spreading of diseases or even a desire to show off one's family wealth. However, one of the undeniable reasons for this concern had to do with what a burial could do for not only the dead but also the living (Garland 1985, 21; Klauck 2003, 72; Evans 2005). A proper burial, as it was generally believed by people of that time, would honor the dead and assure their successful transit to the next world. This was for the good of the dead, as they would not be left wandering between worlds and in limbo. This was, however, also good for the living, as unburied, unsatisfied, and unsettled dead souls could be intrusive and dangerous to the human world. They could, in other words, haunt us. As Derrida (1994, 9, 120) explains, people mourn properly "by *identifying* the bodily remains and by *localizing* the dead"; that is to say, people need to "make sure that the dead will not come back: quick, do whatever is needed to keep the cadaver localized, in a safe place, decomposing right where it was inhumed, or even embalmed" (emphasis original).

Much has been written and debated about what the Romans did with the corpses of the crucified in general and that of Jesus in particular. On one side are scholars who argue that Jesus and other crucified criminals were left unburied by the Romans and exposed to carrion-eating creatures (e.g., Crossan 1994, 123–27, 152–58). A poem from the Hellenistic period, for example, talks about crucified corpses becoming "an ugly meal for birds of prey and grim scraps for dogs" (cited in Sloyan 1995, 15; see also Horace, *Ep.* 1.16.48). Eusebius also mentions how Christians in the early church complained that they "could not bury the [crucified] bodies in the earth," how "neither ... money or prayers move[d]" the Romans, "for in every possible way they kept guard as if the prevention of burial would give ... great pain" (cited in Brown 2004, 242). Other scholars would refer to Roman jurists like Ulpian or Julius Paulus to suggest that the Romans would grant corpses after capital punishments to people who sought their burials, so what we read about Joseph of Arimathea going to Pilate to ask for Jesus's corpse in Mark 15 is not unimaginable (e.g., Evans 2005). Philo, for instance, was aware of "cases when ... people who have been crucified have been taken down and their bodies delivered to their kinsfolk, because it was thought well to give them burial and allow them the ordinary rites" (Philo, *Flacc.* 10.83 [Colson]).

Suffice it to say that much of this debate is concerned with what factually happened to the corpse of Jesus, but this is not my interest here.[17] Whatever the historical facts were, I am more interested in thinking about what sense I can make of Mark's Gospel as a text. Let us remember that reasons for giving a burial could be multiple and that doing so was about not only the dead but also the living. In addition to humiliating and dishonoring the dead and hence giving pain to their associates, as Eusebius mentions, is it thinkable that the Romans were denying a proper burial to their crucified criminals, especially those accused of treason, to also promote and protect their *pax Romana* propaganda by covering up their own tracks, as victims of their acts of violence would be without a tomb to mark their presence and death and hence would disappear without a trace, so to speak? If so, Joseph of Arimathea's decision to give Jesus a tomb and a burial and the women's desire to anoint his corpse might be attempts to honor and remember Jesus's life and Jesus's death. In this case, the empty tomb and the subsequent announcement of Jesus's resurrection might signal that what was destroyed by the death-dealing Roman Empire would nevertheless be remaining, returning, remembered, and reanimated, just as these women who remain after the desertion of Jesus's male disciples are reanimated by terror and amazement and told to return to those same disciples so these male disciples would remember a message that Jesus had told them previously (Mark 14:28; 16:7). Denying someone a tomb, or emptying someone's tomb, would not be able to void or erase the evidence. Traumatic memory of colonialism cannot be repressed but "presents itself only as that which could come or come back" (Derrida 1994, 48).

The same is true if Joseph of Arimathea's burial of Jesus is an attempt to both honor Jesus and quarantine Jesus. That is to say, Joseph might be burying Jesus to ensure "a clear demarcation between the realm of life and the realm of death" (Klauck 2003, 72) and hence peace from ghostly haunting for the living. If so, the empty tomb might signify that traumatic remembrance is recalcitrant memory; it always returns to haunt and cannot be buried, locked up, hemmed in, or filed away. As Mark says about Jesus in 7:24, "He [Jesus] could not be hid" (RSV).

---

17. Note that there is also a kind of middle-ground position regarding the burial of the historical Jesus, namely, he was buried but his burial was a dishonorable one. See, for example, McCane 2004.

What is unspeakable in Mark, I argue, is these women's simultaneously unnerving and uplifting recognition—that is, their traumatic enjoyment—that there is something that exceeds even the cruelest and most traumatic discipline of the Roman Empire, as well as resists the understandable human desires to put trauma to rest through various forms of forgetfulness. Such "cultural hauntings," to borrow the words of Kathleen Brogan (1998, 4, 7), "re-create ethnic identity through an imaginative recuperation of the past" with a collective traumatic history so that what seem like "pathologies of memory take on a cultural and political significance." That significance is the Markan secret about not only the abusive and violent system behind and beneath *pax Romana* (i.e., Gordon's "unacknowledged" or buried past), but also the (re-)creation of a resistant and subversive identity against the Roman Empire (i.e., Derrida's "unknown" and open future). Memories of colonial violence and resistance to empire may be fragmented, but these painful and yet prized memories may also be encrypted and exchanged, as Gordon mentions (2011, 15), in ways akin to what James C. Scott (1992) calls "hidden transcripts."[18]

Mark's Haunting (Memory or Narrative of) Trauma

The women in Mark are told in the tomb that Jesus has been resurrected from the dead and that he will also return like a ghost or a zombie to meet his disciples in Galilee. While the time of this reunion is set beyond Mark's story world, many scholars, including myself, have read this as Mark's reference to Jesus's parousia and hence, in light of the first words that Mark has put in Jesus's mouth about time being fulfilled and God's kingdom having

---

18. Andrew P. Wilson (2004) has also used Derrida's work about realizing (1) one's own impending death as a most intimate, individual, and singular experience that both confirms and threatens one' sense of self and hence as something that is irreducible to language or shared meaning (Derrida 1995a), and (2) the possibility of letters not arriving at their intended destination and hence the potential for subversion, incompletion, and endless dissemination that is represented by the "dead letter office" (Derrida 1987) to argue for his reading of the women's fearful silence in response to the empty tomb as their awareness, through Jesus's death and the absence of Jesus's body, of an infinite lack that threatens or subverts any full confidence in or sense of selfhood, presence, and meaning. While Wilson (2004, 200, 203–4) also mentions Derrida's reference to encountering one's impending death as a "secret" and describes Mark's ending as possibly a kind of continuous mourning, his provocative reading takes into consideration neither Derrida's hauntology nor Mark's colonial context.

come near (Mark 1:15), emphasized Mark's Gospel as an "apocalyptic drama" (Duling 2003, 293–327; cf. Liew 1999). Reading Mark's ending in terms of trauma and haunting or in between trauma and haunting has led me to rethink these "foregone conclusions," to borrow the title of a book on "apocalyptic history" (Bernstein 1994). Rambo (2010, 18, 21) suggests that the enigma of trauma involves "alterations in time, body, and word" and that alterations in body are often tied to alterations in word. If we take the women's silence as their alterations in body and word, what about this alteration in time of which Rambo speaks? Freud's exploration of trauma emphasizes a nonlinear understanding of time; trauma simply will not stay put within the past and let us move on without it. For Derrida (1994, 10), a full comprehension of the end, or what he calls at times "extremity" or "extreme," is related to illusions of utopian and epistemological certainty. Likewise, Gordon's (2011, 5) haunting realigns time through a reference to George Marcus that resources for resistance may have already been buried in the past. According to Stephen J. Binz (1989, 37), the women's silence at the empty tomb does not signify an abrupt ending but is a sign that "Mark leaves his Gospel open-ended." Maria Gemma Victorino (1999, 55), however, suggests that the youth's message to the women at the tomb in Mark 16:7, with the emphasis on meeting Jesus in Galilee, means that this ending of Mark is actually a call to return to Mark's beginning. While Victorino reads this as Mark's call to his original and future readers, including Victorino herself, to read and reread the gospel so Mark's story is ongoing and dependent on the responses of its future readers, I would suggest that if one reads between the lines of Mark's Gospel through the lens of trauma and haunting, one may see Mark's Gospel as "attesting to the temporal distortions and epistemological ruptures ... that [exceed] a radical ending yet has no pure beginning" (Rambo 2010: 15).

Many Markan scholars, after all, have wondered if Mark's abrupt ending at 16:8 implies that its "real ending ... has been lost" (Williams 1999, 21; cf. Croy 2003). One can say, then, in a sense Mark's ending is "radical" because it actually has *no* ending. Not only do the women leave the empty tomb—and the stage—in silence, but Jesus, supposedly the protagonist of Mark's story (Mark 1:1), is also left off the stage despite the youth's report of his resurrection. Mark's drama of trauma closes therefore not with a sole and sharp focus on Jesus (Kotrosits and Taussig 2013, 35–36); instead, it just stops with the enigmatic youth as the only figure left on stage, and its audience is left hanging with various loose ends about the women, the disciples, and the risen Jesus. The beginning of Mark's

Gospel is also less than clear, since its focus on Jesus as the protagonist is equally diffused. The fact that Mark begins his story of Jesus with a reference to a seemingly random patchwork of Hebrew Scripture (Mark 1:1–3) means that the beginning of Jesus's good news actually has other more obscure beginnings.[19]

As Eric L. Santner (1992) and Dominick LaCapra (1994) have suggested separately, narratives of trauma may be simultaneously demonstrating *and* displacing traces of a trauma or loss. In other words, it is basically impossible for readers of traumatic memories or narratives to identify a so-called original or originating trauma. Furthermore, with or without the term "postmemory," critics such as Marianne Hirsch (2012) as well as David L. Eng and Shinhee Han (2000) have enlarged the ripple effects and affects of traumatic memory across generations: a younger generation may experience memories of trauma even if they themselves did not experience that trauma firsthand (see also Chang 2012, 24). In Nora Okja Keller's (1997) novel *Comfort Woman*, for example, the Korean American daughter is haunted by experiences of traumatic effects and affects that she does not understand, even or especially because her Korean mother never shared or spoke of a secret with her daughter: the mother was forced to provide sexual service to Japanese soldiers who occupied her country during the Second World War. As the ambivalent and recursive nature of Freud's writing on trauma describes *and* displays, memory of trauma is unspeakable and repressed but will also resurface, repeat, renew, and ripple itself through different manifestations.[20] To help us return to the idea of haunting in general and Mark's Gospel in particular, Nicolas Abraham and Maria Torok (1994, 128–29, 171–86) use the term "phantom" to refer to this transindividual and transgenerational secret that is kept alive among a group of people covertly and "when *words* fail" (emphasis original).

---

19. Most scholars have suggested that Mark 1:1–3 is a combination of Exod 23:20; Mal 3:1; and Isa 40:3. If readers take the attribution of these verses to Isaiah in Mark 1:1 literally, then they may be led by Mark onto a wild-goose chase within the book of Isaiah that would never end or result in anything, since they will never be able to locate Mark 1:2 in Isaiah.

20. Although R. Radhakrishnan (2003, 8, 49) is not addressing Freud's work in particular, what he says about "radical theory ... function[ing] as a form of forgetfulness" and how "the past has to be corrected in certain ways and remembered 'counter-mnemonically' before an egalitarian future for all can be envisioned" is nevertheless relevant to my exploration of Mark here.

The convoluted nature and the transgenerational aspect of traumatic memories open for us a window to also rethink the Gospel of Mark as a whole. Its beginning use of the term "gospel" or "good news" aside (Mark 1:1), the content and context of Mark's Gospel are both rather traumatic. It is about the crucifixion of a colonized Jew written, as most Markan scholars agree, toward the end of or right after the First Jewish-Roman War, when Jews were overwhelmingly defeated and their temple burned. This traumatic story from a traumatic time also ends, as I have been arguing, with the women's haunting and traumatic enjoyment at the empty tomb in silence and fear. Besides this telling of the women's aborted speech at the end of Mark, Mark's Gospel has itself been criticized for its language. Scholars have long commented on or lamented Mark's elementary and paratactic Greek, as Mark's sentences tend to be brief and linked by a simple Greek conjunction *kai* ("and"). Put differently, Mark's language appears to be strung together like a bare skeleton. The entire gospel itself reads like an abbreviated if not aborted speech. Trauma and memory of it are often so overwhelming and haunting that one struggles to put it into words and voice.

Traumatic haunting as failed orality and *jouissance*. Never going away or resting but returning in complicated and confusing ways, sometimes even across generations, to demand for justice as a reckoning. Why would Mark write during or shortly after the national trauma of the First Jewish-Roman War about the trauma of Jesus's crucifixion, which had happened a generation earlier? Is this story of "messianic secret," to use Wrede's terminology, that ends in silence not simultaneously expressing and displacing a trauma? The relationship between Mark's Jesus and the historical Jesus is, of course, far from being straightforward; that is to say, Mark does not "index the 'real' of history via representation" as much as it "locates the 'real' in the realm of affect" (Siddiqi 2008, 211–12). In addition, the relationship between Mark's story and Mark's history is similarly convoluted, because the locus of Mark's trauma, as I mentioned, is also fleeting, unstable, elusive, and cannot be encapsulated in a single event or in time.[21] This

---

21. While Kotrosits and Taussig (2013, 29) also discuss the First Jewish-Roman War as the context of Mark's writing, they seem to see this as Mark's "way of borrowing the language and images of a past trauma in order to make sense of the present trauma," or "provid[ing] important resources for processing pain and devastation." In other words, rather than seeing this as the convoluted working of one's (political?) unconsciousness in response to trauma as psychoanalysis would, Kotrosits and

is perhaps because colonial trauma is never an isolatable event or incident, and empire is—to borrow the words of Walter Benjamin (1968, 257)—"a single catastrophe which keeps piling wreckage upon wreckage" in ways that we cannot adequately represent. This gospel does not just talk about a messianic secret; it is itself a messy secret that is nevertheless telling. As Mark's parable of the wicked tenants (Mark 12:1-11) shows, Mark's secret has to do with—but not exclusively with—Jesus's trauma.

In addition, biblical scholars have tried to figure out the so-called Synoptic problem since the nineteenth century and developed the method we call redaction criticism around the time of the Second World War, largely because of Wrede's work and its argument that Mark was a worked-over document of the church rather than a documentary of facts. Can we think of this issue *not* in terms of who is using whom or who is more historically accurate but in terms of Freud's almost palimpsestic text about repetitive, almost compulsory, behaviors as symptoms of traumatic haunting?[22] Can we, for the purpose of a more explicitly ethical end, read the redaction history of the Synoptics—or Mark's, Matthew's, and Luke's compulsion to keep returning and rewriting the memory of Jesus—as failed orality and thus haunting attempts to remember, report, relate, and reveal the always unfolding history of empire, war, and other traumas, particularly the symptoms of colonial ills and failures?

Conclusion

I am suggesting that we must read Mark's Gospel in general and Mark's ending in particular not only at the level of formalism, characterization, and literary relations but also at the level of colonialism, imperialism, as well as psychopolitical effect and affect. To read Mark as a memory or

---

Taussig seem to see it as an intentional move by Mark to make sense of one particular known trauma (namely, the First Jewish-Roman War).

22. Scholars have long debated the relationship between the Synoptic Gospels and John; see, for example, D. Moody Smith (2001) for what is arguably the most comprehensive discussion of this subject. Regardless of what one thinks of this relationship, Rambo (2010, 81-110) has proposed a reading of John in terms of trauma and witness. I should point out that Rambo's reading, as part of her project on what she calls "a theology of remaining," does not address the issue of empire and colonization; her only mention of this issue appears in a reference to the work of Joerg Rieger (see Rambo 2010, 14 n. 18). Rambo's provocative reading of John also does not engage the work of haunting by Gordon.

narrative of traumatic haunting is not to see the women's silence at the end of Mark or Mark's paratactic Greek as merely a matter of rhetorical or writing skills to be judged. Neither is the focus on the women disciples and Mark as characters to be blamed or praised. Silence in Mark, in this reading, does not communicate a lack of courage or agency; instead, it points to an encrypted secret about colonial traumas, and Mark's Gospel becomes a productive site to interrogate, illuminate, and expose the underside of imperial peace.

Works Cited

Abraham, Nicolas, and Maria Torok. 1994. *The Shell and the Kernel: Renewal of Psychoanalysis*. Edited and translated by Nicholas T. Rand. Chicago: University of Chicago Press.

Ahmed, Sara. 2004. *The Cultural Politics of Emotions*. Edinburgh: Edinburgh University Press.

Alexiou, Margaret. 2002. *The Ritual Lament in Greek Tradition*. Revised by Dimitrios Yatromanolakis and Panagiotis Roilos. 2nd ed. New York: Rowman & Littlefield.

Benjamin, Walter. 1968. *Illuminations*. Translated by Harry Zohn. New York: Schocken.

Berger, James. 1999. *After the End: Representations of Post-apocalypse*. Minneapolis: University of Minnesota Press.

Binz, Stephen J. 1989. *The Passion and Resurrection Narratives of Jesus*. Collegeville, MN: Liturgical Press.

Bernstein, Michael André. 1994. *Foregone Conclusions: Against Apocalyptic History*. Berkeley: University of California Press.

Bhabha, Homi K. 1994. *The Location of Culture*. New York: Routledge.

———. 1997. "The World and the Home." Pages 445–55 in *Dangerous Liaisons: Gender, Nation, and Postcolonial Perspectives*. Edited by Anne McClintock, Aamir Mufti, and Ella Shohat. Minneapolis: University of Minnesota Press.

Blanco, María del Pilar, and Esther Peeren, eds. 2010. *Popular Ghosts: The Haunted Spaces of Everyday Culture*. New York: Continuum.

Borch-Jacobsen, Mikkel. 1991. *Lacan: The Absolute Master*. Translated by Douglas Brick. Stanford, CA: Stanford University Press.

Brennan, Teresa. 2004. *The Transmission of Affect*. Ithaca, NY: Cornell University Press.

Brogan, Kathleen. 1998. *Cultural Haunting: Ghosts and Ethnicity in Recent American Literature*. Charlottesville: University of Virginia Press.
Brown, Raymond E. 2004. "The Burial of Jesus (Mark 15:42–47)." Pages 241–52 in *Jesus' Mission, Death, and Resurrection*. Vol. 3 of *The Historical Jesus: Critical Concepts in Religious Studies*. Edited by Craig A. Evans. New York: Routledge.
Carter, Warren. 2000. *Matthew and the Margins: A Socio-political and Religious Reading*. Sheffield: Sheffield Academic.
Caruth, Cathy. 1996. *Unclaimed Experience: Trauma, Narrative, History*. Baltimore: Johns Hopkins University Press.
Chang, Juliana. 2012. *Inhuman Citizenship: Traumatic Enjoyment and Asian American Literature*. Minneapolis: University of Minnesota Press.
Cheung, King-kok. 1993. *Articulate Silences: Hisaye Yamamoto, Maxine Hong Kingston, Joy Kogawa*. Ithaca, NY: Cornell University Press.
Chin, Frank, Jeffrey Chan, Lawson Fusao Inada, and Shawn Wong, eds. 1991. "An Introduction to Chinese and Japanese American Literature." Pages 3–38 in *Aiiieeeee! An Anthology of Asian American Writers*. Edited by Frank Chin, Jeffery Paul Chan, Lawson Fusao Inada, Shawn Wong. New York: Mentor.
Cho, Grace M. 2008. *Haunting the Korean Diaspora: Shame, Secrecy, and the Forgotten War*. Minneapolis: University of Minnesota Press.
Choi, Jin Young. 2015. *Postcolonial Discipleship of Embodiment: An Asian and Asian American Reading of the Gospel of Mark*. New York: Palgrave Macmillan.
Chow, Rey. 2014. *Not Like a Native Speaker: On Languaging as a Postcolonial Experience*. New York: Columbia University Press.
Crossan, John Dominic. 1994. *Jesus: A Revolutionary Biography*. San Francisco: HarperSanFrancisco.
Croy, Clayton. 2003. *The Mutilation of Mark's Gospel*. Nashville: Abingdon.
Delaney, Carol. 1998. *Abraham on Trial: The Social Legacy of Biblical Myth*. Princeton: Princeton University Press.
Derrida, Jacques. 1987. *The Post Card: From Socrates to Freud and Beyond*. Translated by Alan Bass. Chicago: University of Chicago Press.
———. 1994. *Specters of Marx: The State of the Debt, the Work of Mourning and the New International*. Translated by Peggy Kamuf. New York: Routledge.
———. 1995a. *The Gift of Death*. Translated by David Wills. Chicago: University of Chicago Press.

———. 1995b. *On the Name*. Edited by Thomas Dutoit. Translated by David Wood, John P. Leavey Jr., and Ian McLeod. Stanford, CA: Stanford University Press.

———. 1999. "Marx and Sons." Pages 213–69 in *Ghostly Demarcations: A Symposium on Jacques Derrida's "Specters of Marx."* Edited by Michael Sprinker. New York: Verso.

Dinkler, Michal Beth. 2013. *Silent Statements: Narrative Representations of Speech and Silence in the Gospel of Luke*. Berlin: de Gruyter.

Donaldson, Laura E. 2005. "Gospel Hauntings: The Postcolonial Demons of New Testament Criticism." Pages 97–113 in *Postcolonial Biblical Criticism: Interdisciplinary Intersections*. Edited by Stephen D. Moore and Fernando F. Segovia. New York: T&T Clark.

Duling, Dennis C. 2003. *The New Testament: History, Literature, and Social Context*. 4th ed. Belmont: Wadsworth Thomson.

Dwyer, Timothy. 1996. *The Motif of Wonder in the Gospel of Mark*. Sheffield: Sheffield Academic.

Elliott, Neil. 1994. *Liberating Paul: The Justice of God and the Politics of the Apostle*. Minneapolis: Fortress.

Eng, David L., and Shinhee Han. 2000. "A Dialogue on Racial Melancholia." *Psychoanalytic Dialogues* 10:667–700.

Evans, Craig A. 2005. "Jewish Burial Traditions and the Resurrection of Jesus." *JSHJ* 3:233–48.

Fenichel, Otto. 1967. "Psychoanalysis as the Nucleus of a Future Dialectical-Materialistic Psychology." *American Imago* 24:290–311.

Foley, Helene P. 2001. *Female Acts in Greek Tragedy*. Princeton: Princeton University Press.

Freud, Sigmund. 1953–1974. *The Standard Edition of the Complete Psychological Works of Sigmund Freud*. Translated by James Strachey. 24 vols. London: Hogarth.

Garland, Robert. 1985. *The Greek Way of Death*. Ithaca, NY: Cornell University Press.

Gordon, Avery F. 2008. *Ghostly Matters: Haunting and the Sociological Imagination*. Minneapolis: University of Minnesota Press.

———. 2011. "Some Thoughts on Haunting and Futurity." *Borderlands* 10.2:1–21. http://tinyurl.com/SBL0684a.

Gregg, Melissa, and Gregory J. Seigworth, eds.. 2010. *The Affect Theory Reader*. Durham, NC: Duke University Press.

Halliday, W. R. 1925. *The Pagan Background of Early Christianity*. Liverpool: University Press of Liverpool.

Hirsch, Marianne. 2012. *The Generation of Postmemory: Writing and Visual Culture after the Holocaust*. New York: Columbia University Press.
Homer, Sean. 2005. *Jacques Lacan*. New York: Routledge.
Horsley, Richard A. 2003. *Jesus and Empire: The Kingdom of God and the New World Disorder*. Minneapolis: Fortress.
Hurtado, Larry W. 2009. "The Women, the Tomb, and the Climax of Mark." Pages 427–51 in *A Wandering Galilean: Essays in Honour of Seán Freyne*. Edited by Zuleika Rodgers, with Margaret Daly-Denton and Anne Fitzpatrick McKinley. JSJSup 132. Leiden: Brill.
Joyce, James. 2007. *A Portrait of the Artist as a Young Man*. Edited by John Paul Riquelme. Norton Critical Editions. New York: Norton.
Keller, Nora Okja. 1997. *Comfort Woman*. New York: Viking.
Klauck, Hans-Josef. 2003. *The Religious Context of Early Christianity: A Guide to Graeco-Roman Religions*. Translated by Brian McNeil. Minneapolis: Fortress.
Koosed, Jennifer L., and Stephen D. Moore, eds. 2014. "Affect Theory and the Bible." Special Issue, *BibInt* 22.4–5.
Kotrosits, Maia, and Hal Taussig. 2013. *Re-reading the Gospel of Mark amidst Loss and Trauma*. New York: Palgrave Macmillan.
LaCapra, Dominick. 1994. *Representing the Holocaust: History, Theory, Trauma*. Ithaca, NY: Cornell University Press.
Lardinois, André, and Laura McClure, eds. 2001. *Making Silence Speak: Women's Voices in Greek Literature and Society*. Princeton: Princeton University Press.
Liew, Tat-siong Benny. 1999. *Politics of Parousia: Reading Mark Inter(con)textually*. Leiden: Brill.
Lincoln, Andrew. 1989. "The Promise and the Failure: Mk. 16:7, 8." *JBL* 108:283–300.
Martin, Dale B. 2012. *New Testament History and Literature*. New Haven: Yale University Press.
Marx, Karl, and Frederick Engels. 1968. *Selected Works: In One Volume*. New York: International Publishers.
McCane, Byron R. 2004. "'Where No One Had Yet Been Laid': The Shame of Jesus' Burial." Pages 253–71 in *Jesus' Mission, Death, and Resurrection*. Vol. 3 of *The Historical Jesus: Critical Concepts in Religious Studies*. Edited by Craig A. Evans. New York: Routledge.
Moore, Stephen D. 2006. *Empire and Apocalypse: Postcolonialism and the New Testament*. Sheffield: Sheffield Phoenix.

Moule, Charles F. D. 1955–1956. "St. Mark XVI.8 Once More." *NTS* 2:58–59.

Parham, Marisa. 2009. *Haunting and Displacement in African American Literature and Culture*. New York: Routledge.

Philo. 1941. *Every Good Man is Free; On the Contemplative Life; On the Eternity of the World; Against Flaccus; Apology for the Jews; On Providence*. Translated by F. H. Colson. LCL. Cambridge, MA: Harvard University Press.

Radhakrishnan, R. 2003. *Theory in an Uneven World*. Oxford: Blackwell.

Rambo, Shelly. 2010. *Spirit and Trauma: A Theology of Remaining*. Louisville: Westminster John Knox.

Rogers, Annie G. 2006. *The Unsayable: The Hidden Language of Trauma*. New York: Random House.

Scarry, Elaine. 1985. *The Body in Pain: The Making and Unmaking of the World*. New York: Oxford University Press.

Schwab, Gabriele. 2010. *Haunting Legacies: Violent Histories and Transgenerational Trauma*. New York: Columbia University Press.

Santner, Eric L. 1992. "History beyond the Pleasure Principle: Thoughts on the Representation of Trauma." Pages 143–54 in *Probing the Limits of Representation: Nazism and the Final Solution*. Edited by Saul Friedländer. Cambridge: Harvard University Press.

Scott, James C. 1992. *Domination and the Arts of Resistance: Hidden Transcripts*. New Haven: Yale University Press.

Sedgwick, Eve Kosofsky. 2003. *Touching Feeling: Affect, Pedagogy, Performativity*. Durham, NC: Duke University Press.

Siddiqi, Yumna. 2008. *Anxieties of Empire and the Fiction of Intrigue*. New York: Columbia University Press.

Sloyan, Gerard S. 1995. *The Crucifixion of Jesus: History, Myth, Faith*. Minneapolis: Fortress.

Smith, Anne-Marie. 1998. *Julia Kristeva: Speaking the Unspeakable*. London: Pluto.

Smith, D. Moody. 2001. *John among the Gospels*. 2nd ed. Columbia: University of South Carolina Press.

Spivak, Gayatri Chakravorty. 1988. "Can the Subaltern Speak?" Pages 271–313 in *Marxism and the Interpretation of Culture*. Edited by Cary Nelson and Larry Grossberg. Urbana: University of Illinois Press.

Stoler, Ann Laura. 1995. *Race and the Education of Desire: Foucault's History of Sexuality and the Colonial Order of Things*. Durham, NC: Duke University Press.

———. 2002. *Carnal Knowledge and Imperial Power: Race and the Intimate in Colonial Rule*. Berkeley: University of California Press.

———, ed. 2006a. *Haunted by Empire: Geographies of Intimacy in North American History*. Durham, NC: Duke University Press.

———. 2006b. "Intimidations of Empire: Predicaments of the Tactile and Unseen." Pages 1–22 in *Haunted by Empire: Geographies of Intimacy in North American History*. Edited by Ann Laura Stoler. Durham: Duke University Press.

———. 2009. *Along the Archival Grain: Epistemic Anxieties and Colonial Common Sense*. Princeton: Princeton University Press.

Tolbert, Mary Ann. 1989. *Sowing the Gospel: Mark's World in Literary Historical Perspective*. Minneapolis: Fortress.

Tomkins, Silvan S. 1995. *Exploring Affect: Selected Writings of Silvan S. Tomkins*. Edited by E. Virginia Demos. New York: Cambridge University Press.

Victorino, Maria Gemma. 1999. "Mark's Open Ending and Following Jesus on the Way." Pages 53–64 in *The Personal Voice in Biblical Interpretation*. Edited by Ingrid Rosa Kitzberger. New York: Routledge.

Wengst, Klaus. 1987. *Pax Romana and the Peace of Jesus Christ*. Translated by John Bowden. Philadelphia: Fortress.

Wiegman, Robyn. 2012. *Object Lessons*. Durham, NC: Duke University Press.

Wilson, Andrew P. 2004. "Trembling in the Dark: Derrida's *Mysterium Tremendum* and the Gospel of Mark." Pages 199–213 in *Derrida's Bible: Reading a Page of Scripture with a Little Help from Derrida*. Edited by Yvonne Sherwood. New York: Palgrave Macmillan.

Williams, Joel F. 1999. "Literary Approaches to the End of Mark's Gospel." *JETS* 42:21–35.

Wrede, William. 1971. *The Messianic Secret*. Translated by J. C. Greig. Greenwood: Attic.

Žižek, Slavoj. 2006. *How to Read Lacan*. New York: Norton.

The Gospel of Bare Life:
Reading Death, Dream, and
Desire through John's Jesus*

Tat-siong Benny Liew

Jacques Lacan (2001, 341) has famously declared that "it is not enough to decide on the basis of its effect—Death. It still remains to be decided which death, that which is brought by life or that which brings life." Of course, for Lacan, whose psychoanalysis has much to do with one's relations to death and the dead (Luepnitz 2003, 232), there is a difference between biological and psychic death and hence between mortality and vitality. Nevertheless, his statement does highlight, in a delightfully ironic way, how talk about death can—or should—be both specific and ambiguous at the same time. This is, in short, my proposal for reading Jesus's death in the Gospel of John. The more specific one gets, the more complicated and, yes, ambiguous it becomes in relation to Jesus's life and his offer of life.

To elaborate on my reading of Jesus's death in John, I will begin by situating and clarifying both my methodological assumptions and my chosen topic of study vis-à-vis *Anatomy of the Fourth Gospel*, by R. Alan Culpepper (1983). I hope that the subsequent directions this essay will take will also become more understandable in light of this opening discussion.

---

* This essay is a slightly expanded version of one that appears in Tom Thatcher and Stephen D. Moore, eds., *Anatomies of the Fourth Gospel: The Past, Present, and Futures of Narrative Criticism*, RBS 55 (Atlanta: Society of Biblical Literature, 2008), 167–93.

Beyond Anatomy and before Autopsy

It is by now well known that Culpepper's "classic" study is a formalist analysis that focuses on how the Fourth Gospel as a whole makes sense through the internal workings of its literary parts. Imaging or imagining John's text as a body, Culpepper's choice to call, and thus categorize, his own study as an "anatomy" is most apt. Knowing that Culpepper's book burst into a critical landscape that was more or less dominated by historical-critical methods and that it did so before all the readings with a "post-" prefix further altered the field, I want to be clear that what I have to say should in no way be read as a devaluation of its moment. As I hope the rest of my essay will show, formalism's emphasis on close reading continues to play an important role in my own work. Since, however, formalism is for me "an *approach*, not an allegiance" (Spillers 2003, 85, emphasis original), let me address *Anatomy*'s limits.

Focusing on the structure or design of an anatomy, it becomes easy to forget that a body, whether textual or biological, is more than bones, muscles, nerves, organs, veins, and how each part functions in relation to the others. More than that, a body functions in context(s). In other words, a focus on anatomy can fall prey to what may be called the "autonomy fallacy," the misconception that a body can be taken in isolation from or independent of its environment, its surroundings, or other bodies. The assumption of autonomy leads, then, not only to anatomy but also to atomization. Zeroing in on the anatomical features of a solitary body out of site means that numerous relations that may exist around this body are also out of sight. When relations are overlooked, anatomy and—or *as*—atomization turn(s) easily into objectification, and questions of ethics and politics become the concerns only of those who toil outside the (scientific?) laboratory.

Stephen D. Moore (1996, 57–58) has made similar criticisms of *Anatomy of the Fourth Gospel* by comparing Culpepper's formalism to an "eyeagram," for which issues of context and ideology are peripheral—hence the blind spots of Culpepper's reading practice. Moore goes on, however, to compare Culpepper's exegetical method to prosection, or anatomization of cadavers, and reads *Anatomy* as an autopsy (58–72). Moore does this not only to link Culpepper's formalist analysis with the critical dissection or amputation that historical-critical practitioners perform on biblical texts but also to question the effects of modern biblical scholarship through its development. I would, however, like to direct Moore's insights and incisions toward a related but different direction.

Whether it is John's corpus as corpse or Jesus's corpse in John's corpus, Moore reveals that Culpepper's ocular obsession is also a postmortem preoccupation. In *Of Grammatology*, Jacques Derrida (1976, 157–64) uses the word "exorbitant" to talk about the need to "open" a reading and hence the need to go beyond the necessity of and respect for "commentary." With this word, which implies what is outside the orbit of the eye ("ex-*orb*-itant") or off the beaten track, Derrida seems to suggest—especially in light of his later writings (e.g., Derrida and Dufourmantelle 2000; Derrida 2001)—a reframing of one's reading with the purpose of being excessive or extravagant in opening up to the vulnerable other.[1] My reading of death in the Gospel of John, then, is not only set within an ideological and a sociopolitical framework but also pursued out of a concern for the other, particularly the displaced or colonized, both past and present. Instead of a formalist fascination with the postmortem in and of the Fourth Gospel, this essay will look at John's production and politics of both life and death within a larger colonial frame. For lack of a better term, it will consider the "extraformal," or what is historical and contingent—particularly the displacement and movements of colonized bodies—to destabilize reading anatomies.

Death Threats and Death Bound

Johannine scholars have long observed that John's Jesus is very conscious of his impending death and that he seems to have come to this consciousness very early. After a couple days of recruiting disciples and before he performs his very first sign at Cana, Jesus already talks about his coming "hour" (2:4). As John will make crystal clear, Jesus's "hour" is none other than his time of crucifixion (see, e.g., 7:30; 8:20; 12:23, 27; 13:1). While the mortality rate was significantly higher in the Greco-Roman world of the first century CE than in today's geopolitical West, it is also well known that life expectancy became relatively "decent" for those who managed to survive the first five or ten years of life (Frier 1999, 86–88; Kelly 2006, 102–6).[2] If death was most threatening to infants and children, why do

---

1. Instead of getting into Derrida's complex argument, let me simply point to the headings of the sections that immediately precede Derrida's discussion of the "exorbitant," like "Writing and Man's Exploitation of Man" (1976, 118–40) or "From/Of Blindness to the Supplement" (1976, 144–52).

2. In a debate with Jesus, some characters in John express the view that Jesus is

we find John's (adult) Jesus being so conscious of, or obsessed with, his own death?[3] Instead of the theological responses conventionally given by Johannine scholars—whether in terms of Jesus's divinity and/or soteriology—I will follow Derrida's suggestion and attempt an exorbitant reading.

Frier (1999, 90), in his essay on Roman demography, correctly points out that the so-called law of average must not blind us to the differences that existed within Roman society. Although Frier himself focuses on class difference—or how the Roman elites generally enjoyed a longer (and better) life than the lower classes—one should keep in mind that while class/status and race/ethnicity are not collapsible, they do have a tendency to intersect. This is particularly so in colonial situations, in which an entire population may be put into a limbo zone of "included exclusion" or "excluded inclusion." That is to say, the colonized, being generally impoverished and/or racially/ethnically marked, are a part of but also apart from the empire. They form and belong to a somewhat separate but surely secondary social stratum. Being "secondary," as I will now proceed to argue, they are also more vulnerable to death.

The paradox of being simultaneously included and excluded—or, more accurately, being included on the premise of exclusion—is precisely how Giorgio Agamben (1998) characterizes what the Romans categorized

---

not yet fifty years old (John 8:57). If one goes by the projection that Bruce W. Frier (1982, 245) develops on the basis of Justinian's *Digest*, a person between the age of thirty and forty-five in the Roman Empire of the third century CE would have an average life expectancy of between twenty-three to fifteen years.

3. Given (1) Martin Heidegger's existentialist philosophy on the need for *Dasein* to acknowledge the certainty of death to be authentic and (2) Rudolf Bultmann's interests in and indebtedness to Heidegger's philosophy, I wonder if Bultmann's (1971) interest in the Fourth Gospel is not at least partially related to the prominence of death in John's story of Jesus, even if there is no entry under "death" in Bultmann's English index. One should not forget either that Heidegger (1971, 107–8) advocates such an essential relation between language and death that he thinks animals just "perish" and are incapable of experiencing death as humans do. If so, John's Jesus, as the Word (1:1–14), would have an even more particular relation to death.

Of course, the whole idea of a life-and-death struggle between master and slave goes back to *Phenomenology of Spirit*, by Georg Wilhelm Friedrich Hegel (1977), within the European philosophical traditions. Mikkel Borch-Jacobsen (1991, 12), in his insightful reading of Lacan, has suggested that Hegel's *Phenomenology* is itself "a speculative version of the Passion," although Borch-Jacobsen's reference is Paul's letter to the Philippians instead of the Gospel of John.

as the *homo sacer*, or "sacred person."[4] Pointing to a reference to one "who may be killed but not sacrificed" in Pompeius Festus's second-century-CE Roman text *De verborum significatione*, Agamben locates not only an act that is beyond law and sacrifice but also a zone where rule and "exceptions to the rule" become indistinguishable. This zone is that of the sovereign, where power can suspend the very judicial order that it itself establishes. The powerless subjects within that same zone, being liable to the whims and under the threats of the sovereign, are all potentially excludable or killable without recourse to law or sublation to the sacred. As such, they also reside in a zone of indistinction as *homo sacer*, which Agamben further glosses as "bare life." Putting sovereign power and bare life as two sides of the same coin or as uncanny doubles within the same zone, Agamben aims not only to show how sovereignty is always already reliant on its death threats and executions but also to stress that more and more people are falling into the category of *homo sacer* or bare life today. Rather than thinking that bare life is the state or fate only of, say, Holocaust victims, political refugees, or those imprisoned in Guantanamo Bay, Agamben (1998, 115) points to the comatose patient—one who is kept in a zone of indistinction between life and death by contemporary medical technology, yet subject to the fluctuating criteria of death given by the medical and legal establishments—to suggest that "today there is no longer any one clear figure of the sacred man … because we are all virtually *homines sacri*."

Agamben's argument about the widening or expansion of the bare life zone should not, however, lead one to forget that historically some people have indeed been more vulnerable as bare life than others. Writing about the experiences of African Americans, Sharon Patricia Holland (2000, 3–5) has suggested, for example, that blacks in the United States have been living in a "space of death"—a death zone, if you will—for five hundred years and that the story of African Americans is basically one of "death-in-life."[5] Citing John Edgar Wideman's mournful assertion that "black lives

---

4. Agamben (1998, 90) also describes such a person as "dwell[ing] in the no-man's-land between the home and the city." As we know, this spatial characteristic of being "in-between"—if not exactly that of "included exclusion" or "excluded inclusion"—is also significant for John's world-traveling Jesus.

5. One can, of course, add to this, as Holland does, Native Americans, or even Asian Americans. Anne Anlin Cheng (2001, 69), for instance, has proposed that Asian Americans suffer a "phantom illness" and occupy a "ghostly," "unstable position in the ethnic-racial spectrum" in the national imagination of the United States because of,

are expendable, can disappear, click, just like that," Karla F. C. Holloway (2002, 1–3, 7–8) argues that untimely deaths among African Americans in the twentieth century were so pervasive and persistently "color-coded" that what she calls "black death" has become nothing less than a "cultural haunting" within African America. This kind of haunting is arguably best expressed by Richard Wright (1969, 83–84), who writes that by the time he was eleven, "[although] I had never in my life been abused by whites, … I had already become as conditioned to their existence as though I had been the victim of a thousand lynchings," because he knew that "there existed men against whom I was powerless, men who could violate my life at will." Using Agamben's work as a lens to read the writings of Wright, Abdul R. JanMohamed (2005), in a thesis that resonates with the work of both Holland and Holloway, presents Wright as one who writes *as* and *about* a "death-bound-subject." JanMohamed uses this term to describe a black subjectivity that is "formed, from infancy on, by the imminent and ubiquitous threat of death" (2).

Within an empire, whether that of ancient Rome or that of the modern United States, a particular segment of the population under colonial "sovereignty" tends to become particularly vulnerable to death, and such a susceptible segment is often singled out on the basis of class/status and/or race/ethnicity.[6] For these groups, being who they are and being dead

---

say, "our" being racialized as "foreign." Being Asian American, or "foreign American," is to find oneself in a zone of indistinction that may bring about deadly consequences.

I have, however, intentionally chosen not to focus on Asian American experiences because I want to pursue a minority subjectivity that is not tied to identity politics. Given this essay's "exorbitant" focus on death, allow me to quote from the late Edward W. Said, who said in an interview, "What is much more interesting is to try to reach out beyond identity to something else. *It may be death*. It may be an altered state of consciousness that puts you in touch with others more than one normally is" (Rose 2000, 25 [emphasis added]). Perhaps the experience of being in the "death zone" will help bring minorities beyond identity politics to be in touch and in coalition with each other. For an attempt to bring biblical scholars from different racial/ethnic minority groups in the United States into a conversation, see Bailey, Liew, and Segovia 2009.

6. The connection between first-century Jews and slavery is also not without warrant, since one major source of Greco-Roman slavery came from war captives (Glancy 2002, 77–79). In fact, Jews of the first century CE could be and often were presented as "born slaves" (Isaac 2004, 463–64). In addition, they, at least as Josephus's representation indicates, did compare their colonial existence to slavery (*A.J.* 20.120). This link between Roman colonization and slavery can also be connected with Agamben's readily killable "bare life" by way of Latin etymology within ancient Roman legal discus-

are almost always one and the same, because their vulnerability to death—whether in the form of fear or of direct experience—is not only known but also deeply internalized (Holloway 2002, 58–59). The applicability of this theory across time and locations can be seen in the early work of Frantz Fanon (1967, 8), where he described black men in the Caribbean and Africa under French colonization as living in "a zone of nonbeing, an extraordinarily sterile and arid region."[7] Later in the same work, Fanon stresses that his fellow blacks are colonized with "a sense of nonexistence" rather than one of inferiority (139).[8] He also specifically mentions in a footnote that he began working on *Black Skin, White Masks* with a view to writing about "death wish among Negroes" (218 n. 6).

Following Agamben's argument that sovereignty turns more and more people into bare life should not lead one to forget that there have always already been specific groups or communities that are more exposed than others. In fact, Agamben (1998, 179) himself states that "the Jews are the representatives par excellence and almost the living symbol of the people and of the bare life that modernity necessarily creates within itself, but whose presence it can no longer tolerate in any way." Keeping in mind, however, that (1) Agamben traces *homo sacer* back to the Roman Empire of the second century CE and (2) that Jews and their land were colonized

---

sion: "Slaves [*servi*] are so-called, because generals have a custom of selling their prisoners and thereby preserving [*servare*] rather than killing them: and indeed they are said to be *mancipia*, because they are captives in the hand [*manus*] of their enemies" (*Digesta* 1.5.4.2–3; cited in Harrill 2006, 30). In other words, slaves were "spared" life and hence bare life. Here is an even more definitive statement by Moore: "The Roman Empire, as is commonly noted, had as its fundamental enabling condition the institution of slavery" (Moore 2006, 61).

7. Paul Gilroy (2005, 11, 22), commenting on current colonial and racial relations, also writes, "The natives, whose bodies are comparatively worthless, already exist in a space of death, ... [and] the colonial insurgent, rather like the slave in earlier phases of imperial dominance, already [belongs] among the socially dead" (see also 48, 50).

8. Kelly Oliver (2004, 4, 13–17) suggests that these statements in Fanon should be read as allusion to and disagreements with Jean-Paul Sartre's existential phenomenology. Oliver's helpful observations do not necessarily, in my view, mean that Fanon does not see black (male) existence as "death bound." Perhaps the difference or disagreement between Fanon and Sartre lies less on the concern with "nonbeing," but more on whether "nonbeing" is an imposition or a choice. One may say the same about Fanon and Hegel; while Hegel needs conflict or struggle to have self-consciousness, Fanon argues that black self-consciousness is always already intruded by a hostile force from the outside (Marriott 2000, 67).

by the Romans during this same period of time, I would contend that the treatment of Jews as bare life should not be conceived as only a *modern* phenomenon. Since codification generally lags behind lived reality, I would go further to argue that what Agamben identifies, highlights, and explains in terms of bare life is helpful in thinking about Jewish life within the Roman Empire of the first century CE. If so, John's portrayal of Jesus's death-consciousness may be inseparable from John's awareness of the bare life status of most Jewish people.

Jews and John within the Death Zone of the Roman Empire

As illustrated by its gladiatorial combats, the Roman Empire was capable not only of violence but also of cleverly combining punishment with entertainment for the sake of empire building. While Rome was never shy in executing its own when "treasonous" or "rebellious" acts were involved,[9] gladiator shows and other similar "game[s] of death" (Plass 1995) generally doubled as, and perhaps had their origins in, the empire's machinations to rid itself of its enemies and captured aliens. According to Polybius, the Roman parades of booty and captives known as the "triumphs" were basically re-creations of military victory (*Hist.* 6.15.7–8). Such a parade could be performed, however, only if the victory had registered five thousand enemy casualties and parades specifically included, as part of the performance, the public execution of the enemies' captured leader (Kyle 1998, 42). By the time Julius Caesar hosted his "mock battle" in the circus in 46 BCE, the pretend fighting had become the occasion in which captives were actually executed in mass (Dio Cassius, *Hist. Rome* 43.23.3–6; Suetonius, *Jul.* 39.4; Appian, *Bell. civ.* 2.102). Captives, along with criminals and slaves, were also condemned to be the "original" gladiators, though later on other persons desperate for a chance of fame and fortune were also recruited to perform voluntarily in this kind of "indirect" death sentence

---

9. I placed "treasonous" and "rebellious" in quotation marks here to connote that what counts as treason and rebellion is often based on the arbitrary decisions of those in power. For an example of what Romans would do to even one of their own on the count or suspicion of conspiracy, Juvenal has the following to say about the abusive killing of Sejanus despite his birth as an equestrian: "Sejanus is being dragged by a hook—a sight worth seeing. Everyone's celebrating" (*Sat.* 10.66–67). Unless indicated otherwise, English translations of Greco-Roman sources are taken from the Loeb Classical Library of the Harvard University Press.

(Coleman 1990, 54–56, 61–62). As Seneca points out, gladiators were not necessarily armed, armored, or trained; as feeble and pitiful victims of mass murder, they brought out the entertainment-seeking crowds' frustration and even rage rather than compassion (*Ep.* 7.3–5). In addition, the Roman Empire employed a variety of "direct" death penalties, such as decapitation, crucifixion, or immolation. Not all direct death penalties were equal, however. By the time of Hadrian, the difference between "simple death" (*capite puniri*) and "ultimate punishment" (*summa supplicia*) was clearly articulated, with the latter—which would include crucifixion and immolation—generally reserved for those who had low or no status, particularly noncitizens (Garnsey 1970, 122–36).

In other words, the Roman Empire not only made torturous and aggravated death a routine (see also Glancy 2005) but also targeted foreign victims of Roman military conquests and colonial enterprise for such a routine. It is important to point out also that there was nothing routine about these deaths, since the Roman Empire made it a point to "ritualize" them into public and stylized displays, or what Donald G. Kyle (1998) tellingly calls "spectacles of death." Like Fanon's "Look, a Negro" (1967, 111–12) or Pilate's "Behold the man" (John 19:5; see also 19:14), these performative sights simultaneously assailed and confined the colonized. While the spectacle nature of indirect death penalties such as the gladiatorial shows is obvious, even direct death sentences in the Roman Empire—like crucifixions—were rarely, if ever, executed without an audience. This is clear in the Fourth Gospel's references to persons near Jesus's cross (19:25–27), the proximity of Golgotha to the city, and the number of people who read the trilingual inscription (19:20). Killing, especially of aliens, was a "satisfying spectacle" (Seneca, *Ep.* 95.33) because it was a ritual that revealed and reinforced Rome's imperial power (Martial, *Spect.* 5.65).[10] While many in the Greco-Roman world joined voluntary associations to partly ensure a proper burial (Kloppenborg 1996, 18–21; Klauck 2003, 47–48, 52), imperial Rome would deny the bodies it executed a proper burial as a sign of deep disrespect or disdain for these often-alien bodies in life *and* in death. Again, John seems to be alluding to this when he has Joseph of Arimathea ask Pilate for permission to give Jesus's body a proper Jewish burial (19:38–42). The torment, torture, and finally death

---

10. For instance, the authority of Caesar was displayed not only in his power to decide on the fate of the gladiator but also in the seating arrangement of the amphitheater (Edwards 2007, 54).

suffered by the victims functioned, then, as threatening object lessons and as a kind of visual terror that a similar fate would await anyone who dared to question or challenge the empire; as such, these spectacles were vital to its order and security.

To put the discussion above in Agamben's vocabulary, Rome's imperial sovereignty was built on the definition of its subject populations—particularly its colonized populations—as bare life. Seeing the colonized as disposable by-products, damaged goods, or abject leftovers of its imperialist projects, Rome placed them under a death sentence that might be commuted at will and at any time, without legal or religious consequence. Like the lynchings Wright witnessed as he was growing up, the public display of death is—but is also more than—a trauma for the colonized and a simultaneous "gala" or even a "gallery" for the colonizers. The display actually also positions bare life as both victim and spectator; or, more accurately, it victimizes bare life also *as* spectator (Marriott 2000, 4-6, 14; see also Holloway 2002, 62-64). That is to say, "death bound" subjectivity comes into being precisely in the move from looking *at* to looking *away from* these various spectacles of death, when these spectacles turn into specters of death. Roman spectacles of death were, in other words, ritual acts that interpellate subjectivities on both sides of the colonial divide.

Jews of the first century CE were no strangers to Rome's imperial sovereignty. They were, in other words, bare life that was readily or always already killable. Unlike Plato, who famously declared philosophy as a necessary means to practice death (*Phaed.* 64a, 80e), Jews of the first century CE seemed to live almost necessarily under death threats and executions. Philo, for instance, says that in 38 CE, under the governorship of Flaccus, Alexandrians were given free rein to take Jewish homes, shops, and lives (*Flacc.* 6.41-43; 8.53-57; 10.73-75). Philo goes on to report that even during the celebratory season Jews were flogged, hung, run over, tortured, and executed at a theater (*Flacc.* 10.81-85). Of course, things were not much better in Judea. Pilate, as the procurator of Judea from 26 to 36 CE, killed many Jews who protested his use of resources from the Jewish temple treasury for public works (Josephus, *A.J.* 18.60-62). When a Roman soldier "flashed" himself during one Passover in front of, and thus enraged, the gathering Jewish pilgrims flocking into Jerusalem for the festival, another procurator, Cumanus (48-52 CE), decided to send in the Roman troops as a precaution. The mere sight of these troops caused so much panic and pandemonium that twenty thousand Jews died in a stampede (*A.J.* 20.105-122).

Perhaps one can say, on the evidence of Philo and Josephus, that the Romans basically adopted a "kill deal" as their default policy with Jews during the first century CE. Whenever there was any sign of unrest—even when it involved a conflict between Jews and their non-Jewish neighbors, not to mention any form of disrespect or challenge of Roman authority, including any prophecy or promises that stirred up popular imagination or yearning—the Romans would tend to respond with a military crackdown to ensure or enforce the so called *pax Romana*. Cumanus, for instance, did so more than once. Immediately after the Passover debacle noted above, he unleashed a military show of force when a slave of Caesar's was robbed outside Jerusalem and again when a conflict broke out between the Samaritans and some Jews of Galilee (*A.J.* 20.113–114, 118–122). But Cumanus was hardly unique. According to Josephus, procurators like Fadus (44–46 CE), Felix (52–60 CE), Festus (60–62 CE), as well as Roman officers who had jurisdictions beyond Judea, like Quadratus (Syria) and Catullus (Libyan Pentapolis), all employed the mighty Roman armies to kill and threaten Jewish lives (*A.J.* 20.2–4, 97–98, 125–133, 167–178, 188; *B.J.* 7.443–446). Of course, the best-known mass killings of Jews happened during the First Jewish-Roman War in 66–72 CE (Josephus, *B.J.* 2.457–468, 487–498, 5.446–451, 6.403–406, 418–420, 7.23–24, 37–40, 96, 142–157, 407–419; see also Tacitus, *Hist.* 5.13).

These threats and realities of death are particularly significant in view of the general scholarly convention to date the Fourth Gospel near the end of the first century, which effectually situates John between the two Jewish-Roman Wars (66–72 and 132–135 CE, respectively). While Louis H. Feldman and Meyer Reinhold (1996, 306) are surely correct that there were various attitudes toward the colonized Jews not only at any given time but also over time, the fact that there were three major Jewish revolts against the Romans within a seventy-year period—the two Jewish-Roman Wars plus the Lukuas-Andreas Rebellion or the "War of Quietus" in 115–117 CE—certainly indicates that things were particularly tense during this time span.[11] Perhaps the death anxiety with which first-century Jews lived

---

11. The Jewish death toll in these two later revolts were also significant, if we can assume the accuracy of our extant records. Supposedly 220,000 Jews were killed in Cyrene and 240,000 more were killed in Cyrus during the Lukuas-Andreas Rebellion (Dio Cassius, *Hist. Rome* 68.32). Again, according to Dio Cassius, during the Second Jewish-Roman War, 985 Jewish villages were razed, 580,000 Jews were killed in battles, and countless more died because of thirst, disease, and fire (69.12–15). Judea was like

was analogous to that articulated by the late Norman Mailer for modern Jews in his post-Holocaust manifesto, "The White Negro."[12] According to Mailer (1959, 338), "we will never be able to determine the psychic havoc … upon the unconscious mind of almost everyone alive in these years.… We have been forced to live with the suppressed knowledge that … we [are already] doomed to die." Under the Roman machination of death threats and executions as a result of "games," penalties, and wars, the Jews of John's time can be understood to have lived within a collective experience that became increasingly similar to Mailer's description.

Writing about the slave trade to the so-called New World, Hortense J. Spillers (2003, 206–7) states that "flesh"—rather than "body"—is a particularly helpful term for registering and reflecting on the violence suffered by African Americans.[13] "Flesh," Spillers's moniker for the "cultural *vestibularity*" of being captured, displaced, colonized, violated, and always already vulnerable, is related or comparable to Agamben's "bare life" (Agamben 2003, 207 [emphasis original]; see also JanMohamed 2005, 10).[14] John, of course, famously introduces Jesus with the phrase "the Word became *flesh*" (1:14). How may John's story of this "flesh" or bare life that straddles between "worlds" come across in light of Rome's colonization of Jews in general and Rome's "spectacles of death" in particular? Is there a space to talk about Jesus's death in John *as* a human condition?[15]

---

a desert, while "the Jewish community in Alexandria and throughout the rest of Egypt became virtually extinct" (Feldman and Reinhold 1996, 291).

12. The Middle Passage and the Holocaust point to the nation building of the United States and Germany respectively. As such, both speak to Agamben's relations between bare life and sovereignty.

13. For Spillers (2003, 206–7), "flesh" is a (more?) "primary narrative" that is also "the concentration of 'ethnicity' that contemporary critical discourses neither acknowledge nor discourse away." Spillers suggests that African American "flesh," having received and registered all kinds of violence, continues to haunt African America even if the captured bodies appear to have been liberated.

14. As something primary to or before "body," Spillers's "flesh" can also be compared or connected to Julia Kristeva's (1982) "abject" as an "not-yet-object" or an "in-between-ness" that threatens boundaries. The connection between Agamben's bare life and Kristeva's abject should require no elaborations, especially if one thinks about bare life in terms of "included exclusion" and abject in terms of being "in between."

15. This is a play on the title of a recent essay by Craig R. Koester (2005), "The Death of Jesus and the Human Condition: Exploring the Theology of John's Gospel," which is developed within the framework of four traditional theological concepts (love, sacrifice, evil, and divine revelation).

Is there room to read the Fourth Gospel without making close reading and history—and I mean here the historical contexts of both John and his twenty-first-century interpreters—mutually exclusive?

Dying, Dreaming, and Dreamreading

In addition to Jesus's obsession with his "hour," other references to death appear in the Gospel of John. In fact, keeping in mind that John presents Jesus's death as the slaughtering of the Passover lamb (19:13–16, 31–37), one may say that death already makes its appearance in the gospel's very first chapter, when the Baptizer presents Jesus as "the lamb of God" (1:29, 36).[16] After Jesus's first reference to his own "hour" before the performance of his first "sign" (2:1–11), he later heals—as his "second sign" (4:54)—a royal official's son who is about to die (4:47, 49). In the aftermath of yet another of Jesus's signs, he will contrast his living bread that leads to eternal life with manna that cannot keep one from dying (6:49–50, 58), while his dissenters will accept death as an inevitable reality even for Abraham and the prophets (8:53).[17] In light of the protracted trial and controversy over the healing of the one born blind (9:1–41), John's Jesus will talk about how thieves and robbers, in contrast to a good shepherd who dies for his flock, come to steal, kill, and destroy, as well as how wolves snatch and scatter the sheep (10:10–18). Then, of course, John narrates the story about Lazarus (11:1–44) to transition to the last week of Jesus's life (13:1–19:42). Even in the epilogue, one finds a "prediction" of Peter's martyrdom (21:18–19; see also 13:36–38) and an "explanation" of the Beloved Disciple's death (21:20–23). One can say, then, that John's

---

16. Alexandre Kojève (1965, 28), commenting on Hegel's death struggle, suggests that constant death threats can cause one to come across to others as a mad person or a menace to society. It is interesting that although Holland does not mention Kojève, her work on reading death and black subjectivity does devote quite a few pages to the Hollywood picture *Menace II Society* (Holland 2000, 6, 19–28, 122–23). I wonder if one cannot read Jesus's cleansing of the temple in John (2:13–22) as an expression of this rebellion or aggression, especially since John does make a point to link this episode to Jesus's own awareness of his imminent death.

17. This reference to food and other related references to hunger and feeding in John may also function as signals of death (4:8, 31–34; 6:1–15, 22–35, 55; 21:9–17). John's statement that the people, after getting fed, want to make Jesus king (6:15) may also serve as an indirect attack on Rome's inability to take care of those under its sovereignty.

Gospel, or "good news," ironically begins and ends with death, or that it moves from Jesus's death to the deaths of his followers.

Instead of thinking that the Gospel of John is a direct and unproblematic reflection of a historical situation—after all, Derrida (1976, 3) makes a point to distance his exorbitant reading from the referential fallacy—I would like to see the Fourth Gospel as an ideological product *and* production that comes out of, as well as seeks to act on, the ideological structure of its time (see also Conway 2002). Catherine Edwards (2007, 20–21, 46–77, 131), in her book on death in Rome, has suggested that literary accounts of deaths were popular inspirational readings in the first two centuries CE and that gladiatorial combats were not only spectacles of death but also occasions of "death as spectacle." That is to say, these literary and live performances of death taught and disciplined Roman citizens how to face death as military men; this explains why, for instance, the first gladiator shows were connected with aristocratic funerals before they became monopolized by the imperial family (47, 49, 52–53). What if we treat the threat and reality of death that we have identified thus far as an ideology that works its way into the gospel's structure like (or better yet, *as*) both a nightmare that haunts and a dream that works out Mailer's (1959, 338) "suppressed" or repressed "knowledge"?

To unpack the relations between death and dream in the Fourth Gospel, I will need to look at how its changing narrative pace correlates with its changing narratives about death, as well as how this narrative unfolding—in terms of both speed and complexity—is a manifestation of the unconscious in dream work.

It has been well recognized in Johannine scholarship that time slows down in the Fourth Gospel. While it takes only eighteen verses to move from a time beyond time to the time of the Baptizer (1:1–18), John spends the first half of his gospel moving through three Passovers (1:19–12:50) and almost the entire second half on the last week of Jesus's life (13:1–20:31). This slowing down of time is, I propose, accompanied by a heightening depiction of death that not only gives coverage to the death of more characters but also becomes more nuanced about the causes of Jesus's death. As noted above, in the first ten chapters of the gospel, John refers to (1) Jesus's awareness of his coming but not-yet-arrived "hour" (2:4); (2) unfulfilled desires or attempts to kill Jesus (7:1, 19, 25; 8:37, 40, 59; 10:31–33); (3) Jesus's discussions and debates that bring up the reality, inevitability, or finality of death (5:21, 24; 6:49–50, 58; 10:10–18); and (4) the near-death experience of the royal official's son (4:47, 49). Henry Staten (1993, 38) has suggested that Jesus's earlier signs, in comparison to his raising of Lazarus, "do not concern the bestowal of life directly but rather the preservation and repair of a life already in existence." Moreover, these references tend to be isolated and, perhaps more importantly, Jesus and the royal official's son are able to avoid death.

In contrast, beginning with the story of Lazarus in chapter 11, John will have different characters actually experience death (Lazarus and Jesus) or be "foretold" of their deaths (Peter and the Beloved Disciple). Not only are the narratives about death—especially those of Lazarus and Jesus—lengthy and detailed, but they are also given in explicit relation to one another. For instance, John's narrative literally goes for overkill in stressing that Lazarus is dead (11:4, 13–14, 17, 21, 32, 39, 44), but in the process of doing so John also weaves in Thomas's statement to the disciples that they should accompany Jesus to die with him (11:7–8, 16). Similarly, the prediction of Peter's upcoming martyrdom leads to the question surrounding the death of the Beloved Disciple (21:18–23). In spite of, or in contrast to, Jesus's statement that Peter should not be concerned with the fate of another (21:22), Jesus's own death is presented as closely tied to that of Lazarus. Lazarus's death and resurrection renew the determination of some to kill Jesus (11:46–53), and Jesus's raising him from the dead leads to a desire to kill Jesus as well as to rekill Lazarus (12:9–11). There is therefore a kind of ripple effect in this latter part of the Fourth Gospel, where death becomes more like a chain reaction than just an individual experience.

Since John, unlike Matthew, Mark, and Luke, has Jesus cleanse the temple early (John 2:13–22) rather than late in his gospel, some scholars describe his raising of Lazarus as the last straw that causes the Jewish authorities to resort to murder. This description is, however, not very accurate, since John has narrated desires or attempts to kill Jesus before chapter 11 (7:1, 19, 25; 8:37, 40, 59; 10:31). What is strategic about Jesus's raising of Lazarus is thus not the desire or even determination to murder Jesus, but a new revelation of what is behind this desire to murder. Previously, the desire to murder Jesus had something to do with an inability or unwillingness to accept Jesus's words (8:37), because those words sound blasphemous (10:32–33). But after Jesus's raising of Lazarus, John suddenly introduces—if one does not count the ambiguous "royal official" (4:46–54)—a new set of characters into the narrative: the Romans.[18] We

---

18. I am not counting the "royal official" of John 4:46–54 as Roman because his

learn from Caiaphas that the Jewish authorities need to keep the Jewish people calm and under control so as not to arouse suspicions and bring about preemptive strikes from the Romans (11:47–53). In other words, the high priest and the authorities want to eliminate Jesus to protect not only their own privilege but also the Jewish people and nation.[19] Obviously, in Caiaphas's estimation, Roman attention and intervention must be avoided at all costs, since the Romans are bound to engage in a "shock-and-awe" operation if they detect any smell of trouble. Not only is Caiaphas's reasoning repeated in 18:14, but Roman characters—from the cohort that arrests Jesus to Pilate who tries him—also begin to play a more direct and explicit role in the gospel. Their appearance leads, in turn, to the open acknowledgment—not once, but twice—that the sovereign right to kill belongs to the Romans and the Romans alone (18:31–32; 19:10). This sequence of two different reasons for killing Jesus—first, because his words offend the sensibilities of certain Jewish authorities, and second, because of the need or desire of some Jewish leaders to demonstrate their loyalty to Rome—is repeated in a condensed form in 19:7–16, after an indirect and ironic allusion to the exclusive Roman right to crucify (19:6).

I would suggest that these two movements—(1) from scattered and isolated references to death to more pervasive and connected descriptions of death and (2) from describing Jesus's death as a result of an intra-Jewish power struggle to framing it within Roman colonialism—are comparable to the movement in dream work, in which a latent content struggles to work its way through the unconscious to manifest itself. Fanon (1963, 52) has suggested that the muscles, emotions, and psyches of the colonized are paralyzed during the day but can run free in dreams at night.[20] The latent

---

identity is simply too ambiguous. Moore would also see John's passion narrative as heavily foregrounding the Romans; see Moore 2006, 54.

19. Pilate, in contrast, is willing to kill Jesus to show his own loyalty to Caesar, as well as to both reveal and reinforce the power of Roman sovereignty (19:12–22). See also Koester 2005, 143. Caiaphas's statement in John actually also echoes a sentiment that can be found in Greco-Roman writers like Polybius (*Hist.* 6.54.1–4), Cicero (*Phil.* 10.20), and Lucan (*Phar.* 2.306–325). For the Romans, this "one-death-for-many-lives" rationale was often presented as a potentially productive way to end civil war (Edwards 2007, 39).

20. As L. William Countryman (1994, 2) comments, there is a long tradition of understanding the Fourth Gospel as "mystical." I am, however, suggesting that we read this "mystic" quality of John in terms of dream work. If texts or narratives

content here is a Roman ideology of death that formed, informed, and deformed Jewish existence, especially in the period between the two Jewish-Roman wars. While J. B. Pontalis (1978) makes a connection between the workings of death and dream in Sigmund Freud, and Said makes a distinction between a latent and a manifest content in colonial ideology (Said 1978, 201–25), I would like to talk about how death can become a latent, nightmarish structure that haunts colonial subjectivity (see also JanMohamed 2005, 22–27).[21] This structure is latent not only because being "death bound" is, as Mailer (1959, 338) points out in "The White Negro," a "suppressed knowledge," but also because manifesting one's own station as bare life involves a complicated spec(tac)ular crossing on the part of the colonized (Spillers 2003, 397). As W. E. B. Du Bois points out in *The Souls of Black Folk*, colonized or displaced people live with a "double consciousness," or "this sense of always looking at one's self through the eyes of others" (1953, 2–3). Seeing oneself as a "spectacle of death" means that living as bare life may become what Pierre Bourdieu (1977) calls *habitus*, those socialized actions and reactions that one acts out more or less unconsciously or subconsciously. To articulate or explain this *habitus*, one will need to go beyond Du Bois's "double consciousness" to develop a third

---

also have to do with, as I have been arguing, fear, desire, or generally domains of the psyche (see Brooks 1994), then perhaps "anatomy" or anatomical dissection is not entirely adequate for the task of interpretation. The motif of misunderstanding in John that Culpepper (1983, 152–65) has helpfully summarized can also be read in light of dream work.

21. In addition to Freud's work on dream and death, which both Pontalis and JanMohamed have sought to put together in their theorization and practice of reading Freud and with Freud, I would suggest that when it comes to John, there is a third aspect of Freud's work that may be put in the mix. Since the Fourth Gospel is a retelling of Jesus's life and death several decades after the fact—thus a sort of memorial of or for Jesus—Freud's work on memory would also seem appropriate to the task. It is well beyond the scope of this essay to go any further into this direction, but let me simply suggest two more thoughts. First, psychoanalysis is in many ways an intriguing lens through which to read John, since it is also concerned with resurrecting a burial of the past. Second, I need to differentiate my own interest in reading John in terms of memory work from the approach employed by Tom Thatcher (2006). While Thatcher's approach focuses on the politics of memory vis-à-vis textuality (i.e., texts that are written down) within the Christ-following communities, I have in mind something not only more psychoanalytical but also more broadly sociopolitical, a model that is closer to what I have in mind can be seen in Assmann (1997), although its focus is not on a biblical book per se, let alone the Gospel of John.

eye: one will need to see oneself seeing as one is seen. This need for the third eye may also help to explain why John slows down his narrative and devotes a total of nine chapters (John 12–20) to the last week of Jesus's life. These chapters not only follow his raising of Lazarus but also contain a significant amount of soliloquy on the part of Jesus. They can be read as the site or the process through which John works out and clarifies his understanding of (Jesus's) death.

Just as this complicating of the spec(tac)ular may be helpful or even necessary to manifest a latent structure, reading John's manifest content as a struggle to express a latent content can also help to complicate—or even make a different sense out of—passages that would otherwise seem rather anti-Jewish. When one reads Jesus's accusation that his Jewish opponents have a devilish human-killer as their "father" (8:44), one may well detect a latent or veiled reference to none other than Rome, given that (1) John gradually comes to articulate killing as exclusively a Roman prerogative (18:31–32; 19:10); (2) John nuances the move or motive to kill Jesus beyond blasphemy to the threat of Roman interventions (11:47–53); and (3) Roman ideology presented Caesar as the empire's paternal patron or even paterfamilias (Agamben 1998, 88–89). In addition, John shows, although in the circuitous ways of a dream, that Roman imperialism is not only (following Agamben) contingent on turning colonized Jews into bare life or potential victims of its machination of death, but also (supplementing Agamben) relies on making them extensions of that machination, or living appendages of its killing machine. For the sake of self-preservation—whether the "self" here is referring to a personal or a collective life—subjects who are themselves "death bound" may end up binding others to death. Put differently, the desire to live in a colonial situation can easily turn into a desire to kill even one's own. The perverse logic of colonialism means that it is often through murder that a colonized person or people may concretize their own desire to live. The Roman machination of death, then, "not only shapes one's view of things but demands an endless response" that predisposes relations between Jews and Romans as well as poisons relations among Jews (Spillers 2003, 378). Imperial death threats and sentences can make the colonized collaborate in oppressing their own and hence in their own oppression. In other words, it is tunnel vision or short-sighted to see John's depiction of some Jews—particularly their attitudes and actions toward Jesus—as "anti-Jewish." One must not fail to see the Roman Empire always already looming and lurking in the background.

John's Improvisations and Inventions of Death

If one reads the Gospel of John in terms of both death work and dream work, one must remember that, according to Freud (1953–1974, 4:124), every dream is also a wish. That is to say, the Fourth Gospel is not only a site through which John works out and makes manifest—no matter how laboriously or obliquely—the latent structure of death that binds the colonized, but also the representation of a desire to get out of the "death zone" to which the colonized have been confined. Hence, one finds in John's Gospel no narrative of the Last Supper before Jesus's crucifixion, but only a postcrucifixion and postresurrection meal (21:1–14) to remember the dead and restore the living to life (see Lucian, *Luct.* 24; Morrison 1993, 142–43).[22] Likewise, one finds more than a Jesus returning to demonstrate the physical scars of his crucifixion, a show-and-tell that may be read as similar to Emmett Till's mother deciding to have an open casket during his son's funeral "so that the world could see what they had done to my child" (cited in Holloway 2002, 25, see also 130) and to "pass on" the "cultural haunting" of being African American (Holloway 2002, 136). In addition, one reads in John—besides the resurrection of Lazarus and Jesus—numerous promises of and references to "life," whether in terms of its resurrection, eternality, or abundance (2:19–22; 3:14–15; 5:21, 24–29; 6:39–40, 44, 54; 8:51; 14:19). Given John's portrayal of Jesus as the Passover lamb, it should also be noted that (1) the Passover sacrifice is about not only death but also *deliverance* from death (Koester 2005, 145), and (2) this deliverance from death is set within a context of Israelites being displaced and enslaved in Egypt.

According to Michael Taussig (1987, 4), "the space of death is important in the creation of meaning and consciousness, nowhere more so than in societies where torture is endemic and where the culture of terror flourishes. We may think of the space of death as a threshold that allows for illumination as well as extinction." Virgil, who also figures regions of the dead as places of revelation and inspiration, would have agreed (Edwards 2007, 17). It is important to point out here that even Bourdieu (1977, 79),

---

22. In fact, I tend to see Toni Morrison's other novel (1987) about the return of a dead beloved as sharing many of the dynamics and topics with the Gospel of John, including colonial oppression, death as a cultural haunting *and* awakening, as well as the movement of dream work in literary texts that end up speaking the unspeakable or unspoken.

in his theorization of *habitus*, insists on making room for improvisation within the socialized repertoire that one inhabits. I would suggest that John's Jesus, in a way that parallels those in gay communities who lived in the shadow of the AIDS epidemic at the end of the twentieth century, ends up improvising a subversive and threatening way of life. According to J. Halberstam (2005, 2), many gay persons, as a result of and in response to the threat and reality of AIDS, improvise to produce a "queer time," or "alternative temporalities ... [and] futures [that] can be imagined according to logics that lie outside of those paradigmatic markers of life experience—namely, birth, marriage, reproduction, and death." They do this, Halberstam suggests, in spite or perhaps because of how often and how much they are considered to be expendable bodies whose premature deaths are taken for granted rather than taken seriously by mainstream society. Yet, "by rethinking the conventional emphasis on longevity and futurity, and by making a community in relation to risk, disease, infection, and death," there arises "the potentiality of a life unscripted by the conventions of family, inheritance, and child rearing" and one that "show[s] little or no concern for longevity" (Halberstam 2005, 2, 4).

Since I have already argued for reading John's Jesus as a colonized Jew who lives knowingly in the shadow of death,[23] let me now point to his belief in the *productive potential* of death. John's Jesus not only looks at his life in light of his imminent death but also reinterprets death for the purposes of life. The best expression of this theme is arguably when, in response to a group of Greeks who come looking for him after his raising of Lazarus and several days before his last Passover, Jesus makes the somewhat enigmatic statement that "unless a grain of wheat falls into the ground and dies, it remains alone; but if it dies, it bears much fruit" (12:24). Immediately after this, Jesus gives what I take to be his key improvisation in making death productive. Like Halberstam's description of those who live life with abandon in the shadow of AIDS, John's Jesus suggests that "the one who hates his life in this world will keep it into life eternal" (12:25). In other words, if imperial sovereignty controls its subjects via a threat of death, one way to begin resisting this control is to let go of one's fear of death and be willing to die. Is this why John says that this dying and resurrecting Jesus is "the truth" and that "the truth will make you free" (8:32;

---

23. I have also argued elsewhere for a reading of John's Jesus as a queer or transgender subject; see Liew 2009.

14:6)? Is this what Fanon (1967, 227) is referring to when he talks about Vietnamese who have an "Asiatic attitude toward death" that confounded Europeans? Not only does John present Jesus's crucifixion as glorification (3:14; 8:28; 12:32)—and thus as Jesus's "triumph" in a sense (Koester 2005, 141–42)—but John also surprises many Johannine scholars by presenting Jesus as one who seems to remain in control during his arrest and passion (Ashton 1991, 489).

I think Helen C. Orchard (1998) is onto something when she suggests that John's Jesus is not only a victim of violence but also a colluder or conspirator in his own betrayal and death. But rather than following Orchard in pitting these two views as mutually exclusive, I would propose that what is in fact most impressive is how John implies a change of Jesus from bare life to one who is in control of his own death and life. Midway through the gospel, Jesus announces that he will willingly lay down his life "on his own accord and in his own authority" (10:17–18). Instead of stopping Judas from betraying him, Jesus lets Judas go from his "light" (1:4–5, 9; 8:12; 9:5; 12:46) into the "night" (13:27–30; see also 11:9–10; 12:35–36) even though he is fully aware of Judas's intentions (13:21–26). During his arrest, Jesus not only stops Peter from attempting to fight back with a sword (18:10–11) but also seems to welcome rather than avoid his coming captors. John says that Jesus, "knowing everything that was coming upon him, *went out* and said to them, 'Whom are you looking for?'" (18:4). As if this were not enough to emphasize Jesus's agency and initiative, the Johannine Jesus "surrenders" himself in this fashion not once but twice (18:7–8). I put "surrender" in quotes here because it is really an inaccurate description of what happens in light of the strange phenomenon that occurs between John 18:4–5 and 18:7–8. When Jesus voluntarily identifies himself as the very one whom the Jewish delegates and Roman cohort are coming for, John tells us that these captors, despite their "lanterns, lamps, and weapons" (18:3), "withdrew backward and fell to the ground" (18:6).

This dramatic or even unrealistic contrast of Jesus stepping up to speak and his captors stepping back to fall is in line not only with what Norman R. Petersen (1993) has called the "special language" or "anti-language" in John but also with the often expressionist or fantastical characteristic of dream work (JanMohamed 2005, 27).[24] Whatever else this strange event

---

24. Koester (1995, 27) has also noticed this dramatic or unrealistic characteristic in John's rhetoric, although Koester chooses to make sense of this difficult characteristic by referring to the workings of symbols or symbolism.

may signify, it shows how Jesus gains control over the death zone set by the Romans by being willing to step right up to and into death. A similar instance appears at John 14:25–31. While the reference to the Holy Spirit—particularly its function in reminding and elucidating—intimates the dynamics of the gospel in terms of dream work (14:25–26; see also 15:26; 16:13–15), Jesus's emphasis that "the ruler of the [Roman?] world … does not have any power over me" (14:30) shows that at issue in John is not just the affirmation and the gift of life but also the ownership of death. Jesus's consistent claim that he himself is laying down his own life is nothing less than a declaration of choice and agency. John's Jesus is not only detached but also *deliberate* in death.

In contrast to reading the Fourth Gospel as providing some kind of "pie in the sky" to overcome death (e.g., Reinhartz 2001, 113–15), JanMohamed's work on what he calls the "death-bound-subject" is particularly helpful here. Linking Agamben's bare life with Orlando Patterson's (1982) work on slavery as a form of powerlessness, natal alienation, and social death, JanMohamed suggests that bare life signifies social death. Even if such a person is physically alive, the fact that he or she can be killed at any time and for any reason means that such a person does not really count and has no legitimate place in the social body (JanMohamed 2005, 16). JanMohamed (2005, 19) goes on to propose that bare life, or the life of a "death-bound-subject," is "*defined by the need to avoid the possibilities of life as well as the possibility of death*" (emphasis original). Feeling the threat of death and not wanting to die, a "death-bound-subject" ends up controlling or repressing his or her desires for a fuller life. As a result, he or she stays within this death or deathly zone of "neither quite alive nor quite dead" (19). I think John can be read as alluding to this position also in a dreamlike—that is to say, an indirect and inexact—manner. John says adamantly and repeatedly that Jesus comes to give (eternal) life (1:4; 3:15–16, 36; 4:14, 36; 5:21–26, 39; 6:27–68; 10:10, 28; 11:25; 14:6; 17:2–3; 20:31). John also says, however, that some Jewish persons who come into contact with this giver of life decide to keep a certain distance because they are fearful of being "put away from the synagogue" (9:22; 12:42; see also 16:2). The reason for this fear can be seen in the comparison that Patterson (1982, 5) makes between what he calls the slave's "natal alienation"—that is, being socially dead with no rights or claims of birth—and a "secular excommunication." Being separated from a synagogue was a particularly severe form of social death for a Jew living under Roman colonization, since, as noted earlier, living under Roman rule in the aftermath of the

First Jewish-Roman War was in itself already a form of social death. Yet, being distant from Jesus—ironically, for John—is itself death (8:21, 24). John is therefore pointing to a situation in which certain Jews are choosing one form of death to avoid another form of death.

This situation is, in effect, what JanMohamed describes as the conundrum of a death-bound-subject or bare life. One settles for living a social death in order to avoid a physical death, since one knows that one tiny step out of the circumscribed death zone will result in a literal death. To break out of this conundrum, a "death-bound-subject" must become aware of this nonchoice but then proceed to choose to fight back with a counterthreat. If sovereignty's control over bare life is contingent on a threat of death, what may break that control is the threat on the part of the bare life to "'actualize' his [sic] potential or postponed death" (JanMohamed 2005, 17; see also Agamben 1998, 184–85). JanMohamed (2005, 17) calls this willful counterthreat—this willingness on the part of bare life to risk actualizing the death threat of the colonial master—"symbolic death." More specifically, JanMohamed (2005, 17) defines this "symbolic death" as being "constituted by the death of the slave's subject-position as a socially dead being and his *rebirth* in a different subject-position" (emphasis added). It is a switch from "living within death" to "dying within life" (128, 275), or to making a life out of re/signing death. By "re/signing death," I mean here the doubled sense of resigning to die and deconstructing the death zone in terms of Agamben's connection between sovereignty and bare life.

Jean Baudrillard seems to be saying something similar with a vocabulary of the economy: gift and countergift. According to Baudrillard (1993, 40), if power consists in a unilateral giving and taking of life, then "the power of the master has to unilaterally grant life will only be abolished if this life can be given to him—*in a non-deferred death*" (emphasis original). In fact, there is a strand of Greco-Roman philosophy that seeks to embrace death as a response to or cure of one's fear of death, like Lucretius by way of Epicureanism or Seneca through Stoicism (Edwards 2007: 78–112). We have from these resources a different lens to read and think about John's emphasis on being "born anew" or "born from above" (3:1–8), as well as the two resurrections that are recorded in the Fourth Gospel.[25] The symbolic nature of Lazarus's resurrection is, in my view, particularly perti-

---

25. Despite their similarity in emphasizing liberation from death *through* death, I must emphasize the need to keep in mind that a colonized Jew and a Greco-Roman philosopher occupied very different location of exploration in the first century CE.

nent. While most Johannine scholars would read Lazarus's resurrection as a symbolic foreshadowing of Jesus's resurrection, I would suggest doubling its symbolic function to include the sense that is being proposed by JanMohamed. Put differently, Lazarus's death and resurrection may signify a change of subject position rather than something literal, and this may be the case not only for Lazarus but also for Jesus. Thus John's Jesus clarifies from the beginning of the episode that Lazarus's sickness does not lead to death (11:4) and refers later to Lazarus's state as "having fallen asleep" (11:11). Although it is conventional within Johannine scholarship to read these as references to Lazarus's resurrection, it is important to keep in mind that John also makes a specific reference to a desire to (re)kill Lazarus after his resurrection (12:10–11). In other words, Lazarus can die (again).[26] If so, his (first) death *and* resurrection may well be symbolic in the way JanMohamed describes it, especially if one considers the workings of death in terms of and through dream.

This altering of subject position is an improvisation, or even an invention, like a discovery produced by death. It is so decisive, important, and influential that one can only compare it to a new birth. Death, in other words, is understood by John as actually a ground for being, or a new being who cannot be easily recognized (20:14; 21:4). Derrida (1993) has made a similar suggestion in *Aporias*, where he further compares death to border: both, for Derrida, are figures of passage and nonpassage involving a certain "step" and "not" (3–11). John will likewise present Jesus's death and resurrection as involving his passing of numerous borders. John's Jesus passes from the "world above" to the "world below." He also crosses the Jordan back into Judea to raise a dead Lazarus, a crossing that is in many ways a "step" into his own death despite his disciples' initial "not" (10:40–11:16). These "steps" that Jesus takes into death will ironically, according to John, also provide Jesus a ticket back to the "world above" and his followers a path or a way through the death zone (13:1; 14:2; 16:5, 7). Instead or in protest of being circumscribed to a death zone—a state of "living within death" that is also a liminal space between life and death—John dreams

---

26. Koester (1995, 110) argues that Lazarus's resurrection functions to foreshadow Jesus's resurrection rather than the resurrection to be experienced by believers, because Lazarus obviously will die again. But if Lazarus's second death disqualifies it from being a model for the promised resurrection of believers, why is it acceptable for Jesus's resurrection? In other words, why is the implication of a second death not agreeable for believers but agreeable for Jesus?

and writes of a Jesus who cannot only defy death but also travel between worlds and go through closed doors (20:19, 26). Since part of the rationale for providing a proper burial has to do with safeguarding the realm of life from that of the dead (Klauck 2003, 72), Jesus's resurrection and his ghost- or phantom-like appearances seem to suggest that—the good intentions of Joseph and Nicodemus notwithstanding (19:38–39)—nothing can secure a space from Jesus's intrusions and egressions. Mark Stibbe (1991) has helpfully pointed to John's Jesus as an elusive character, since other Johannine characters often find themselves playing "hide and seek" with Jesus (1:38; 5:13–14; 6:15–25; 7:1–11, 30, 44; 8:20–22, 59; 9:12, 35; 10:39–40; 11:1–6, 46–57; 12:36; 18:4, 7; 20:15). There is a politics of mobility here that must not be overlooked.[27] Jesus will continue to haunt the world below with his return, whether in his own bodily form, the form of the Holy Spirit (7:39; 14:15–27; 15:26; 16:7; 20:22), or the bodies of his disciples (16:16–22).

Derrida (1976, 73) is, of course, known for suggesting that writing spells both the death of *and* the resource for logos. Linking, then, death with resource or invention, one may further point to Derrida's (1989) understanding of invention as an opening to the other and ask if the death of the Word in John functions also inventively as such an opening. John's Jesus has declared himself a "gate" or "door" (10:9). I have argued elsewhere that building community is one of John's purposes and that Jesus, while dying on the cross, facilitates a new adoptive relation between his mother and the Beloved Disciple to signify the coming together of such a community (19:25b–28; Liew 2002, 195–96). If one can read Jesus's so-called high priestly prayer before his suffering and death (17:1–26) as his will, and if Seneca (*Ep.* 26.6) and Pliny the Younger (*Ep.* 8.18.1) are correct to suggest that one's will tells the truth of a person's character and commitment, then the community of his followers is of utmost importance to John's Jesus.[28] He sees his life and his work continuing in the community that survives him.

---

27. The rhetoric of this politics is extremely "dreamy" or dreamlike in John. Within this state of being in-between consciousness and unconsciousness, we read about a Jesus whose spacing in between worlds functions to represent both the liminal state of a bare life and the liberating freedom of an uncircumscribed life.

28. According to Roland Barthes (1982, 166), death in Tacitus's *Annals* functions similarly and "symbolically as the purest moment of life." They are, for Barthes as they are for Edwards, sites or sights for inspiration and instruction (163). Spillers (2003,

Jesus prays for his community in John 17 because it is not enough for Jesus to be reborn or resurrected from the death zone alone. As shown by both Lazarus and the Beloved Disciple, re/signing oneself to death—or "symbolic death"—does not necessarily mean that one will not literally die. Jesus needs to create and continue a community to keep his fight against the colonial master alive.[29] According to the late classics scholar Nicole Loraux (1986), funeral oration had a role in the "invention of Athens." Loraux argues that as a didactic speech, the funeral oration "does not so much console as it explains and exalts" heroic deeds, militaristic virtue, and, most of all, fidelity to the polis (48). In doing so, the funeral oration provides the crucial bridge or transition through which a person's primary loyalty would move from one's family to the city of Athens: "When the mothers, as members of the family, are moved away from the funeral pyre, they are integrated for the first time into the civic universe. Referring to their sons as *kleinotatous en Argeiois* (the most illustrious of the Argives), they recognize at last the rights of the city over the children whom they had wanted entirely for themselves" (49).

Loraux's work not only provides another perspective to read the new relation that the crucified Jesus facilitates between his mother and his Beloved Disciple (19:25b–28) but also reinforces a political reading of Jesus's death in John. It is as if John is insisting, through his writing of Jesus and Jesus's death, that despite threats of social death, physical death,

---

217–18), writing about the bare reality of flesh, conveys that displacement of people often includes a displacement of genitalia. Her argument that displacement in general and slavery in particular lead to a crisis of blood relations and hence the threat of kinlessness becomes even more alarming if one factors in the threat and reality of death. That is to say, Spiller's displacement of genitalia signals a danger of not only an orphan people but also a crisis of "progency *and* ethnicity or 'race'" (Holland 2000, 47 [emphasis original]). In other words, the bare life and death zone that are associated with displacement and colonialism often augur or bespeak genocide, especially in the eyes of the victims (Holland 2000, 79; see also Roberts 1997). In this light, John's insistence on Jesus creating a community through his death is all the more striking.

29. For Emmanuel Levinas (1969; 1996, 50), community—or more specifically, fecundity—is one way to overcome death. While Levinas's suggestion is meant to address Heidegger's (1962, 281–311) existentialist understanding of death as one's own and hence individualistically nonrelational or not related to others', Levinas's (1969, 56) sex-specific, or even sexist, definition of fecundity as a resurrection of a son not only echoes what we have in John's Gospel but also resonates with the concern over genocide that I am referring to through the work of Spillers.

and even genocide, a new community will come into being and keep generating and regenerating. By embracing his impending death, John's Jesus ends up reentering life in the "world above" *and* regenerating life as well as conceiving a fictive family in the "world below." Again, given the fluidity between the deaths and resurrections of Lazarus and Jesus in the Fourth Gospel, one may say that Jesus's death and resurrection function to "unbind" the (biological) bindings—and hence also the imperial ties—that keep Lazarus (socially) dead, entombed, and separate from other human beings, family, and community (11:44). This exchange of adoptive love and relations over social death through symbolic death can also be seen in the conversation between Jesus and Peter after Jesus's resurrection (21:15–19). Love for Jesus after his resurrection is expressed by caring for others, but doing so necessitates one's awareness or acceptance of one's own death in the manner of Jesus.[30]

---

30. The ironic relation between life and death, or life through death, that I have been arguing for John may also be seen in the way John associates food and drink with both life and death. We see John's Jesus getting thirsty and promising the Samaritan woman "living water" (4:1–14; see also 6:35; 7:37–39); when we find Jesus thirsty again in John, he is hanging and dying on the cross (19:28–30). John's Jesus also proclaims himself the "bread of life" in contrast to Moses's manna that cannot prevent death (6:1–59). The next time we read about "bread," it has become a means to identify Jesus's betrayer who will facilitate Jesus's death (13:10–30). "Bread" appears again in the last chapter of John, when Jesus cooks a postcrucifixion and postresurrection meal for his disciples, which leads to the commission to Peter to feed Jesus's flock (21:9–17). The offering of food and commission to feed are, however, followed by the references to the death of both Peter and the Beloved Disciple (21:18–23). Referring to both literary texts and material culture (including monuments, mosaic, and other artifacts), Edwards (2007, 161–78) suggests a connection between dining and dying in the Roman world, whether in terms of one's inevitability to leave life as one needs to leave a dinner party, or one's self-destruction (i.e., death) because of one's overindulgence in food and other bodily cravings. If so, the fish barbecue or funeral banquet in John 21 plays a curious function. It may double as a resolution of Jesus's death as well as an introduction to his followers' death. Their eating or consuming of food, just like Jesus's drinking of the sour wine on the cross, ends up anticipating the consummation of their lives. Peter's feeding of Jesus's flock would then not only lead to Peter's martyrdom as Jesus implies but also signal the death of those whom Peter will feed or has fed. Reading John 21 in light of the relations of dying and dining, one may exegete the mysterious "these" in Jesus's question to Peter (21:15) as referring to the fish he ate through the provision of Jesus; that is to say, Jesus wants to know if Peter loves him more than bodily cravings so Peter, like Jesus, would be willing to give up feeding his own life for the feeding or nourishing of others (see also 4:31–38; 6:25–27). Not

Community, or caring for one another *within* the community (John 13:34–35; 15:12, 17), is another well-recognized theme in Johannine scholarship. Again, I would suggest that reading John in the colonial framework that I have outlined here provides a distinctive rationale for this emphasis. As intimated earlier, the Roman machination of death could turn bare life into extensions of that machination and thus poison relations among the colonized. This reality is evident in the desire of some Jewish authorities to kill Jesus, perhaps for the sake of pacifying their Roman masters. James Baldwin (1967, 213) seems to be alluding to a similar dynamic when he writes, "For who has not hated his black brother? Simply *because* he is *black, because* he is brother" (emphasis original). Something similar to this transference of what David Marriott (2000, 82) calls "negrophobic fantasies" by blacks to other blacks may also have taken place among late first-century Jews, given what Peter Schäfer (1997) calls "Judeophobia" in the Greco-Roman world. When the African American author and gay activist Joseph Beam (1986, 239) "dare[s] *us* to dream that we are worth wanting each other" (emphasis original), he is writing to counteract two hostile fronts simultaneously: heterosexism within the black movement and racism within the gay movement. In other words, Beam's *dream* is not unrelated to the intracommunal love commanded by John's Jesus. In emphasizing how the "world" will hate him and his followers (15:17–16:3; 17:14), Jesus's love command for his community may well have something to do with his recognition that hate can be both internalized and transferred. Fanon (1967, 190–91) has repeatedly alluded to this dynamics of "projection" and "transference" with what he calls "the racial distribution of guilt" (103), particularly how Antilleans would not only distance themselves from but also denigrate other blacks, particularly Senegalese (26, 38, 101–3, 113, 148, 162–64 n. 25, 180–83; see also Marriott 2000, 82–84). Competing for the colonizers' recognition and possessions, colonized people often end up committing violence against one another (Fanon 1963, 307–9; see also Willett 2001).

It is, in this light, significant that Jesus's community of followers in John is made up of not only Jews but also Samaritans, Greeks, and potentially many others. The (potentially?) wide base of Jesus's community in John, however, does not invalidate my suggestion that Jesus's love command is

---

to forget here is Jesus's proclamation in John that completing his Father's work is his consumption of food (4:34).

partly based on the need to address the psychic transference of and among "death-bound-subjects." While John acknowledges coverage limits (20:30; 21:24–25), he nevertheless devotes considerable space to detailing the relations between Samaritans and Jesus. Jesus's encounter with the Samaritan woman ends not only with many Samaritans coming to believe in Jesus (4:39–42) but also with Jews mistaking Jesus himself as a demon-possessed Samaritan (8:48). Jesus's inclusion of and identification with the Samaritans are even more striking because John makes a point to say not only that Jesus is a Jews but also that "Jews do not associate with Samaritans" (4:9; see also 19:21). Instead of projecting or transferring the hatred of the (Roman) world toward Samaritans (as most Jews have supposedly done) or toward other Jews (as some Jews are doing to Jesus), John's Jesus dies to bring the colonized into a unified and loving community (11:51–52), or what Holloway (2002, 57, 67) calls "a macabre fraternity."

Dreaming Ambiguities

For John's Jesus to build this community of love and resistance among the colonized, his dream or desire must be recognized. John seems to recognize the difficulty of this recognition, given his own repeated references to the teaching role of the Holy Spirit after Jesus's departure (7:39; 14:26; 15:26; 16:13; 20:22). John's dream of life and death, or life through death, is difficult because it is full of complications and ambiguities. As noted above, community may allow one's work of resistance to continue beyond one's own death, as seems to be the case with the Beloved Disciple (21:18–24). At the same time, Jesus's conversation with Peter about Peter's upcoming death, as well as John's somewhat veiled comments about the Beloved Disciple's death, seem to indicate that one's change of subject position—that is, one's embrace of one's own symbolic death—must be so pervasive and deep that one must, like Jesus, be ready to embrace even the deaths of one's family, fictive *and* otherwise. If it is through willingness to die that one may live on an individual level, a similarly ironic and difficult dynamic is true on a communal level. One's life may perpetuate through one's "siblings" and "offspring" only if one resists the desire to protect them from dying.

While the potential efficacy of John's invention can be seen in a couple of examples from Josephus, where the willingness of Jews to die actually caused Pilate and Petronius, a Roman governor of Syria, to turn back from carrying the image of the emperor into Jerusalem or the temple (*A.J.*

18.55–59, 261–283), there is no guarantee that what JanMohamed calls "symbolic death" may not entail actual or literal death. After all, some studies have shown that the border between the symbolic and the literal in the Fourth Gospel is far from stable—they leak, flow, and evolve into each other (Staten 1993; Moore 2003)—so one should not metaphorize the materiality in John's narrative too quickly or too completely. In a sense, one may say that the proximity and fluidity between symbolic and literal death make community indispensable to the continuation of one's life and work. John's dreamy distinction between symbolic and literal death turns out, then, to be a disturbing one, for it implies also a very fine line between murder and suicide. If symbolic death means being unafraid or even willing to die and literal death is not only possible and probable in a colonial situation, then John's Jews actually have good grounds to read Jesus's action and articulation as an intent to commit suicide (8:21–22). When Thomas, in response to Jesus's decision to go to Judea for Lazarus despite the known danger ahead, suggests to the other disciples that they should accompany Jesus to die with him, he is in fact also reading Jesus's proposed action as suicidal.

Holloway (2002, 91, 94, 98), writing about "black death," points to a similar ambiguity that exists between suicide and accidental death or even homicide, because blacks who die in living risks or risking life may well be committing "suicide-by-other-means." If Agamben sees death as political and not just biological, Emile Durkheim (1951) showed years ago that suicide is social instead of merely individual. Perhaps JanMohamed can help to pull all these threads together by explaining how Agamben's "bare life" is stuck with the choice of killing or being killed. Since a bare life cannot really kill the colonizer, one can only kill another colonized person, kill oneself symbolically or literally, or continue to live under the killing threats of the colonizer. That is why JanMohamed (2005, 21, 229, 277) also sees rebellion, suicide, and murder as a mixed bag. It is noteworthy in this regard that Agamben (1998, 136–37) himself, in discussing bare life, also mentions suicide, although he insists on differentiating bare life from sacrifice in a ritual or religious sense (113–14). John shows, however, that sacrifice in a different sense may yet be factored into this already complicated and ambiguous mixture of rebellion, suicide, and murder. When Caiaphas suggests that Jesus "should die on behalf of the people rather than to have the entire nation perish" (11:49), he is in effect understanding the murder of Jesus as a sacrifice, in at least the sense of surrendering or destroying someone or something for the sake of a larger or higher goal.

More disturbing is the fact that John not only supports Caiaphas's understanding but also proceeds to further enlarge this higher purpose from benefiting a single nation to the greater gathering of all God's dispersed children (11:51–52; see also 18:8). Durkheim (1951, 217–40) would call this an example of "altruistic suicide."

Paul Plass (1995) has interestingly compared Roman political suicides to game theory. Like Jean Baudrillard (1993), who links death with economic exchange, Plass argues that Roman suicides, as political games, were governed by implicit rules and were hence uncertain or ambiguous in how things would turn out. With moves and countermoves, those who threatened suicide as a political protest against the emperor might actually find clemency, or they might end up paying the heavy price of losing their life. Plass's metaphors, whether game theory or gift exchange, underscore what John's Caiaphas and narrator both point to: the politics of death is often a matter of mathematics.[31] Whether the numbers are John's "one" against "many," symbolic death involves a calculation—and hence always already the possibility of miscalculation—of costs and returns. One may, of course, understand symbolic death, especially its "suicidal" or "sacrificial" aspect, as but a desperate means to make sense of bare life; it is done, in other words, out of an already passive rather than an active position in relation to life. However, even this absence of choice, nonchoice, or what looks like a number zero may itself be an inaccurate entry that will make all the difference on a balance sheet. As with challenge and compliance, there is an ambiguity between choice and coercion. The stakes are admittedly high when a miscalculation may lead to not only a literal loss of life but also a waste of death.

Starting with feminist voices, various scholars have articulated hesitations and reservations with this kind of ideology of sacrifice, particularly within the so-called Judeo-Christian traditions (for recent examples, see Boyarin 1999; Castelli 2004). To go back to Loraux's work, this ideology can be read in terms of what Jean François Lyotard (1988, 100) calls the "Athenian 'beautiful death,'" which he glosses as the "exchange of the finite for the infinite, the *eschaton* for the *telos*: the *Die in order not to die*" (emphasis original). John's ambiguity between symbolic and literal death—or the fine line between dying well, being willing to die, and wishing to die—becomes

---

31. According to Edwards (2007, 99), "[the] term *ratio*, in the sense of calculation, recurs frequently in Seneca's discussion of when is the right time to die."

even more questionable given the Romans' celebration of suicide as not only a heroic act but also a continuation of Rome's military and masculinist traditions (Edwards 2007, 1, 7, 32, 97). The problem then is more than just what John thinks, but if and how his thinking may be duplicating the ideologies of his colonial master.

In addition, even Jesus's agency in embracing his own "hour," which supposedly signifies a change in his subject position from being a bare life to one that features will and choice, is ambiguous in light of his ubiquitous references to his "Father." While John makes it a point to distance Jesus's own choice from the desire of Jesus's mother in the wedding at Cana (2:3–4), the same cannot be said about the relation between Jesus and his Father. There is a sense, of course, that John's appeal to the Father may function to resist the power of imperial Rome. This is evident, for example, in Jesus's response to Pilate's claim that Pilate's own power is derivative of another (19:8–11). In addition to highlighting the guilt of Caesar and hence the entire Roman apparatus in 19:11, Jesus's reference to "from above" may also refer to the existence of an authority even above that of Rome (3:31; 8:23). A helpful picture here is the familiar one of the Roman magistrate with the imperium and the lictor who always accompanied and went before him. On one level, Jesus is pointing out that Pilate is but a lictor who executes the sentence in the power of Caesar; on another level, Jesus may be suggesting that the entire Roman Empire is but a lictor under the power of his Father (see also Moore 2006, 64). As good as this latter meaning may sound to an anti-imperial ear, Agamben (1998, 89) points out that the only reason why Roman custom would allow a son to place himself between the magistrate and the lictor is because the son was always already "subject to a power of life and death with respect to the father." In other words, the son's presence does not contradict but rather confirms the sovereign power of the magistrate as father or father as magistrate.

The Father's role, then, not only makes Jesus's own agency ambiguous but also doubles that of the Roman master. Aside from the Roman ideology of paterfamilias, John's emphasis on a relation with this Father that is not based on blood and biology but on *obedience* makes it all the more troubling (1:12–13; 8:31–32, 51; 14:15–15:11; 17:6–9). Not only is such a paternalistic relation similar to the one that exists between colonizer and colonized, but it also, considering its emphasis on obedience, implies a view of others as infants at best and instruments at worst. John's insistence on the Father's invisibility (1:18; 5:37; 6:46) further implies that, unlike Jesus and Jesus's followers, the Father is not flesh (4:24). This contrast implies an even more significant differential in power in light of Spillers's and Agamben's work, despite John's characterization of the Father's relation with Jesus and Jesus's followers as one of love (3:35; 5:20; 10:17; 14:19–23; 15:9–11; 16:26–27; 17:20–26). The politics of mobility referred to earlier is also framed in terms of a world of light above and a world of darkness below (1:9; 3:3–8, 18–21, 31; 8:12, 23–24; 9:1–5; 11:7–10; 12:44–50; see also Dube 1998). Therefore, John's rhetoric and logic are, despite small doses of more horizontal or fraternal expressions (10:30; 15:15), hierarchically conceived, and, given Jesus's emphasis on returning or going to the Father, vertically oriented.

Take, for instance, the intracommunal love command discussed earlier. Since John's Jesus declares that laying down one's life for another is love par excellence (15:13; see also Levinas 2000, 216) and since Jesus immediately specifies obedience to his commands as prerequisite of friendship with him (15:14), love and death seem to be always already mingled in John. More importantly, it is hard not to conclude that being willing to die is not a command performance, as seems to be the case with Jesus (10:18).[32] If John's Jesus, as well as those who follow John's Jesus, are supposed to be fully subjected to the will of the Father to the point of death (6:35–64; 10:1–18; 15:1–16:4; 21:15–19), then are we not back to a scenario in which a Caesar-like head sits comfortably in a choice seat and watches bare life performing death for his purposes and his enjoyment? This is all the more troubling since John apparently feels no need to explain or account for this hierarchical relation between Jesus and his Father; in other words, John basically takes a hierarchical paternal function for granted. Similar

---

32. Levinas, in arguing for an ethical rather than a Heideggerian or existentialist reading of death, sees community, fecundity, or sacrificing oneself for others as a "meaningful" death. Although Levinas (1998, 126) is adamant that no one has the right to ask another person to sacrifice for others, "voluntary" sacrifice is also problematic on at least two fronts: (1) what appears "voluntary" is not necessarily without force; and (2) even "true" volunteering may still be a sincere wrong.

I do not have the space here or the ability to work through all the questions surrounding death, sacrifice, and suicide, but I do need to point out that these are indeed postcolonial questions. From her early work on the problematic reading of a young Indian revolutionary's death in 1926 as suicide in terms of *sati*, Gayatri Chakravorty Spivak (1988, 294–308) has been concerned with not only the reading of death of the colonized in the binary terms of "victimage versus cultural heroism" but also how ignoring "the role of violence in the development of [colonial] conscience is to court the repetition of suicide as accountability" (1999, 291–92).

to the way some Jews present Jesus's challenge as a contest between a king and a Roman emperor (19:12, 15), John seems to see his situation as a struggle between two paternal and paternalistic authorities who reward obedience with life and reprove disobedience with death (6:50; 8:21, 24; see also Moore 2006, 50).

Reading Anatomies and the Art of Mourning

I think the mixture of rebellion, murder, sacrifice, and suicide in the Gospel of John points to the depth of death within John himself as a death-bound-subject. He sees his choices as but different types of death: social, symbolic, and/or actual. These are severely limited choices, if they are choices are all. Not only is John "caught up in an infinite labyrinth of death" (JanMohamed 2005, 265) even in resistance, but the structure and logic of imperial sovereignty and bare life also seem to be so pervasive and deep-seated that John is consciously and unconsciously subjected to them even as he dreams of a different subject position. Perhaps more accurately, John's dream of a changed subject position is possible or thinkable only within the structure and logic that bind, subjugate, and "subjectify" him. To use a vocabulary familiar to both Johannine and Derridean studies, John's "aporias" or inconsistencies actually—and ironically—reveal the consistent and constitutive power of colonial sovereignty. It must be remembered that John, just like his Jews, is a colonized—thus victimized—agent, even or especially when we point to the inadequacies of his invention of or intervention over death. At the same time, as the term "victimized agent" implies, John is not only a victim: his invention or intervention not only shows that others, including the colonial masters, are constitutive of his own subjectivity but also points to the need to remain open to the other. After all, John reminds us that there are not only many deeds of Jesus that he has failed to record or tell but also that even all the books in the world cannot contain every act of Jesus (21:25). Since this concluding statement is given right after references to the death of both Peter and the Beloved Disciple (21:18–23)—the latter of whom is also credited as the source of John's book about Jesus living and giving life in the shadow and experience of death (21:24)—I would suggest that John ends by foregrounding his corpus as but traces of the departed. Like the wounds and scars that Jesus shows his disciples after his resurrection (20:19–28), John also makes visible the cuts that he has performed on his gospel. In a sense, then, one can say that even his gospel emerges as a corpse; it is declared an aborted text immediately upon its birth. Our attention is thus turned away from the corpus back to, shall we say, the corpses. Instead of seeing reading as anatomizing or analyzing the corpus, perhaps it is more appropriate to think of "reading [the Fourth Gospel] ... as an ... interminable and unforeclosable work of mourning" (Michaud 2002, 83).

In retelling Jesus's story, John honors and portrays the struggles of one colonized and departed Jew or Jewish community. Earlier I referred to Derrida's exorbitant reading; let me now point to his suggestion of mourning as "a *politics* of memory, of inheritance, and of generation" (Derrida 1994, xix [emphasis original]). This memory or mourning politics must involve, for Derrida, both a respect and a betrayal of the other, since betrayal is necessary to welcome and to make room for what this other has been awaiting (see also Derrida 1999; Krell 2000). What John awaits is life beyond bare life. In memory of John's memory of Jesus, we must not only recall but also rework what John has written.

After all, learning about one who has departed or seeing another's corpse may remind one of one's own mortality as well as one's vitality. In other words, knowing that you are, unlike the departed or the corpse, still here and alive can become a moment of empowerment. As John 20:30–31 indicates, we are empowered or at least asked to think about our own life and perhaps even to rehearse our own death. If so, then John's Jesus is, like a Roman gladiator, dying for an audience, and John is performing the role of a master of ceremonies. Since John's Jesus needs witnesses and John needs readers, so John's portrayal of Jesus's life and death is every bit as spectacular as other Roman spectacles of death. But how will his audience respond? Will they mourn as Derrida suggests, and/or will they objectify the departed or the dead as passive and hence feminized (Bronfen 1992, 30, 65, 102, 120; Edwards 2007, 43–44)? What may this second potential response imply about female readers of John? All these questions must remain open, and the responses ambiguous. This element of ambiguity should not be surprising if one considers not only John's own specialization in double-speak but also the agency of the reader or spectator. Just like John, who internalizes and improvises on the death-bound subjectivity given to him by his colonizers, we who live under the "effective history" (Gadamer 1994, 301–2) of colonialism and the Fourth Gospel can also invent a different future. While we are grateful that John's Jesus does not say anything about "letting the dead bury their own dead" (Matt 8:22; Luke 9:60), we also need not be stuck in John's accounting or algebra of life and death in our own understanding and practice of living, reading, and writing.[33]

As Friedrich Nietzsche suggests, critical students of the past "must possess the strength, and must at times apply this strength, to the destruction and dissolution of the past in order to be able to live" (cited in De Man 1983, 149). To mourn the dead is to keep engaging, including disagreeing with them. After all, to reanimate the dead is to give them "new," and hence at least a partially different, life. Agamben (1998, 186), in his work on bare life, mentions in passing the difference between "anatomy" as a description of inert organs by dissecting a dead body and "physiology" as an explanation of functioning organs in a living and moving body. Likewise, John's text is for me a mediating zone of intersubjective interaction that is sociohistorically based, rather than an autonomous or isolated aesthetic object. In and through the Fourth Gospel, I find and participate in movements between worlds so as to be in touch with others—including the memory, mourning, and betrayal of the dead—for the hope of life.

Works Cited

Agamben, Giorgio. 1998. *Homo Sacer: Sovereign Power and Bare Life*. Stanford, CA: Stanford University Press.
Ashton, John. 1991. *Understanding the Fourth Gospel*. Oxford: Clarendon.
Assmann, Jan. 1997. *Moses the Egyptian: The Memory of Egypt in Western Monotheism*. Cambridge: Harvard University Press.
Bailey, Randall C., Tat-siong Benny Liew, and Fernando F. Segovia, eds. 2009. *They Were All Together in One Place? Toward Minority Biblical Criticism*. Atlanta: Society of Biblical Literature.
Baldwin, James. 1967. *Nobody Knows My Name: More Notes of a Native Son*. New York: Dial.

---

33. I see this as one way to move, as Said does, from a "rhetoric of blame" to a "contrapuntal reading" that makes connections not only between a work of culture and its larger sociopolitical world but also between a work of the past and its reader in the present (Said 1993, 51, 66, 96; 2004). My point about improvisation—for both John and those who read John—is also meant to dispute the criticism of some that new historicism inevitably "reduces" a writer to his or her historical circumstances to the point of making authorial agency an oxymoron (Posnock 2007, 144, 164). In my view, there is a lot of space between a liberal humanism that advocates an extreme form of individual freedom or autonomy and a determinism that eliminates human agency.

Barthes, Roland. 1982. "Tacitus and the Funerary Baroque." Pages 162–66 in *A Barthes Reader*. Edited by Susan Sontag. New York: Hill & Wang.

Baudrillard, Jean. 1993. *Symbolic Exchange and Death*. Translated by Iain Hamilton Grant. Thousand Oaks, CA: Sage.

Beam, Joseph. 1986. *In the Life: A Black Gay Anthology*. Boston: Alyson.

Borch-Jacobsen, Mikkel. 1991. *Lacan: The Absolute Master*. Translated by Douglas Brick. Stanford, CA: Stanford University Press.

Bourdieu, Pierre. 1977. *Outline of a Theory of Practice*. Translated by Richard Nice. Cambridge: Cambridge University Press.

Boyarin, Daniel. 1999. *Dying for God: Martyrdom and the Making of Christianity and Judaism*. Stanford, CA: Stanford University Press.

Bronfen, Elisabeth. 1992. *Over Her Dead Body: Death, Femininity and the Aesthetic*. New York: Routledge.

Brooks, Peter. 1994. "The Idea of a Psychoanalytic Literary Criticism." Pages 20–45 in *Psychoanalysis and Storytelling*. Cambridge: Blackwell.

Bultmann, Rudolf. 1971. *The Gospel of John: A Commentary*. Translated by G. R. Beasley-Murray. Philadelphia: Westminster.

Castelli, Elizabeth A. 2004. *Martyrdom and Memory: Early Christian Culture Making*. New York: Columbia University Press.

Cheng, Anne Anlin. 2001. *The Melancholy of Race: Psychoanalysis, Assimilation, and Hidden Grief*. New York: Oxford University Press.

Coleman, Kathy M. 1990. "Fatal Charades: Roman Executions Staged as Mythological Enactments." *JRS* 80:44–73.

Conway, Colleen M. 2002. "The Production of the Johannine Community: A New Historicist Perspective." *JBL* 121:479–95.

Countryman, L. William. 1994. *The Mystical Way in the Fourth Gospel: Crossing Over into God*. Rev. ed. Harrisburg, PA: Trinity Press International.

Culpepper, R. Alan. 1983. *Anatomy of the Fourth Gospel: A Study in Literary Design*. Philadelphia: Fortress.

De Man, Paul. 1983. *Blindness and Insight: Essays in the Rhetoric of Contemporary Criticism*. New York: Routledge.

Derrida, Jacques. 1976. *Of Grammatology*. Translated by Gayatri Chakravorty Spivak. Baltimore: Johns Hopkins University Press.

———. 1989. "Psyche: Inventions of the Other." Pages 25–65 in *Reading de Man Reading*. Edited by Lindsay Waters and Wlad Godzich. Minneapolis: University of Minnesota Press.

———. 1993. *Aporias: Dying—Awaiting (One Another at) the "Limits of Truth."* Translated by Thomas Dutoit. Stanford, CA: Stanford University Press.

———. 1994. *Specters of Marx.* Translated by Peggy Kamuf. New York: Routledge.

———. 1999. *Adieu to Emmanuel Levinas.* Translated by Pascale-Anne Brault and Michael Naas. Stanford, CA: Stanford University Press.

———. 2001. *On Cosmopolitanism and Forgiveness.* Translated by Mark Dooley and Michael Hughes. New York: Routledge.

Derrida, Jacques, and Anne Dufourmantelle. 2000. *Of Hospitality.* Translated by Rachel Bowlby. Stanford, CA: Stanford University Press.

Dube, Musa W. 1998. ""Savior of the World, But Not of This World: A Postcolonial Reading of Spatial Construction in John." Pages 118-35 in *The Postcolonial Bible.* Edited by R. S. Sugirtharajah. Sheffield: Sheffield Academic.

Du Bois, W. E. B. 1953. *The Souls of Black Folk.* New York: Modern Library.

Durkheim, Emile. 1951. *Suicide: A Study in Sociology.* Translated by John A. Spaulding and George Simpson. Glencoe, IL: Free Press.

Edwards, Catharine. 2007. *Death in Ancient Rome.* New Haven: Yale University Press.

Fanon, Frantz. 1963. *The Wretched of the Earth.* Translated by Constance Farrington. New York: Grove.

———. 1967. *Black Skin, White Masks.* Translated by Charles Lam Markmann. New York: Grove.

Feldman, Louis H., and Meyer Reinhold, eds. 1996. *Jewish Life and Thought among Greeks and Romans: Primary Readings.* Minneapolis: Fortress.

Freud, Sigmund. 1953-1974. *Standard Edition of the Complete Psychological Works of Sigmund Freud.* Edited and Translated by James Strachey. 24 vols. London: Hogarth.

Frier, Bruce W. 1982. "Roman Life Expectancy: Ulpian's Evidence." *HSCP* 86:213-51.

———. 1999. "Roman Demography." Pages 85-109 in *Life, Death, and Entertainment in the Roman Empire.* Edited by David S. Potter and David J. Mattingly. Ann Arbor: University of Michigan Press.

Gadamer, Hans-Georg. 1994. *Truth and Method.* Translated by Joel Weinsheimer and Donald G. Marshall. 2nd ed. New York: Continuum.

Garnsey, Peter. 1970. *Social Status and Legal Privilege in the Roman Empire.* Oxford: Clarendon.

Gilroy, Paul. 2005. *Postcolonial Melancholia*. New York: Columbia University Press.
Glancy, Jennifer A. 2002. *Slavery in Early Christianity*. New York: Oxford University Press.
———. 2005. "Torture: Flesh, Truth, and the Fourth Gospel." *BibInt* 13:107–36.
Halberstam, J. 2005. *In a Queer Time and Place: Transgender Bodies, Subcultural Lives*. New York: New York University Press.
Harrill, J. Albert. 2006. *Slaves in the New Testament: Literary, Social, and Moral Dimensions*. Minneapolis: Fortress.
Heidegger, Martin. 1962. *Being and Time*. Translated by John Macquarrie and Edward Robinson. New York: Harper.
———. 1971. *On the Way to Language*. Translated by Peter D. Hertz. New York: Harper.
Hegel, Georg Wilhelm Friedrich. 1977. *Phenomenology of Spirit*. Translated by A. V. Miller. New York: Oxford University Press.
Holland, Sharon Patricia. 2000. *Raising the Dead: Readings of Death and (Black) Subjectivity*. Durham, NC: Duke University Press.
Holloway, Karla F. C. 2002. *Passed On: African American Mourning Stories*. Durham, NC: Duke University Press.
Isaac, Benjamin. 2004. *The Invention of Racism in Classical Antiquity*. Princeton: Princeton University Press.
JanMohamed, Abdul R. 2005. *The Death-Bound-Subject: Richard Wright's Archaeology of Death*. Durham, NC: Duke University Press.
Kelly, Christopher. 2006. *The Roman Empire: A Very Short Introduction*. New York: Oxford University Press.
Klauck, Hans-Josef. 2003. *The Religious Context of Early Christianity: A Guide to Graeco-Roman Religions*. Translated by Brain McNeil. Minneapolis: Fortress.
Kloppenborg, John S. 1996. "Collegia and *Thiasoi*: Issues in Function, Taxonomy and Membership." Pages 16–30 in *Voluntary Associations in the Graeco-Roman World*. Edited by John S. Kloppenborg and Steven G. Wilson. New York: Routledge.
Koester, Craig R. 1995. *Symbolism in the Fourth Gospel: Meaning, Mystery, Community*. Minneapolis: Fortress.
———. 2005. "The Death of Jesus and the Human Condition: Exploring the Theology of John's Gospel." Pages 141–57 in *Life in Abundance: Studies of John's Gospel in Tribute to Raymond E. Brown*. Edited by John R. Donahue. Collegeville, MN: Liturgical Press.

Kojève, Alexandre. 1965. *Introduction to the Reading of Hegel: Lectures on the Phenomenology of Spirit*. Edited by Allan Bloom. Translated by James H. Nichols Jr. Ithaca, NY: Cornell University Press.

Krell, David Farrell. 2000. *The Purest of Bastards: Works of Mourning, Art, and Affirmation in the Thought of Jacques Derrida*. University Park: Pennsylvania State University Press.

Kristeva, Julia. 1982. *Powers of Horror: An Essay on Abjection*. Translated by Leon S. Rudiez. New York: Columbia University Press.

Kyle, Donald G. 1998. *Spectacles of Death in Ancient Rome*. New York: Routledge.

Lacan, Jacques. 2001. *Ecrits: A Selection*. Translated by Alan Sheridan. New York: Routledge.

Levinas, Emmanuel. 1969. *Totality and Infinity: An Essay on Exteriority*. Translated by Alphonso Lingis. Pittsburgh: Duquesne University Press.

———. 1996. "Meaning and Sense." Pages 33–64 in *Emmanuel Levinas: Basic Philosophical Writings*. Edited by Adriaan T. Peperzak, Simon Critchley, and Robert Bernasconi. Translated by Alphonso Lingis. Bloomington: Indiana University Press.

———. 1998. *Otherwise Than Being, or, Beyond Essence*. Translated by Alphonso Lingis. Pittsburgh: Duquesne University Press.

———. 2000. *Entre Nous: Essays on Thinking-of-the-Other*. Translated by Michael B. Smith and Barbara Harshav. New York: Columbia University Press.

Liew, Tat-siong Benny. 2009. "Queering Closets and Perverting Desires: Cross-Examining John's Engendering and Transgendering Word across Different Worlds." Pages 251–88 in *They Were All Together in One Place? Toward Minority Biblical Criticism*. Edited by Randall C. Bailey, Tat-siong Benny Liew, and Fernando F. Segovia. Atlanta: Society of Biblical Literature.

———. 2002. "Ambiguous Admittance: Consent and Descent in John's Community of 'Upward' Mobility." Pages 193–224 in *John and Postcolonialism: Travel, Space and Power*. Edited by Musa W. Dube and Jeffrey L. Staley. Sheffield: Sheffield Academic.

Loraux, Nicole. 1986. *The Invention of Athens: The Funeral Oration in the Classical City*. Translated by Alan Sheridan. Cambridge: Harvard University Press.

Luepnitz, Deborah. 2003. "Beyond the Phallus: Lacan and Feminism." Pages 221–37 in *The Cambridge Companion to Lacan*. Edited by Jean-Michel Rabaté. New York: Cambridge University Press.

Lyotard, Jean François. 1988. *The Differend: Phrases in Dispute*. Translated by Georges Van Den Abbeele. Minneapolis: University of Minnesota Press.

Mailer, Norman. 1959. "The White Negro." Pages 337–58 in *Advertisements for Myself*. New York: Putnam's Sons.

Marriott, David. 2000. *On Black Men*. New York: Columbia University Press.

Michaud, Ginette. 2002. "Literature in Secret: Crossing Derrida and Blanchot." *Angelaki: Journal of the Theoretical Humanities* 7:69–90.

Moore, Stephen D. 1996. *God's Gym: Divine Male Bodies of the Bible*. New York: Routledge.

———. 2003. "Are There Impurities in the Living Water That the Johannine Jesus Dispenses?" Pages 78–97 in vol. 1 of *A Feminist Companion to John*. Edited by Amy-Jill Levine with Marianne Blickenstaff. Cleveland: Pilgrim.

———. 2006. *Empire and Apocalypse: Postcolonialism and the New Testament*. Sheffield: Sheffield Phoenix.

Morrison, Toni. 1987. *Beloved*. New York: Knopf.

———. 1993. *The Bluest Eye*. New York: Random House.

Oliver, Kelly. 2004. *The Colonization of Psychic Space: A Psychoanalytic Social Theory of Oppression*. Minneapolis: University of Minnesota Press.

Orchard, Helen C. 1998. *Courting Betrayal: Jesus as Victim in the Gospel of John*. Sheffield: Sheffield Academic.

Patterson, Orlando. 1982. *Slavery and Social Death*. Cambridge: Harvard University Press.

Petersen, Norman R. 1993. *The Gospel of John and the Sociology of Light: Language and Characterization in the Fourth Gospel*. Valley Forge, PA: Trinity Press International.

Plass, Paul. 1995. *The Game of Death in Ancient Rome: Arena Sport and Political Suicide*. Madison: University of Wisconsin Press.

Pontalis, J. B. 1978. "On Death-Work in Freud, in the Self, in Culture." Pages 85–95 in *Psychoanalysis, Creativity, and Literature: A French-American Inquiry*. Edited by Alan Roland. New York: Columbia University Press.

Posnock, Ross. 2007. "Planetary Circles: Philip Roth, Emerson, Kundera." Pages 141–67 in *Shades of the Planet: American Literature as World Literature*. Edited by Wai Chee Dimock and Lawrence Buell. Princeton: Princeton University Press.

Reinhartz, Adele. 2001. *Befriending the Beloved Disciple: A Jewish Reading of the Gospel of John*. New York: Continuum.

Roberts, Dorothy. 1997. *Killing the Black Body: Race, Reproduction, and the Meaning of Liberty*. New York: Vintage.

Rose, Jacqueline. 2000. "Edward Said Talks to Jacqueline Rose." Pages 9–30 in *Edward Said and the Work of the Critic: Speaking Truth to Power*. Edited by Paul A. Bové. Durham, NC: Duke University Press.

Said, Edward W. 1978. *Orientalism*. New York: Pantheon.

———. 1993. *Culture and Imperialism*. New York: Knopf.

———. 2004. *Humanism and Democratic Criticism*. New York: Columbia University Press.

Schäfer, Peter. 1997. *Judeophobia: Attitudes toward the Jews in the Ancient World*. Cambridge: Harvard University Press.

Spillers, Hortense J. 2003. *Black, White, and in Color: Essays on American Literature and Culture*. Chicago: University of Chicago Press.

Spivak, Gayatri Chakravorty. 1988. "Can the Subaltern Speak?" Pages 271–313 in *Marxism and the Interpretation of Culture*. Edited by Cary Nelson and Larry Grossberg. Urbana: University of Illinois Press.

———. 1999. *A Critique of Postcolonial Reason: Toward a History of the Vanishing Present*. Cambridge: Harvard University Press.

Staten, Henry. 1993. "How the Spirit (Almost) Became Flesh: Gospel of John." *Representations* 41:34–57.

Stibbe, Mark W. G. 1991. "The Elusive Christ: A New Reading of the Fourth Gospel." *JSNT* 44:20–39.

Taussig, Michael. 1987. *Shamanism, Colonialism, and the Wild Man: A Study in Terror and Healing*. Chicago: University of Chicago Press.

Thatcher, Tom. 2006. *Why John Wrote a Gospel: Jesus—Memory—History*. Louisville: Westminster John Knox.

Willett, Cynthia. 2001. *The Soul of Justice: Social Bonds and Racial Hubris*. Ithaca, NY: Cornell University Press.

Wright, Richard. 1969. *Black Boy: A Record of Childhood and Youth*. New York: Harper & Row.

Psychoapocalypse:
Desiring the Ends of the World

Tina Pippin

"Do not start that. Miracles are getting more common, mate. We knew this was coming." He cried with gruff emotion, touched his chest near his heart. "It's the ends of the world."
"End of the world?"
"Ends." (Miéville 2010, 84)

The Means Justify the Ends

In the ticket line to see *2012* with my "The Politics of Apocalypse" class one semester, we met a woman who was returning for a second viewing of the film because she found it so believable. "This is the way it's really going to happen," she shared. "This movie shows exactly how the world is going to end; I have to see it again to catch all the details. After you see it you just want to be nice to people." This viewer had crossed over into the film's fantastic vision of the end; in fact, she was an enthusiastic evangelist for the earthquakes and the shifting tectonic plates that flood and reorder the earth's continents. Desire for the end, this particular ending of the world, was addictive for her and necessitated a repeat visit. As in the *Left Behind* books and films (which this woman told us she also believed), the packaging of apocalypse makes the end-time violence accessible and desirable. The final fictional scenes and aftermath of the world-as-we-know-it become the soon-to-happen fulfillment of (secular and/or biblical) prophecies. But this kind of prophecy warns humanity: it may be too late to stop the endings of the world, but it is not too late to be nice and hopefully gain a coveted spot in the next world(s).

This strange pull of apocalypse emerges like the biblical beasts, suddenly and with abandon. Apocalypse is a force that gathers strength in colluding with the Real.[1] Rapture, Mayan millennium, climate change, and biblical apocalypses all converge into the narratives of the ends of the world. The gods of apocalypse do not scatter humans like in the Babel story; they seize control, destroying the Other in flood, fire, and other (un)natural disasters. Ironically, the manifold fictions become truth, making the fantasies of the ends into the tower of bricks again. The desire for destruction is not that far removed from the desire for Babel and, ultimately, the longing for Eden. I read biblical apocalyptic literature,[2] especially the largest chunk of it in the Apocalypse of John, as consuming this desire and reflecting it back in bold and startling ways. It is as if the text asks, "Are these the endings you really desire? Are these the endings you imagine your God needing?" Here I want to investigate some psychological interweavings of the fantastic narratives, especially as they unfold into utopian, neocolonial dreams in a recent apocalyptic film, *2012*. My hunch about apocalyptic literature and other forms has been to agree with many others that it provides a release (a catharsis) of emotions.[3] I think apocalyptic urges a certain violent political desire that actualizes in the present. I am also working with the premise that there is no singular apocalypse in the Bible, despite all the efforts to merge the scraps of end-time dreams. Readers encounter apocalyptic in infinite ways, often dragging, as did the biblical prophets, their political agendas and struggles along, brick by brick, to rebuild the tower and, quite often, "Western" superiority and imperialism.

Taking China Miéville's suggestive question in his 2010 novel—what if there are multiple end*s* of the world—I want to play with the reality in the Bible and beyond that there are already ends that have been pieced together. Certainly there are discordant parts (millennial movements such as Heaven's Gate, Jonestown, Waco, and too many others), yet there are shared threads among the many different seams. Other prospective

---

1. For an excellent overview of Žižek and Lacan on the concepts of desire, trauma, and the Real, see Runions 2003, 19–25. See also Žižek 1991 for Žižek's reading of Lacan

2. The traditional definition of biblical apocalyptic literature is as follows: "An apocalypse is defined as 'genre of revelatory literature with a narrative framework, in which a revelation is mediated by an otherworldly being to a human recipient disclosing a transcendent reality which is both temporal, insofar as it envisages eschatological salvation, and spatial insofar as it involves another, supernatural world'" (Collins 1979, 9). Such a definition holds fast to a neutral position and does a disservice to the very ideological nature of apocalypses.

3. See, for example, Collins 1984.

ends include human-made and natural catastrophes. These ends are in competition with each other to be the "first apocalypse," and not only the first but also the sole end. As Miéville subversively asks in his novel, what would happen if more than one apocalypse happened at once? A meteorite or comet or nuclear holocaust at the same time as the Christian rapture would surely mess up the plans for the rise of the antichrist and the tribulation. Or how disappointed one would be if one's idea of apocalypse turns out to be wrong. Miéville's logic seems to be that imagining that only one scenario is possible opens up the possibility that all endings are possible. Miéville muses: "What happens if two apocalypses are scheduled to happen at the same time? How cosmologically embarrassing!" (Lyall 2010, C8).

Miéville is working out of a conviction that fantasy and science fiction are both important conversation partners with Marxist criticism and political analysis. The debate among theorists of fantasy and science fiction has traditionally focused on their differences. One of the main science fiction theorists, Darko Suvin (1979, 9), set the tone for the debate by privileging science fiction and calling fantasy "just a subliterature of mystification." Suvin (2000, 211) later shifted his initial negativity toward fantasy literature: "The divide between cognitive (pleasantly useful) and non-cognitive (useless) does not run between SF and fantastic fiction but inside each." Miéville (2002, 44), drawing on both Suvin and science fiction theorist Carl Freedman, carries this point further to note that fantasy and science fiction share common characteristics and that "unscientific but *internally plausible/rigorous*, estranging works share crucial qualities of cognitive seriousness." Both literary forms have a connection with the "impossible." Science fiction is the "not-yet-possible," while the fantastic is "the never-possible" (44–45). Fantasy is no less ideological than science fiction; thus the hierarchy cannot stand (Miéville 2009, 242–43).

Fredric Jameson enters the conversation here to engage both science fiction and fantasy on his way to a study of utopia and its political effects. Jameson (2005, 74) remarks that there is "something like a binary alternation between the reality principle of SF and the pleasure principle of fantasy," with utopia as a synthesis of the two as "the supreme creativity or shaping impulse of fantasy marshalling the most recalcitrant raw material of all, in the state and the social order." Jameson privileges more complex science fiction and fantasy, that is, those works that move away from the binary of good versus evil (e.g., works such as those by J. R. R. Tolkien, J. K. Rowling, and others). Jameson draws on Freud's concept of wish-fulfillment in daydreaming in noting that this kind of binary fantasy draws out "the essentially infantile spirit of an opposition between heroes and villains which reconfirms the narcissistic perspective of the self on other people and other realities" (58). In this way, biblical apocalyptic functions to set the stage for the reader's journey into these ends. In a Freudian sense this fear of the end drives apocalyptic dreams. In a Marxist sense, "whatever threatens the system as such must be excluded," and that means a blatant disregard for the individual (205). Thus science fiction and fantasy both show repressed desires for some utopian or dystopian future worlds. There are apocalyptic narratives that mark us, whether or not we are "believers" in any of these ends.

Of course in his fictional writings, Miéville, like many contemporary apocalyptic films (e.g., *The Day after Tomorrow, 2012*), merges science fiction and the fantastic in creative ways. As a Marxist, Miéville is committed to utopian desire in different ways than these films; for him, the dominant system has many cracks and crevices. He also holds fast to a main mantra of fantasy: "The defiantly fantastic—the never-possible—will not go away" (Miéville 2002, 45). Both the awful and not-so-awful apocalyptic films hold to this premise. It is hard to shake the horror of these ends, for they break us out of our "psychic numbing."[4] The apocalypse is fantastic, both in biblical accounts and in popular cultural retellings, but it is also a chaotic mix of the never-possible (e.g., angel armies defeating evil beasts) and the not-yet-possible but possible at any moment. The apocalypse is the ultimate "inconvenient truth." Biblical apocalyptic, as well as its contemporary iterations, breaks down our sense of safety, but just momentarily. We can close the books or walk out of the theater into the sunlight.

Yet the apocalyptic dream sticks; we cannot wish it away and may in fact have some emotional investment (religious, economic, political) in keeping the dream active. This active dream can translate into real politics, such as support for nuclear build-up and mutually assured destruction (MAD). As documentaries such as *Countdown to Zero* show, we are living out an apocalyptic dystopia; unless we act quickly to eradicate nuclear weapons (to get to zero), the future of the planet is doomed. Postapocalyptic films (*A Boy and His Dog* [1975], *Mad Max* [1979], *The Road* [2009], *The Book of Eli* [2010]) play on this inevitability of some form (nuclear or

---

4. The phrase "psychic numbing" is used by Joanna Macy and Robert Jay Lifton in their work on raising awareness about nuclear weapons. See Macy 1983, 7, 13; and Lifton 1982; 1991, 500–506.

otherwise) of destruction of the earth and the sad lot of the survivors who eke out hope in the end.[5] Jameson (2005, 199), bringing in Freud again, comments that "the Apocalypse [of John] is neither dialectical (in the sense of its Utopian 'opposite') nor some mere psychological projection, to be deciphered in historical or ideological terms" but a religious text with a "secret Utopian vocation." Jameson elaborates:

> But as with Freud's reading of dreams about one's own death, the end of the world may simply be the cover for a very different and more properly Utopian wish-fulfillment: as when ... the protagonist and a small band of other survivors of the catastrophe go on to found some smaller and more livable collectivity after the end of modernity and capitalism ... and construe certain kinds of apocalypse as the expression of the melancholy and trauma of the historical experience of defeat. (199 n. 32)

I am not so sure biblical apocalypse is so secretive about its utopian vocation; in fact, I find great clarity in its hatred for the imperial rule, especially in the Apocalypse of John (with the tale of the destruction of the whore of Babylon). Utopia is set up in grand style in this book—a bejeweled, wealthy city with an elite membership. It would be anachronistic to say the Apocalypse of John is about the escape from capitalism. God's empire is wealthier than any earthly one (e.g., Babylon/Rome).[6] Does God mine the earth for these treasures, bringing them into the gates to hoard for all eternity? There is no capitalist industrial society in the new Jerusalem, but there are riches to be desired. There is no capitalist exchange, but there are commodities. The glitter is alluring, as is the fabulously adorned bride

---

5. Wheeler Winston Dixon (2003, 97) notes that post-9/11 apocalyptic films, like post–Pearl Harbor ones, step up the desire for worldly destruction: "Time is running out. I can feel it. The romance of Armageddon is being replaced by the spectre of inevitable destruction."

6. See Robert Royalty's (1998, 125–49) discussion of "Wealth and Rhetoric in Revelation." He writes, "As slaves of God, the Christians are slaves of the most powerful and wealthiest monarch. Their God is not only wealthier than Caesar, but the wealth of heaven is superior to the wealth of Rome" (149). Wes Howard-Brook and Anthony Gwyther (1999, 265) see the new Jerusalem as an alternative to Babylon, and as a place of harmony and divine economics; for them, "the alternative to global capital is not Marxism or some form of state control. It is, according to the Bible, local community grounded in God's provident care." This is the utopian vision of Christian base communities such as the Catholic Worker houses, but I do not read biblical apocalyptic in this way. I see God setting up a very controlled state, the ultimate gated community.

of Christ whose body becomes the city: "It has the glory of God and a radiance like a very rare jewel, like jasper, clear as crystal" (Rev 21:11). So much desire and an eternity to explore and realize it, but it is only for the lucky survivors.

Jameson (2005, 199) believes "that it is easier to imagine the end of the world than the end of capitalism." Or, as Slavoj Žižek (2010, 335) understands it, "the reproduction of the system [of capital] [is] an end in itself." Maybe this is a reason so many film (and also biblical) versions of the end have the survivors carrying their values (economic, religious, ethical, etc.) with them to rebuild society in the old image (but better, and with fewer people). Miéville further clarifies the relationship between fantasy and capitalism.

> I am claiming that the fantastic, particularly because "reality" is a grotesque, "fantastic form," is *good to think with* [from John Clute]. Marx, whose theory is a haunted house of specters and vampires, knew this. Why else does he open *Capital* not quite with an "immense," as the modern English translation has it, but with a "monstrous" [*ungeheure*] collection of commodities? (Miéville 2002, 46)[7]

So is biblical apocalyptic "good to think with"? Thinking with the fantastic for Miéville (2002, 46) is a way to rethink social conventions: "Changing the not-real allows one to think differently about the real, its potentialities and actualities." He further states that "we need fantasy to think the world, and to change it" (48). But in what ways does fantasy open up doors to change? If indeed fantasy "mimics the 'absurdity' of capitalist modernity" (42), then a Jack Chick comic or the *Left Behind* franchise is deeply embedded in the earthly gold standard that mimics the heavenly one. Or rather, these fictions invest in an exaggerated vision of the standard: streets of gold and a crystal and bejeweled city. In this regard, the Apocalypse of John easily slides into a capitalist cloak.

These narratives support a conservative agenda of (measured) xenophobia and all-out macho heteropatriarchy. Octavia Butler, Philip K. Dick, Ursula Le Guin, Marge Piercy, Joanna Russ, Miéville, and others critique such unified visions in their fiction, yet the filtered and revamped

---

7. Suvin (2000, 211) comments that Marx's "favorite tropes include the fantastic creatures—spectres, vampires, zombies, idolatrous fetishes, sorcerer's apprentices—that pullulate in his writings."

versions of various biblical apocalypses continue to haunt and maintain their trek of domination. As Suvin (2000, 214) comments, "As dogmas go, the Invisible Hand of the Free Market making for universal contentment was no better than being washed in the Blood of the Lamb or the UFOs." In fantasy fiction, there can be critique of the status quo or acquiescence to it; there are the protestors at the Group of Eight (G8) rallies and the Tea Party conventions supporting differing ideologies. Fantasy is about dreaming, about desiring, and Martin Luther King Jr.'s dream of equality and human rights is quite different from the Tea Party's rewriting of the United States Constitution. Each apocalyptic narrative has to be considered in its own context, and that context is partly historical but not just in the largely unknowable past. Apocalyptic fictions jump into our present in a variety of ethical and not ethical ways. Suvin (2000, 238) argues that fantasy literature emerged out of the crisis of capitalism beginning in the mid-1800s. He raises a series of questions.

> Is Fantasy as a tradition and present institution a tool of the reigning ideology of wars for profit, locking out cognition (in [Siegfried] Kracauer's phrase) as workers are locked out when demanding an economic basis for dignity, or is it an induction of cognition, however partial and metaphoric? Hurray for an escape from alienation: but is, or is not, the "escape from the phony" also one into a mirror-image phony.... Isn't very often a degraded pseudo-utopianism at work here? (234)

Suvin is arguing that fantasy knocks the reader back into the status quo. The utopian dream looks a lot like our political (and religious) fantasies. He would probably find my linking of fantasy and horror with biblical apocalyptic anachronistic. Yet Suvin acknowledges the power of a genre he names "Horror Fantasy" to incorporate "a longing for salvation and a homeopathic accommodation" (241). Horror fantasy forms around two poles, "*subversion* and *addiction*" (241). There may be a subversion of the dominant order, a critique of business as usual (see Jackson 1981), but the violence (or gore fest) captivates the viewer or reader. Like the woman in the *2012* movie line, we come back for more, in order to reexperience and memorize the gory details and in order to have our desire magnified and made visual.[8]

---

8. Or as Dixon (2003, 143) relates, "When we dream of the certainty and inevi-

Desire remains a key part of fantasy. But with apocalyptic literature and film, what is the reader or viewer desiring? The ends? A cathartic expulsion of repressed fears? A violent millennial purging of the earth and reinstatement of colonialism? What are these narratives of the ends cloaking? Or do they cover? No, they uncover and reveal (apocalypse or revelation) real desire. As twisted and perverse as this may seem, the fantastic works not only to reveal and revel in these imaginary stories but also to break into other alternative worlds. Thus when we are faced with apocalyptic fantasies, we are faced with imagining and choosing new alternatives. That is, we are not obligated to choose death or even to choose to be nice until our desired global apocalypse occurs. We can choose to work against the violence and destruction of the planet, and we can decide to build coalitions with the oppressed to create new ways of living on our globalized planet. That statement sounds utopian, which apocalypse certainly is, but we can help write different endings for life, not death. The fantasy urges us not to act but to acquiesce to the "inevitable" in the guise of the "not possible." It urges us to dream about the remnant that will survive and imagine ourselves among them.

The Ends Justify the Means

> Kind of galling when you realize that nutbags and cardboard signs had it right the whole time. (Spoken by character Carl Anheuser, chief advisor to the United States president, in *2012*)

> The earth is utterly broken,
> the earth is torn asunder,
> the earth is violently shaken ...
> and it falls, and will not rise again. (Isa 24:19–20)

Since the 1950s science fiction movies of alien invasion or other planetary end, the dream of different endings continues to find a place in the Hollywood lineup. Many films, like *When Worlds Collide* (1951), promise a new creation of humanity. An "Adam" and an "Eve" are needed to continue humanity. They are always white, speak English, and are United States citizens. Roland Emmerich's 2009 film, *2012*, takes up this theme of

---

tability of the apocalypse, we are afraid of life itself." Perhaps the movie-line woman's idea of being nice to people is grounded in these multiple fears—of the end and of life.

destruction and survival but stops short of the need to colonize another planet because the earth is made empty again. This time the central Adam and Eve figures are African American (a government geologist and an art historian). For most of the film there is destruction, the turning of the planet in on itself. There are also some most notable hits; a bank skyscraper in Los Angeles, the Christ the Redeemer statue (Rio de Janeiro), and the Vatican all crumble. In the iconic picture of God creating Adam in the Sistine Chapel, God and Adam separate as the ceiling crumbles. A tsunami hits Washington, DC. As in another film, *Independence Day* (1996), by Emmerich, the White House takes another solid hit. Susan Sontag (1966, 215) in her essay "The Imagination of Disaster" comments on this type of effect: "The lure of such generalized disaster as a fantasy is that it releases one from normal obligations. The trump card of end-of-the world movies ... is the great scene of London or Tokyo discovered empty, its entire population annihilated ... or the vacant city repopulated by a few select survivors." Emmerich plays on deep fears of the demise of "the West" and in particular, of United States superiority.[9]

In a similar vein as in *When Worlds Collide* with their one spaceship ("a modern Noah's ark") to carry survivors into a survivable future, in *2012* the G8 nations build technologically equipped arks to preserve "democracy." Only the G8 leaders and their head staff get tickets, along with a few from the top 1 percent of society who can afford to pay one billion euros for passage. Of course, a few workers are needed to serve the rich and powerful and lend their specialized skills. We only see the first-class cabins of the elite. Nepal, the roof of the world, is the secret location of these arks, but it also suffers the flooding of the earth, and it is Buddhism, namely, Tibetan Buddhist monks, that saves the central (heteropatriarchal) family. The landmass that emerges after the waters recede is Africa; the roof of the world shifts to South Africa (or what were the Drakensberg Mountains in KwaZulu-Natal, South Africa).[10] In a move of ultimate and extreme imperialism, as the film ends the arks of the G8 (Canada, France, Germany, Italy, Japan, Russia, the United Kingdom, and the United States—no African countries!) head toward this new land to settle and recolonize the

---

9. His other films with a similar theme include *Universal Soldier* (1992), *Independence Day* (1996), *Godzilla* (1998), *The Patriot* (2000), and *The Day after Tomorrow* (2004).

10. The Dutch name for the mountain range is Drakensberg, or Dragon Mountains. The Zulu name is Ukhahlamba, or "barrier of spears."

planet. The G8, founded in 1975, serves as an economic council of wealthy nations, the European Union, and, except for Japan, "the West." An additional group of five called the Outreach Five includes Brazil, China, India, Mexico, and South Africa. The larger group is often noted as the G8 + 5; there is also an even larger group, the G20.[11] What is all too obvious from this list is the exclusion of all but one country from the continent of Africa. South Africa is the one country out of the whole continent—and planet—that rises after the floodwaters begin to recede a bit. Africa has been washed clean, purified, and is now a colonizer's dream. The "African Eve" has been left behind for a new set of "'African' Eves" to reset the human genetic future.

Emmerich exaggerates disaster in this film. To say he amplifies apocalypse is probably an oxymoron, since apocalypse is already from the start almost too much to imagine, let alone to bear. Using popular readings of the Mayan calendar cycles along with doomsday predictions and a load of pseudo-science, he throws in outrageous and preposterous scenarios of earthquakes and floods and a total rearrangement of the earth (e.g., Wisconsin is now the South Pole). He explains, "I said to myself that I'll do one more disaster movie, but it has to end all disaster movies. So I packed everything in" (cited in Koban 2009). The special effects of the earth's return to chaos in *2012* are beautifully filmed. Mathias Nilges notes that the difference between Cold War-era apocalyptic films and those made after 9/11 is that instead of seeing our fears enacted onscreen to total destruction (*On the Beach* [1959] and *Dr. Strangelove* [1964] come to my mind), escaping fears is primary. In this way the destruction is beautiful. Nilges (2010, 26) clarifies, "Destruction is, therefore, not beautiful in itself but becomes associated with the beauty it can bring about, the beauty of an existence that is often represented as more enjoyable since simpler—if not more sublime—than our chaotic present: If this is true, what is it about the present we do not enjoy?"[12] The key question for Nilges is, "What is it that disrupts our imagination of the future and

---

11. The G20 (founded in 1999) nations are Argentina, Australia, Brazil, Canada, China, France, Germany, India, Indonesia, Italy, Japan, Mexico, Russia, Saudi Arabia, South Africa, South Korea, Turkey, the United Kingdom, and the United States.

12. Nilges (2010, 26) mentions the documentary *Žižek!* (dir. Astra Taylor) in which Žižek "remarks that it seems strange that we seem to lack the ability to imagine smaller systemic changes that could improve US society while we are easily able to imagine scenarios of complete global destruction."

how is this impasse culturally resolved?" (20). The aesthetics of destruction is for Emmerich on an increasingly larger and larger scale (e.g., the sequencing of disaster from *Independence Day* to *The Day after Tomorrow* to *2012*). This director is resolving the impasse with aliens and fire and flood and ice. He is throwing everything he can on the screen and at the survivors, as well as at the viewers.

Along this line of imagining a hyperapocalypse, Sontag (1966, 224) states, "Ours is indeed an age of extremity." She believes there are two threats in our age: "unremitting banality and inconceivable terror" (224). The greatest psychological terrors must be mitigated by these extreme, apocalyptic fantasies. What changes over the ages is the political and moral context of these fictions (224). The backdrop for *2012* is certainly 9/11, the wars in Iraq and Afghanistan, Sudan, Congo, xenophobia in the United States, and so on.[13] When we allow ourselves to think the unthinkable and see our anxieties played large on the screen, we can reenter the world more calmly. Sontag points out that many science fiction films "reflect world-wide anxieties, and they serve to allay them" (225); she also notes that most science fiction films "bear witness to the trauma, and in a way, attempt to exorcise it" (218). However, this is not what *2012* wants to do, for it is too apathetic to the billions of people and other living things that are completely destroyed in the earthquakes and floods. Paul Willemen (2010, 267) makes the point that many films like *2012* move beyond apathy or indifference to the massive loss of lives: "Most disaster movies and post-apocalypse movies celebrate, in the very display of productive resources that constitutes the 'spectacle,' the kind of organization of social relations that is on course to create the joyous spectacle of global mayhem." Willemen argues that Hollywood is selling us these apocalypse and postapocalyptic utopias, and we are lining up to revel in wars and extreme "acts of God" to end life as we know it. Does 9/11 continue to be a wound that needs healing?[14] Does *2012* destroy the United States (and then the world) before the terrorists do? Is it an infantile way of saying, "You can't have it so we'll destroy it first!" but with an added twist, "And you with it!"

---

13. Charles Strozier (2005, 263) comments, "It is altogether appropriate to place the World Trade Center disaster at the center of any inquiry into the meaning of collective trauma in the contemporary age."

14. Strozier (2005, 263–64) points to "the radical dismemberment of bodies" that occurred in 9/11.

Sontag (1966, 225) goes a bit further with this idea of the lure of apocalyptic fantasies by noting that the effect of end-time fantasies "is to normalize what is psychologically unbearable, thereby inuring us to it.... In one case, fantasy beautifies the world. In the other, it neutralizes it." The survivors can rewrite history and culture in their own terms. The few (about 400,000 people, plus some animals and fine art and other material goods deemed valuable) who make it on the arks in *2012* are seen smiling, like Christopher Columbus and his crew, at the newly emerged land on the horizon.

What are the arks bringing with them to this new African rooftop of the world, around the Cape of Good Hope? They bring the G8, the structure of globalization and the International Monetary Fund and the World Bank. They bring white male supremacy and traces of democracy (the self-appointed United States president and the G8 structure). What is being preserved is the lucky elite and their accoutrements. There are protestors, but all of them are shown only in one brief scene outside of a G8 meeting in British Columbia; their chant, "No G8!" is drowned out in the world flood. There is the idea that this tectonic shifting produced a "good flood," the "flood to end all floods." Now the proper nations and people are in charge, and they all share similar ("Western") values. The "myth of the empty land" is finally a reality; the land really is empty. Only those on the lifeboats survive. Africa emerges as a sort of new Jerusalem to be recolonized; this is the ultimate imperialist dream. There are no pesky, rebellious "native" people on this land to colonize; all Others are on the boat and are de facto assimilated, at least as the film leaves the story. The G8 can seize power and rule the world, and it is the right thing to do, says this film. The multicultural myth on the boats is that some of the human races will survive but all will be part of this new Euro-American "democracy." The class distinctions are maintained—servants and the served remain categories on the boats. So everything is as it was before, only massively pared down and without much dissent. Everyone on the boats is glad to be alive and excited about rebuilding the world. Despite the left-leaning filmmakers, this film winds up servicing Christian right-wing politics and anesthetizing us to the real dangers of climate change and capitalism and colonialism.

This "good hope," this desire for a new world, is the message of the film. It hits the reset button on history, while dragging in and rescuing "the imperialist white-supremacist, capitalist patriarchy" (hooks 2004, xi–xiii). The arks, like the phallic rocket in *When Worlds Collide* or the nuclear bomb in *Dr. Strangelove*, are perverse. Žižek (1999, 94) comments that the "fantasmatic narrative" does not transgress the status quo: "For that reason, fantasy as such is, in its very notion, close to perversion." The irony is that the apocalypse in the case of recent apocalyptic films, and I would argue in the biblical case also, is about such rescuing. When the patriarchy is under threat, human and/or deities, imaging the disaster/s that will wipe out the enemies, the Other, fulfills a certain desire for closure. Only the "purified" will survive.

In the commentary on the *2012* DVD, Emmerich asks, "Who is worth saving?" The self-proclaimed United States president Carl Anheuser (a name based on the company that makes Busch beer, Anheuser-Busch, with a link to President George W. Bush, whom the writers ironically dislike) states, "We need to bring people who can contribute." Herein lies the core conflict in this film for Emmerich, for who decides who lives or dies? The United States president's dead wife wanted a lottery. He bravely stays behind in the White House attending to the injured. Previously he said to the lead geologist, "It's a brave new world you're headed to." Is this an allusion to Aldous Huxley (1932)? Yet the promise of entry onto the ark for the Indian geologist, who first discovered the geological shifting, and his family is broken, and they die in a tsunami. We see the waves coming from their perspective right before they hit them. Does this represent the failed promises of the colonizer to the colonized throughout history?

The "radio host of the apocalypse," Charlie Frost (played by Woody Harrelson), represents the extremes of conspiracy theorists and end-of-the-world prophecy believers. He possesses a valuable map to the location of the arks, which the hero and his family find and redeem. Frost represents the extremity of desire for the end; he has a utopian longing: "Whether you're a Christian or a Buddhist or Muslim or Rastafarian ... by tomorrow we will all be one." He refuses to leave Yellowstone Park as the earthquakes approach. The hero takes off in a plane ironically named "Western Spirit," leaving Frost behind. "It's beautiful! I'm gonna stay!" he shouts as the ground dissolves beneath him. Reporting until the very end he proclaims, "This marks the last day of the United States of America. And by tomorrow, all of mankind." Then a mushroom cloud, like an atomic explosion, engulfs him. The end brought him "goose bumps," the ultimate thrill ride. The thing he had believed in and tracked for years was occurring, and his desire was fulfilled (see Bould 2002).

Apocalyptic films out of Hollywood usually have a happy ending, what Tolkien (1964, 68–73) would call a "eucatastrophe." Disaster is a necessary purifier for the sins of humanity. The apocalypse is never satisfied;

it is never finished, for to finish would mean the end of desire (see Quinby 2009). Continually piling up the bodies (of the damned and of the saved) and bombing the earth with fire and ice and whatever it can imagine is the raison d'être of apocalypse. Apocalypse desires. If desire is part of the apocalyptic imagination, then desire resides not only in the readers/viewers but also in the text itself. The narrative of desire lures, seduces, complicates. What about me doing this essay? In what ways have I allowed apocalypse to pull me in, to engulf me in a cloud of desire? Why do I have the need to continually face off with apocalypse, to do battle as if to reenact some superhero myth in which I am the star actor? I was not trained for this confrontation; my traditional biblical studies education led me to the peace table, to negotiate with these ends, even to argue that what they represent is actually liberating and hopeful, enough so that I am one of their spokespeople. I am surrounded by apocalyptic endings with little chance of winning on my own. Do I desire to be one of the survivors and to have a place (for my family too) on the boat or a house in the gated city? Here lies the powerful hold of apocalyptic (for me, at least): to imagine death so that one may hope to live or as a way of hanging on tighter to life, but also as a way of learning to let go, to let the apocalyptic powers win, now and in the future.

The woman in the *2012* line had obvious premillennial beliefs, into which she was able to incorporate Mayan prophecy and perhaps other unsaid end time beliefs. The Christian framework formed from a heavy colonial past (and present) provided hope in future salvation. I do not know if she believes she would be raptured before the eco-catastrophes in *2012* or if she believed she would be chosen (or be wealthy enough) for the ark. But the weight of this colonial eschatology tells her—and all of us—to wait for God to enact the end in God's own time and that such destruction is part of God's plan for humanity. In *2012* there is the return to Africa, to Zulu land, but rebuilding is in the colonizers' hands. There is no God, but there is the new nation. The remnant resettles "wilderness," but this time without the "savages." The dream of world domination is complete. There is only the imperial regime of the G8 and the kingdom of their gods on earth. There is only the brave new world.

There is no Statue of Liberty sticking out of the beach in *2012*,[15] but there is United States superiority (but questionable democracy), since the

---

15. The reference is to the film *Planet of the Apes* (1968).

self-appointed United States president Carl Anheuser seems to be the one in charge. The film helps to shore up our national identity after the traumas (of the flooding of the earth and of 9/11). The new nationalism creates the new world in the image of the United States. We, and our allies, are the winners. The survivors represent those who control the wealth (means of production). The main point of view in the film is from the hero and his reunited family. There was no one at fault (humans, gods, aliens); the disaster was totally beyond our control. So there was no way to prepare for the cataclysm; only luck and connections and/or money could help one survive. Of course, the G8 nations had an escape plan, and they do great violence by limiting the ways of escape (in a sort of hyper-Katrina way).[16] It is similar to the plan in rapture theology; the end is coming, and the chosen will be lifted away from the violence. Instead of heaven, those rescued in *2012* go on extended safari. The failure of the film, and the failure of heaven, is to build a truly transnational and diverse society.

Conclusion: Heaven Recolonizes Earth

> Then I saw the holy city, the new Jerusalem, coming down out of heaven from God.... "See, the home of God is among mortals. He will dwell with them as their God; they will be his peoples, and God himself will be with them.... And the one who was seated on the throne said, "See, I am making all things new." (Rev 21:2–5)

Are biblical apocalypses anticolonial texts? Yes, but then they reify and mimic the earthly throne/Rome with the heavenly throne. The United States and its values displace God in secular apocalypses such as *2012*. The fantasy of the surviving remnant as the American family, white, middle class (or formerly, before the apocalypse) grabs at the fears of changing racial and class demographics in the United States and Europe (see Monleón 1990; Balasopoulos 2005). There is the fulfillment of the heteropatriarchal family. The point of view in *2012* is from the stereotypical (if slightly complicated) American family—husband, stepfather, wife, older male child, younger female child. But the viewpoint is also from the G8; the survival of the family is tied to the geo-economy of the G8 and their ability

---

16. Erin Runions (2006, 124) notes, "It appears that the use of apocalyptic metaphors to motivate economic ends is not benign; the stakes are deadly, both at home and abroad."

to nation-build. The family is not totally cut off from their former, materialistic lives, for the boats carry more than the basics needed for survival. All former conflicts (family and global) are resolved by the catastrophe. The apocalypse wipes clean any pesky differences, and the central family and the world can start over with a "clean slate." Naomi Klein is instructive on this point.

> This desire for godlike powers of total creation is precisely why free-market ideologues are so drawn to crises and disasters. Non-apocalyptic reality is simply not hospitable to their ambitions.... Believers in a shock doctrine are convinced that only a great rupture—a flood, a war, a terrorist attack—can generate the kind of vast, clean canvases they crave. It is in these malleable moments, when we are psychologically unmoored and physically uprooted, that these artists of the real plunge in their hands and begin their work of remaking the world. (Klein 2007, 24)

The dream of the remnant requires the rupture of the world, a (near) total split with the present but retention of bits and pieces of the past. The arks in *2012* store the past; beyond the art and technology, these boats haul global politics into the future. Recent films such as *2012*, *The Road*, and *The Book of Eli* also intimate a multicultural future, but the terms are governed by the central survivors, those who we know will rebuild "Western" society and uphold its political and moral values. Again, "America" displaces God in *2012*, or rather the two become one (see Davis and Monk 2007).

Christian utopian dreams claim to be about absolute love and a compassionate God, but the irony is that "the saved" are lured into eternal confinement in the new city. Žižek (2010, 117) argues that the injunction to love God above all else, including hating family, leads to terror: "Terror is terror out of love for the universal-singular others and against the particular. This terror names exactly the same thing as the work of love." In this way, the gods of biblical apocalypse terrorize believers and nonbelievers alike as they hold out the hope of the destruction of this world and its re-creation. Žižek warns, "With regard to the social order, this means that the authentic Christian apocalyptic tradition rejects the wisdom according to which some kind of hierarchical order is our fate, such that any attempt to challenge it and create an alternative egalitarian order will necessarily end in destructive horror" (117). In biblical eschatology, there is an inevitability to God ending human history and God's creation; God dreams of flood and fire and seemingly endless ways to knock off the world.

The arrival of the new Jerusalem (Rev 21–22) tells the story of an earth that is totally cleansed and resettled by the "survivors" (in this case the living dead, or resurrected male believers). Such utopian thinking is singular in its perspective and grand designs. The new Jerusalem is a trap; there is a sole ideology and hierarchical structure. As in *2012* one patch of land is habitable (unless you count the Abyss that continues to exist and nag from outside the new Jerusalem's walls), but in the biblical case the city is prefabricated and not some pristine wilderness. The different politics at work here are, of course, the G8's usurping of the role of God; this group brings "Western" values and ingenuity to rebuilding and recivilizing the planet. Even with its imperfections and implied minor conflicts, there is an eerie unity in the group pictured at the end of the film on the ark. They look out together, gratefully and hopefully, but assuredly, toward the "new Africa." In the Apocalypse of John, it is God who holds the ultimate knowledge of the future, engineering a perfect society. Believers are to put their faith in this ending, this city of hope, or in the case of *2012*, this newly virgin land.

Yet the bulk of the biblical apocalyptic stories focus on terror and destruction. There are only short tales (mainly from Ezekiel and John) of the new (urban) space of creation, and no stories of the survivors settling in and interacting. Cinematic apocalypses follow a similar narrative line; the viewer sees the destruction or effect of some unknown disaster and follows a survivor or group to the hope for humanity at the end of the story. According to Žižek (2010, 80), in Lacanian terms watching the erasure of humans from the earth is "the fundamental subjective position of fantasy: to be reduced to a gaze observing the world in the condition of the subject's non-existence." It is the "*impossible gaze,* the gaze by means of which the subject is already present at the scene of its own absence" (84, emphasis original). Žižek notes further that "the core of a Lacanian notion of utopia" is "a vision of desire functioning without an *objet a* [excess or surplus] and its twists and loops" (84). Apocalypses allow us to see our nonexistence in various ways.

I often joke with students, "What if the Rapture has happened and we've been left behind? What if this world is what's left after all the 'believers' go to heaven with Jesus? What if our current world and its violence is the disaster?" There is a moment of hesitation from both believers and nonbelievers. Could this (fiction/inevitability) be true? Žižek (2010, 328) explores this idea further: "The gap which makes these paradoxes possible is that between knowledge and belief: we *know* the (ecological) catastrophe is possible, probable even, yet we do not *believe* it will really happen" (emphasis original). Therein lies the power of the fantasy of the ends, whether they take the form of the unbiblical rapture or the disintegration of the planet or its invasion by alien beings or objects. Complete unbelief is impossible.

What are, then, the psychological effects of end*s*? Every time I hear the radio test of the emergency alert system, I experience the "hesitation" that Tzvetan Todorov (1973, 31, 33, 41, 157) says accompanies the fantastic. Although I rationally know it is "just a test," the test is a stand-in for the possibility, the Real. I imagine all sorts of scenarios that would prompt a real alert. I find these tests a bit creepy, for they remind us that apocalypse is possible. The possibility of more than one ultimate catastrophe is unsettling—that the one end you desired and put all your faith in (1) might not be the only one; (2) might be usurped in power by something(s) greater; or (3) might wind up an "also ran" in the apocalyptic Olympics. Despite the grand efforts of the premillennialists to stake a claim in one ending, these endings of theirs (also plural) are extrabiblical, as extrabiblical as nuclear or environmental disaster. Listen to any week of Hal Lindsey's prophecy news show to witness the shifting narratives. Over the years since *The Late Great Planet Earth* (Lindsey and Carlson 1970), there have been antichrists and beasts. But what determines "biblical"? The canonical borders are blurred. The woman I mentioned earlier could easily hold multiple beliefs of the ends. The biblical apocalyptic prophecies make claims—both all claims and no claims. In filling the void of apocalypse with their noisy narratives, they aim to intimidate and scare. Apocalypse is a green screen that can be filled with any scenario.

As much as one might dismiss the various ends as the irrational dreams of crazy prophets, the apocalypse is accessible—or more accessible than one might first admit. One metaphor is that one does not just read or view the apocalypse; one walks through it or enters into the book or the movie screen and participates in it and shares the dream. In walking through the apocalypse, there are lots of crazy paths. Or consider another version of the metaphor: dreaming of apocalypse (and even engaging in the scholarship) is like flying in a flying dream. There is a wild freedom, a (limited) aerial view, a sense of falling into a bottomless pit. Falling, falling, but maintaining the ability to fly.

Works Cited

Balasopoulos, Antonis. 2005. "Unworldly Worldliness: America and the Trajectories of Utopian Expansionism." *Utopian Studies* 15.2:3–35.

Bould, Mark. 2002. "The Dreadful Credibility of Absurd Things: A Tendency in Fantasy Theory." *Historical Materialism* 10.4:51–88.
Collins, Adela Yarbro. 1984. *Crisis and Catharsis: The Power of the Apocalypse*. Philadelphia: Westminster.
Collins, John J. 1979. "Introduction: Towards the Morphology of a Genre." *Semeia* 14:1–19.
Davis, Mike, and Daniel Bertrand Monk. 2007. "Introduction." Pages ix–xvi in *Evil Paradises: Dreamworlds of Neoliberalism*. Edited by Mike Davis and Daniel Bertrand Monk. New York: New Press.
Dixon, Wheeler Winston. 2003. *Visions of the Apocalypse: Spectacles of Destruction in American Cinema*. London: Wallflower.
hooks, bell. 2004. *We Real Cool: Black Men and Masculinity*. New York: Routledge.
Howard-Brook, Wes, and Anthony Gwyther. 1999. *Unveiling Empire: Reading Revelation Then and Now*. Maryknoll, NY: Orbis.
Huxley, Aldous. 1932. *Brave New World*. London: Chatto & Windus.
Jackson, Rosemary. 1981. *Fantasy: The Literature of Subversion*. London: Methuen.
Jameson, Fredric. 2005. *Archaeologies of the Future: The Desire Called Utopia and Other Science Fictions*. London: Verso.
Klein, Naomi. 2007. *The Shock Doctrine: The Rise of Disaster Capitalism*. New York: Vintage.
Koban, Craig J. 2009. "A Film Review: *2012*." *Craiger's Cinema Corner*. http://tinyurl.com/SBL0684h.
Lifton, Robert Jay. 1982. "Beyond Psychic Numbing: A Call to Awareness." *American Journal of Orthopsychiatry* 52:619–29.
———. 1991. *Death in Life: Survivors of Hiroshima*. Chapel Hill: University of North Carolina Press.
Lindsey, Hal, and Carl C. Carlson. 1970. *The Late Great Planet Earth*. Grand Rapids: Zondervan.
Lyall, Sarah. 2010. "Making Squid the Meat of a Story." *New York Times*. July 24, C1 and 8.
Macy, Joanna R. 1983. *Despair and Personal Power in the Nuclear Age*. Gabriola Island: New Society.
Miéville, China. 2002. "Editorial Introduction: Symposium. Marxism and Fantasy." *Historical Materialism* 10.4:39–49.
———. 2009. "Afterword: Cognition as Ideology: A Dialectic of SF Theory." Pages 231–48 in *Red Planets: Marxism and Science Fiction*. Edited by

Mark Bould and China Miéville. Middletown: Wesleyan University Press.

———. 2010. *Kraken: An Anatomy*. New York: Ballantine.

Monleón, José B. 1990. *A Specter Is Haunting Europe: A Sociohistorical Approach to the Fantastic*. Princeton: Princeton University Press.

Nilges, Mathias. 2010. "The Aesthetics of Destruction: Contemporary US Cinema and TV Culture." Pages 23–33 in *Reframing 9/11: Film, Popular Culture and the "War on Terror."* Edited by Jeff Birkenstein, Anna Foula, and Karen Randell. New York: Continuum.

Quinby, Lee. 2009. "'The Days are Numbered': The Romance of Death, Doom, and Deferral in Contemporary Apocalypse Films." Pages 96–119 in *The End All around Us: Apocalyptic Texts and Popular Culture*. Edited by John Walliss and Kenneth G. C. Newport. London: Equinox.

Royalty, Robert M., Jr. 1998. *The Streets of Heaven: The Ideology of Wealth in the Apocalypse of John*. Macon, GA: Mercer University Press.

Runions, Erin. 2003. *How Hysterical: Identification and Resistance in the Bible and Film*. New York: Palgrave Macmillan.

———. 2006. "Desiring War: Apocalypse, Commodity Fetish, and the End of History." Pages 113–27 in *The Postcolonial Biblical Reader*. Edited by R. S. Sugirtharajah. Oxford: Blackwell.

Sontag, Susan. 1966. "The Imagination of Disaster." Pages 209–25 in *Against Interpretation and Other Essays*. New York: Farrar, Straus & Giroux.

Strozier, Charles B. 2005. "From Ground Zero: Thoughts on Apocalyptic Violence and the New Terrorism." Pages 263–77 in *War in Heaven, Heaven on Earth: Theories of the Apocalyptic*. Edited by Stephen O'Leary and Glen S. McGhee. London: Equinox.

Suvin, Darko. 1979. *Metamorphoses of Science Fiction*. New Haven: Yale University Press.

———. 2000. "Considering the Sense of 'Fantasy' or 'Fantastic Fiction': An Effusion." *Extrapolation* 41:209–47.

Todorov, Tzvetan. 1973. *The Fantastic: A Structural Approach to a Literary Genre*. Translated by Richard Howard. Ithaca, NY: Cornell University Press.

Tolkien, J. R. R. 1964. "On Fairy-Stories." Pages 1–82 in *Tree and Leaf*. London: Allen & Unwin.

Willemen, Paul. 2010. "Fantasy in Action." Pages 247–86 in *Transnational Cinemas, Transnational Perspectives*. Edited by Natasa Durovicova and Kathleen Newman. New York: Routledge.

Žižek, Slavoj. 1991. *Looking Awry: An Introduction to Jacques Lacan*. Cambridge: MIT Press.

———. 1999. "Fantasy as a Political Category: A Lacanian Approach." Pages 91–100 in *The Žižek Reader*. Edited by Elizabeth Wright and Edmond Wright. Oxford: Blackwell.

———. 2010. *Living in the End Times*. London: Verso.

Part 3
Responses

Response:
Disseminations (and/or Sublimations)
of the Death Drive

Theodore W. Jennings Jr.

Psychoanalysis may be viewed (following suggestions by Paul Ricoeur [1970] in *Freud and Philosophy*) as a hermeneutics, specifically as a hermeneutics of desire. It traces or tracks the imprint of desire first in the dream and then in a variety of behavioral symptoms (jokes, slips of the tongue, as well as bodily symptoms). This hermeneutics is, however, never simple since desire is constitutionally conflicted, divided, deflected, and disguised. Thus desire is never only or primarily what it seems. It is constitutionally enigmatic. It is this that necessitates something like a science of desire, an analytics of desire.

The essays in this volume propose to link such a hermeneutics of desire to a reading of biblical texts and to see to what extent such a move can helpfully link up with, or even transform, those biblical hermeneutical projects commonly related to Marxist and/or postcolonial reading strategies. For example, Jeremy Punt suggests that in South Africa postcolonial readings as well as Marxist readings seem not to have attracted widespread understanding or employment, and he wonders whether a psychoanalytic approach might make these other approaches more useful or attractive. If, as he suggests, these former approaches have entered into a certain deadlock, might this in some way be ameliorated by the introduction of psychoanalytic approaches to bridge them with one another and with the South African project of biblical interpretation generally? From the outside, this seems rather a risky move, since it may involve only adding yet a further layer of complexity to an already complex situation. If, as he suggests, Marxist perspectives may be too universalizing, it is surprising that a psychoanalytic tradition that generalizes from

Viennese Victorian families can be of much help or that it can overcome depoliticizing tendencies that he supposes may characterize at least some postcolonial interpretive projects. Of course, the work of Franz Fanon (e.g., 1967a, 1967b) comes to mind as one who has fruitfully explored much of this terrain (though of course not as an interpreter of biblical texts); one would hope that Fanon's texts might be mobilized as a test case for this project.

Roland Boer's essay demonstrates an intriguing connection by tracing the idea of the fetish in Freud and Marx back to the observations of early Western cultural anthropologists (whose work paralleled that of the colonial project of Europe). In locating this common root, Boer is able to show the ways in which the fetish is a sort of repository of disguised desire. One may say that the fetish is that on which alienated desire is fix(at)ed. In ways rather dependent on Feuerbach's (2004) critique or analysis of religion as projected desire/value, the fetish is that which embodies the desire of the subject(s), externalizing it, objectifying it so that it becomes something social. Let us say that it is an object on which is projected the desire for life or well-being. But this in turn takes its revenge on the subject, depriving the subject of what is its own, subjecting the subject to abjection before the disguised token of its alienated desire (money, the commodity, a shoe, or religion itself). The desire for life becomes the instrument of death, the impoverishment of life or its end.

The mechanism for this lethal projection, Boer suggests, is the denial of castration, which I read as constitutive lack. This lack, then, may be compensated for by the projection of what is lacking onto the fetish or, in Marx's terms, the whole fetishistic system that constitutes capitalism. But instead of a mere critique of that system, what if a way were found to short-circuit the entire process? What if, instead of the disavowal of castration, we were to embrace it? This reminds me of a move suggested by Antonio Negri (2003) in his *Time for Revolution*: he suggests that constitutive lack (poverty) is fundamental to existence. It is poverty, recognized and affirmed, that makes love possible (following perhaps the suggestion of Diotima in Plato's *Symposium*). Negri suggests that this love growing out of an affirmed lack engenders the joining together in labor to create the common as a shared world. Thus what follows is not so much an obsessive critique of empire, capital, and so on as the creation together of a different human world. In this sense, embracing castration may be the necessary starting point for a psychic and political economy that eschews the fetish. This may open a way to a biblical hermeneutics that explores the embrace of weakness or lack and critiques the displacement mechanisms that may still operate in the residual phallocentrism of certain ways of speaking of the divine.

Boer carries his argument a step further in "Freud, Adorno, and the Ban on Images," concerning the prohibition found in Exod 20. Freud interprets the rejection of images as provoking the breakthrough into abstract thought, while Adorno insists that it in fact imposes a renunciation of all forms of abstraction, most especially the sorts of reification that fuel commodity capitalism and even utopian politics. The double renunciation of images (Freud) and of concepts (Adorno) may indicate a grim resignation of shortcuts to meaning. I wonder if a somewhat different mood, a more serene acceptance, may be found in Ecclesiastes.

One of the features of Freud's later work (1961) is his postulation (he would say discovery) of the death drive as a complement to and in conflict with the erotic drives that he had located in the libido. It was because of the conflicting character of desire that eros alone did not seem adequate for its analysis. Hence the countervailing death drive. This death drive may function as agressivity toward the other or as directed toward the self. It may also be viewed as the aim of achieving stasis, whose ultimate goal is the return to a mineral state itself.

Several of these essays explore some of the vicissitudes of the death drive, so I will link them via this mechanism. Tina Pippin's essay explores aspects of such a death drive in her essay on "Psychoapocalypse," in which she, focusing primarily on the movie *2012*, discerns the desire for an ending of planetary life in the apocalyptic visions of contemporary cinema. Here we see displayed a desire for an end to civilization somehow combined or in conflict with a (supplemental) desire for the continuation of life, at least for some.

In this connection, it is intriguing that Engels (2008) and Nietzsche (1997) contemporaneously, as well as Freud a few decades later, understood Christianity to emerge in the context of a sort of sickness unto death of the Roman imperium, in which nothing new seemed possible or thinkable. (Hence the notion of an all-consuming destruction that seems to be in the background of certain Pauline formulations in letters to Thessalonica and Rome would have been all too familiar to readers in the Roman Empire.) Do we live in an analogous time, in which history seems to have come to an end and there is nothing left but to distract ourselves with shopping, or weary with what is, to desire the utter destruction of the world? If this fantasy or desire seems intolerable to waking consciousness, then may we seek to console ourselves, as if waking from a nightmare, with the fantasy that something (preferably like us) will somehow escape unscathed? Pippen does provide us with a sidelong glance at the Apocalypse of John as an analogue to our contemporary fascination with or fantasy of global catastrophe. Of course, in that text one might argue that none survive since those who enter the divine polis are those who have already been slain (martyrs), but we must come back to that theme in a bit.

There are three essays in this volume that engage in a close reading of biblical texts and so provide us with test cases for the benefits of including psychoanalytic perspectives in our hermeneutical toolbox and that, among other things, may suggest the death drive as illuminating of this work.

Jione Havea's reading of the encounter of Saul with the medium of Endor is an intriguing example, since it raises the question of what it is that Saul actually desires. His *talanoa* weaves together postcolonial, Marxist, and psychoanalytic perspectives. I will focus on the last and in particular the way in which a certain death drive is decoded in the reading. As Havea notes, Saul seeks Samuel, who is now dead. If we recall that Saul has never had dealings directly with YHWH but only with Samuel, we might even say that he seeks a dead YHWH. It is in any case Samuel who had, on behalf on YHWH, oiled up Saul's masculine beauty as the sign that YHWH had favored him as (surrogate) king or war chief of Israel, just as later Samuel at YHWH's behest had oiled up the boyish beauty of David to supplant Saul in that capacity. Samuel is now dead and having pronounced the sentence of death on those who seek to converse with the dead, Saul (nevertheless) comes to Endor to seek intercourse with Samuel, the true surrogate of YHWH.

But what does Saul desire? It may be worth recalling (as Havea does not in this essay) that this is not the first time that a desperate Saul has sought out Samuel. The earlier time was when Saul was being supplanted by David. Saul sends his minions in pursuit, but they are overcome by the (erotic) frenzy that accompanies Samuel and his company. After the third time, Saul goes himself, is overtaken by that same frenzy, strips naked, and is found lying in a swoon as if dead (1 Sam 19:19–24). If the result of seeking Samuel (to no avail) while alive left him naked and near dead, what, we may wonder, does Saul desire this time? He is told, of course, that he will die (so perhaps joining at least with Samuel)—and he does die in the battle that follows. The desire for death, perhaps (barely) disguised as a yearning for life or love, is the desire that is requited in this melancholy tale.

If the story of Saul is a story of dealing with death, his own and that of the representative of YHWH (Samuel), the essay on the Gospel of Mark by Tat-siong Benny Liew suggests another way in which the death of the other is dealt with in the remarkable narration of the women fleeing the tomb at the end of that gospel. Here Liew contests the interpretations—his own included (see Liew 1999, 133–48; 2003)—that regard the silence of the women in the register of failure; instead, Liew regards the fear and amazement as an appropriate (telling, we might say) response to that which ruptures the boundaries of language and (imperial) law. Using Lacan's notion of *jouissance* as the conjoining of traumatic rupture and unprogrammed pleasure, Liew hears the not-speaking of the women as the fitting indicator of the eruption of *jouissance*.

Levinas (2000) proposed that the first death, the death that is encountered, is the death of the other. In the case of Mark's narrative, that death is the death of Jesus, at least at the level of narration. But it is also a death that will not stay put, stay in its grave, and permit itself to be embalmed. The dead who will not stay dead and so enter into the register of the undead (as Žižek suggested) or become the haunting presence/absence of the living dead. Thus we have to do not only with trauma but also with haunting. Or perhaps with haunting (the "undeadness" of the dead) as itself further trauma, or a trauma of a different sort.

In any case, the nonspeaking of the women who flee the tomb may be favorably contrasted with the response of the disciples to what may be a resurrection appearance earlier in the narrative, when they see the undead Elijah and Moses consorting in a sort of radiance with Jesus. Peter's response seems odd: "Let us make three booths." But the narrator tells us, they "did not know what to say, for they were exceedingly afraid" (Mark 9:6 RSV). Note the conjunction of not-saying and fear that anticipates the last words of the gospel. Perhaps better to say nothing at all than to say something clearly inapt and inept.

If the spectrality of the undead haunts the Gospel of Mark, it is the spectacle of the imperial death-dealing machine that illumines Liew's reading of the Gospel of John. Even more than the essay on Mark, this essay entails a close reading that reaches from the beginning to the end of the narrative while placing it within the context of Roman colonial power. This is enriched by means of contemporary reflections on life as bare life, expendable life, from Agamben as well as by contemporary interpreters of the life of racialized subjects. From the standpoint of Agamben (1998), at least in *Homo Sacer*, humanity as a whole is in process of reduction to bare or expendable life, life under the threat of death, so much so that the death camp can become for him a representation of the place in which we all find ourselves relative to the imperial power (late neoliberal globalization, the surveillance state, etc.) that afflicts contemporary humanity. Here it is not simply a question of mortality (all must die) but of being subjected to a death penalty that makes life already doomed to the machinations of a sort of police power.

In the first century, that police power is present as the Roman Empire itself, and Liew detects in John's narrative a growing disclosure of the murderous force of Roman law. In one of his most interesting interpretive moves, Liew suggests that the Judean opponents are simply the mask or puppets of that Roman power. Thus the inculpation of Judean authorities is not to be read as anti-Semitism or anti-Judaism but as the exposure of the ways that the colonized are led to collaborate with the power that threatens them with death. That is, by siding with Roman imperial power, they seek to escape its menacing grip. (Josephus might be an important case in point.) One seeks to escape death by siding with the death-dealing force.

But if coming to terms with the executioners is not the way to purchase a modicum of life within the context of the omnipresent threat of execution, what then?

One way adopted by this gospel (and I would suppose the other gospels as well) is to transform the threat of death into a willingness to die, thereby depriving the empire of the force of that threat. This move from victimage to agency seems to characterize Jesus's last days in Jerusalem. Thus death becomes not doom but destiny, a destiny that is or seeks to be not death-dealing but life-giving. This, of course, treads very close to the territory of suicide, suicide by cop as some now say. To be sure, the suicidal character of this death is somewhat mitigated not only by the recollection that not-dying is not an option (one will in any case die), but also by the reflection that under empire one's life is already sentenced to die—that is, life as bare life. If the result of a willingness to die is a sort of enhancement of life, life liberated from the threat of death, life lived in the community of love, then perhaps it is not really suicidal after all. For suicide typically despairs of life and of community.

At the end of this rich and complex essay, Liew reflects on the complexity of reading an ancient text that may have much to offer yet that may also convey aspects of the very patriarchal structure that funds the Roman (and other) colonial enterprise. Using to good effect Derrida's reflections on inheriting from a tradition as always entailing a betrayal of that tradition (Derrida 1994), Liew suggests that the Gospel of John remains still a patriarchal text, making necessary a contestation (or perhaps deconstruction) of that aspect of the text if it is to become a living or life-enhancing text. As Derrida had noted with respect to the legacy of Marx, if it is not to be consigned to the tomb of the past it must be appropriated, and this will always entail an affirmation of aspects of the legacy while others are rejected as belonging in the past. This is both fidelity to what is living and betrayal of what may best be seen as the dead hand of the past. In this sense, the death drive may be sublimated as the killing of the (symbolic) Father so as to unleash the community of siblings—something toward which Freud (1955) points in *Moses and Monotheism*. In our world "come of age," in which the God-hypothesis is no longer operative (Bonhoeffer 1954), what is at stake may be less the death or even the deconstruction of the Father as trying to learn to live without what might be termed the "father-function," a function that is very much alive in the world of globalized capital, surveillance, and management. (Living without the "father-function" may indeed bring us back to Boer's suggestion about embracing castration.) If the reading of biblical texts can provide some illumination for us on this journey, then close readings like those offered here that both betray and transmit the legacy may be worthwhile indeed.

A final word of encouragement. In reading essays in this field, I am often struck by the reliance on not only secondary but also tertiary texts to deploy the thought of some of the great intellects to which we refer. This happens when instead of citing, for example, Derrida or Lacan, what gets cited are writers who are themselves dependent on secondary texts about Derrida or Lacan. Thus one sometimes senses a tendency to employ the seminal ideas at something like three degrees of separation. This is often true of other theoretical texts like those of Marx, or Kristeva, or Žižek, and so on. As one afflicted with a double addiction, on the one hand, to the reading of biblical texts and, on the other hand, to the reading of the primary texts of the great innovators of Continental thought, I find this thirdhand use to be uninspiring. Accordingly, I was quite glad to read some of the contributors actually employing readings of Derrida's own writings or those of Freud and Lacan. I hope that example will be salutary for others who take up Derridean, Freudian, or Marxist readings of texts.

Works Cited

Agamben, Giorgio. 1998. *Homo Sacer: Sovereign Power and Bare Life*. Translated by Daniel Heller-Roazen. Stanford, CA: Stanford University Press.
Bonhoeffer, Dietrich. 1954. *Prisoner for God: Letters and Papers from Prison*. Edited by Eberhard Bethge. Translated by Reginald H. Fuller. New York: Macmillan.
Derrida, Jacques. 1994. *Specters of Marx: The State of the Debt, the Work of Mourning, and the New International*. Translated by Peggy Kamuf. New York: Routledge.
Engels, Friedrich. 2008. "Bruno Bauer and Early Christianity." Pages 194–204 in *On Religion*, by Karl Marx and Friedrich Engels. Mineola, NY: Dover.
Fanon, Frantz. 1967a. *Black Skin, White Masks*. Translated by Charles Lam Markmann. New York: Grove.
———. 1967b. *The Wretched of the Earth*. Translated by Constance Farrington. Harmondsworth, UK: Penguin.
Feuerbach, Ludwig. 2004. *The Essence of Religion*. Translated by Alexander Loos. Amherst: Prometheus.
Freud, Sigmund. 1955. *Moses and Monotheism*. Translated by Katherine Jones. New York: Vintage.
———. 1961. *Beyond the Pleasure Principle*. Edited and Translated by James Strachey. New York: Liveright.
Levinas, Emmanuel. 2000. *God, Death, and Time*. Translated by Bettina Bergo. Stanford, CA: Stanford University Press.
Liew, Tat-siong Benny. 1999. *Politics of Parousia: Reading Mark Inter(con)textually*. Leiden: Brill.
———. 2003. "Re-Mark-able Masculinities? Jesus, the Son of Man, or the (Sad) Sum of Manhood." Pages 93–135 in *New Testament Masculinities*. Edited by Stephen D. Moore and Janice Capel Anderson. Atlanta: Society of Biblical Literature, 2003.
Negri, Antonio. 2003. *Time for Revolution*. Translated by Matteo Mandarini. New York: Continuum.
Nietzsche, Friedrich. 1997. *Daybreak: Thoughts on the Prejudices of Morality*. Translated by R. J. Hollingdale. Cambridge: Cambridge University Press.
Ricoeur, Paul. 1970. *Freud and Philosophy: An Essay on Interpretation*. Translated by Denis Savage. New Haven: Yale University Press.

Response:
The Ideology of Universalization

Christina Petterson

This collection of essays sets out to analyze how psychoanalytical approaches may mediate between or engage with either postcolonial and/or Marxist biblical interpretation, producing new ways of understanding all. Judging by the history and end result of this volume, this is easier said than done. Before I begin, I would like to express three hesitations that will inform my response.

My first hesitation is that placing the three approaches (postcolonialism, Marxism, and psychoanalysis) side by side lends a depth and importance to postcolonialism, while in my opinion it has yet to prove its worth. I should emphasize that I am not saying that questions of neo/colonialism and imperialism and their structural effects are unimportant or unworthy of critical interrogation. I am saying that postcolonialism generally seems ill-equipped to deal with such issues, mainly because of its class blinkers, its ahistorical practice, and its overwhelming focus on identity. While Jeremy Punt is confident that psychoanalysis indeed can mediate between postcolonial and Marxist approaches, I am less persuaded. What I think he means is that psychoanalysis can curb the unappetizing aspects of Marxism and give postcolonialism the political clout it is lacking.

My second hesitation concerns my own shortcomings in the field of psychoanalysis. Being generally sympathetic to Marxism and socialism, I have reservations in regard to the individualism of psychoanalysis and its overwhelming focus on the alienated subject as an end in and of itself. It is, however, possible to domesticate this more unpalatable aspect of psychoanalysis within a Marxist framework, as Roland Boer does in his essay "Freud, Adorno, and the Ban on Images."

My final hesitation is that my own preference is for historical biblical interpretation and less the kind that is carried out here. This is not a default position resulting from my background and my white privileges but a conscious preference informed by my politics after dabbling in the poststructural market. My own agenda is to use historical material to think through alternatives to our present system, not to try and accommodate the biblical material to capitalism. This means that from the outset I do not agree with the many of the approaches taken, which inevitably generates a somewhat awkward task.

In working through these articles in order to write a response, the metaphor of herding wild cats came to mind. The three articles that read biblical texts do not engage with Marxism; the contribution that explicitly deals with the theoretical aspect of psychoanalysis as mediator between postcolonialism and Marxism does not engage the Bible; the three contributions that practice the interpenetration of Marxism and psychoanalysis address a subfield of New Testament scholarship (the reception of a biblical theme and the reception of a genre respectively). While less determined and committed people might have thrown the towel in the ring years ago, the editors are convinced that the difficulties signify the importance of the task and not its impossibility.

Having recently reread Richard Rohrbaugh's (1995) response to the *Semeia* collection on autobiographical criticism, I find several of his points very useful and pertinent to the task at hand. For example, if I ask myself what I learned about the Bible after reading these articles, the honest answer is: not much. I did learn things about Pacific Islander culture, the movie *2012*, and fetishism; this echoes Rohrbaugh's (1995, 253) experience when he notes that while he did not learn very much about the Bible, he learned a great deal about its appropriation. A second point, which relates to my second hesitation, is Rohrbaugh's own acknowledged limits in trying to respond to the material in that *Semeia* volume. As is also the case here, there is much literature here with which I am not familiar, nor am I likely to be. But as with Rohrbaugh, my ignorance is not only academic but also one of difference. As Rohrbaugh was baffled as to how to respond to explicitly female or Hispanic readings, I also find it very difficult to engage in any meaningful way with Jione Havea's reading of the Endor medium, which is informed by Pacific Islander cultural practice. One way, however, is in his use of Frantz Fanon.

When the topics in question are those of Marxism, postcolonialism, and psychoanalysis, we should perhaps not be surprised that three of the seven articles in this volume use Fanon: Punt as an example of drawing together the three topics, Havea in his reading of the Endor medium in 1 Sam 28, and Tat-siong Benny Liew in his reading of Jesus and bare life in John. What we encounter in these two latter articles, however, is the "postcolonial Fanon," which as his biographer David Macey (2000, 26–27) points out, is a sanitized version of Fanon, one that relies almost exclusively on *Black Skin, White Masks* and eradicates the specificities of Fanon's colonial experience. Indeed, while Liew justifies his use of Giorgio Agamben's theory of "bare life" across time and location with a reference to Fanon's descriptions of black men as nonbeing and Havea uses Fanon as a universal expression of the experience of the black person, it is necessary to emphasize that Fanon (1967, 14), in his introduction to *Black Skin, White Masks*, notes that his observations and conclusions are valid only for the Antilles.

Punt's article describes Marxism's relationship to postcolonialism as "strained because the latter engages in a (Western) critique of Western civilization that proceeds beyond Marxism's economic paradigms. Poststructuralism is already suspicious of universalism (Eurocentrism), which is an important characteristic of Marxist theory." That may be true from a postcolonial perspective, but from a Marxist point of view, the problem with postcolonialism is its class blindness (Ahmad 1992; Dirlik 1994). This is most evident in the concept of hybridity and its contingency on a middle-class-subject position, which can express this in-between-ness or ambivalence. Hybridity is thus not a feature of the experiences of all postcolonial peoples but limited to the elite or bourgeois postcolonial condition, of which, say, Homi Bhabha is a product. Hybridity is thus conceptualized within relations determined by particular material conditions and yet universalized as a feature of the postcolonial subject.[1] A response to Punt's statement that postcoloniality can hardly be divorced from matters of class should be, "Of course not, but it very often is." I think this must be examined in practice rather than in theory; it must be scrutinized in actual postcolonial analyses of texts rather than inferred from various introductions to postcolonial theory. Punt's optimism in regard to the ability of

---

1. Rey Chow (1993, 35) also draws attention to this feature of Bhabha's conceptual apparatus when she notes that "what Bhabha's word 'hybridity' revives, in the masquerade of deconstruction, anti-imperialism, and 'difficult' theory, is an old functionalist notion of what a dominant culture permits in the interest of maintaining its own equilibrium." I would like to thank Steed Davidson for this reference.

psychoanalysis to mediate between the two is in my opinion also completely unjustified, in that psychoanalysis takes for granted and proceeds from the condition of alienation, which Marxism is committed to combat. Boer's article on the ban on images is particularly instructive on this point.

Liew's "The Gospel of Bare Life: Reading Death, Dream, and Desire through John's Jesus" is a reading of Jesus's death in the Gospel of John within a colonial frame. His main theoretical impulses are Giorgio Agamben's *Homo Sacer* (1998) and Abdul JanMohamed's *The Death-Bound-Subject* (2005), which provide him with the framework to read the Jews in John as "bare life" by way of their status as colonized under the Roman Empire. While I see Liew's point, I am nevertheless very reluctant to go there. Not because of what it means for the reading of the Jews in John but rather the implications for the African American population of the United States. Liew argues that

> within an empire, whether that of ancient Rome or that of the modern United States, a particular segment of the population under colonial "sovereignty" tends to become particularly vulnerable to death, and such a susceptible segment is often singled out on the basis of class/status and/or race/ethnicity. For these groups, being who they are and being dead are almost always one and the same, because their vulnerability to death—whether in the form of fear or of direct experience—is not only known but also deeply internalized (Holloway 2002, 58–59).

My first issue with this quote is the equation of the Roman Empire and that of the United States, because it relegates the actions of the state to a predetermined facet of empire; the practices of the US state, its outrageous economic inequality and ongoing marginalization, population management, granting/refusing civil and political rights are deliberate political choices and not by virtue of empire. My second issue is that it places sovereignty first and then marginalization of "a particular segment" second ("tends to become" and then "is singled out"), because in the case of the African American population, the nonsubject status of the black person is *constitutive* of US state sovereignty in a way utterly unimaginable within the Roman Empire and its distinct socioeconomic and constitutional formation. What takes place here, then, is not only the equation of empires that Boer discusses in his article but also the equation of various minority groups—Liew also mentions gay communities during the AIDS epidemic and the production of "the Jew" as a metahistorical victim of oppression. This practice of juxtaposing various oppressive systems and minority groups seems to be a defining feature of postcolonial analysis, which has a relaxed relationship to nuance and historical difference. But are all minority struggles equal? Are the political and socioeconomic challenges facing the Jewish community in the United States the same as those facing the African American community? Not only are they historically unequal in terms of civil rights, but they also differ in access to cultural and political power in contemporary United States society. Even today, the relations between the two groups constitute a highly sensitive political issue in United States politics.

Tina Pippin's article draws together psychoanalysis, fantasy, and science fiction literature to analyze the genre of apocalypse, more precisely Roland Emmerich's 2009 film, *2012*. Since I have not seen the film nor know anything about fantasy and science fiction, I cannot do full justice to Pippin's multifaceted article, but I found it immensely stimulating. Pippin argues (I think) that the various apocalyptic imaginings do not really offer us alternatives to the world we live in, because their new worlds are just a more simplified version of the one destroyed. Thus what they offer is a reaffirmation of the status quo. Hence, while the *way* the world ends may differ (water and flooding is currently a favored theme—see also *Noah*, which resonates with Havea's article and the threat of rising sea levels for those living in the Pacific Islands), the remnant rebuilding the world after its near annihilation is constant. Looking at how the Apocalypse of John is trying to express the end of Roman imperialism over against the way modern apocalyptic logic normalizes capitalism by envisioning not the end of the economic system but rather the end of the world provides food for thought, not only in relation to the collusion between capitalism and Christianity but also the relation between the Apocalypse of John and the socioeconomic system of its day.

This brings me to Liew's first contribution to this volume, which is a study of the silence of the women in Mark's ending. There was one matter that I found confusing in this article. In note 21 Liew notes that Maia Kotrosits and Hal Taussig discuss the First Jewish-Roman War as the context of Mark's writing and makes this the way in which Mark uses language of a past trauma to understand the current one. Liew then continues, "rather than seeing this as the convoluted workings of one's (political?) unconscious in response to trauma as psychoanalysis would, Kotrosits and Taussig seem to see it as an intentional move by Mark to make sense of one particular known trauma." What puzzles me in this is that Liew seems to place himself in the psychoanalysis group, while to me it looks like he is doing the same as Kotrosits and Taussig, but wanting to extend the particular historical situation of Mark into a universal position. In the section "The Uncanny and the Unhomely Haunting of Colonial Trauma," Liew picks up the corpse of Jesus as Slavoj Žižek's "undead," with which he closed the previous section. This "brings to mind" Freud's concept of the uncanny, which via Bhabha's translation of the term as "unhomely" through Juliana Chang's interpretation becomes connected with colonization and leads us to the Roman Empire. The Roman Empire, as a historical reality with distinct burial practices, is thus installed as the backdrop to psychoanalytic terms such as *trauma* and *haunting*, and Jesus's resurrection becomes a resistance against Roman death practices. On the one hand, this ultimately historicizes Mark, which thus cannot at all be understood outside the framework of the Roman Empire. A Marxist perspective cannot object to such radical historicization. However, the paradoxically concomitant *ahistoricism* in Liew's reading due to the psychoanalytical perspective and the postcolonial inflection seems to suggest that there is little or no room for noncolonial traumas. From a historicist perspective, I have no objection to the contextualization of Mark within the Roman Empire, but the ahistorical consequences seem to be curiously reductive.

In an interesting essay with which I have been working recently, Louis Marin (2001) examines the production of meaning and the missing presence of Jesus at the tomb. He argues that the resurrection narratives liberated an empty place, which interpretive speech occupied, and in which it established a universal message. This particular space is preserved by the text "in its constitutive reality" and is possible only on the basis of the "lack manifested by the empty tomb" (128–29). Because of a hole in lived experience (a missing corpse), the narrative papers over, so to speak, that very hole with spoken words, the words spoken by the young man/messenger/angel. The missing body, then, is substituted by words, and thus the narrative takes the place of the event to which it refers. The absence of the body is exchanged with speech (namely, the message "he has been raised"), and hence being emerges in a different order (i.e., the symbolic order). While Marin's article uses Matthew as point of departure, he regards the resurrection narratives as "constitutive of the symbolic order of our own language" (119). Read against this backdrop, then, the universality in Liew's argument seems to suggest that colonial trauma is constitutive of the symbolic order of our language. As was the case in my discussion with Punt, this seems to exclude all kinds of other violating acts of language (e.g., production of class difference) and privilege that of colonialism.

Finally, I accidentally placed the two Liew articles on either side of Boer's article on fetish, and this made me think of something in relation to fetish and displacement, which is not part of Boer's argument. Liew's emphasis on the Roman Empire in Mark and John does seem disproportionally large when compared with both gospels' (but especially John's) negative focus on the Jewish opponents of Jesus. This made me wonder whether the explosion of empire studies that Boer identifies as a particular New Testament development is perhaps indicative of a displacement of the problem of the anti-Jewish nature of the New Testament texts onto the more politically correct Roman Empire?

Works Cited

Agamben, Giorgio. 1998. *Homo Sacer: Sovereign Power and Bare Life*. Translated by Daniel Heller-Roazen. Stanford, CA: Stanford University Press.
Ahmad, Aijaz. 1992. *In Theory: Classes, Nations, Literatures*. London: Verso.
Chow, Rey. 1993. *Writing Diaspora: Tactics of Intervention in Contemporary Cultural Studies*. Bloomington: Indiana University Press.
Dirlik, Arif. 1994. "The Postcolonial Aura: Third World Criticism in the Age of Global Capitalism." *Critical Inquiry* 20:328–56.
Fanon, Frantz. 1967. *Black Skin, White Masks*. Translated by Charles Lam Markmann. New York: Grove.
Holloway, Karla F. C. 2002. *Passed On: African American Mourning Stories*. Durham, NC: Duke University Press.
JanMohamed, Abdul R. 2005. *The Death-Bound-Subject: Richard Wright's Archaeology of Death*. Durham, NC: Duke University Press.
Macey, David. 2000. *Frantz Fanon: A Life*. London: Granta.
Marin, Louis. 2001. "From Body to Text: Metaphysical Propositions on the Origin of Narrative." Pages 115–29 in *On Representation*. Edited by Louis Marin. Stanford, CA: Stanford University Press.
Rohrbaugh, Richard L. 1995. "A Social Scientific Response." *Semeia* 72:247–58.

"Den Himmel überlassen wir / Den Engeln und den Spatzen": A Tupiniquim Response*

Fernando Candido da Silva

Quo magis res singulares intelligimus eo magis Deum intelligimus. (Benedictus de Spinoza, 1677)

Todas as naus são naus de sonho logo que esteja em nós o poder de (as) sonhar. (Fernando Pessoa)

In August 1549, only a few months after his arrival at what he called "Terras do Brasil" along with Tomé de Sousa's armada (first governor-general), Father Manuel da Nóbrega (1955, 57–67) wrote, from the Baía de Todos os Santos to his brethren in Coimbra, an informative letter regarding the Jesuit endeavor in the Americas. In that letter, the future first provincial of the Jesuits in Brazil did more than describing; he projected the dilemmas of *his civilization* in this land "that has a thousand-league coast all populated by people." The Tupiniquim and Tupinambá—those who "sleep in hammocks made of cotton"—were perceived through the ethnocentric criterion of the absence: "These gentile people adore nothing, nor know God" (62).

By not taking the wild thought *seriously*, as "another image of thought" (Viveiros de Castro 2015a, 74–75), Nóbrega commits to provide what he understands as absence: "Only the thunders are called Tupana, which is what one calls a divine thing. And thus, we do not have another more convenient term to bring them to the knowledge of God, than calling it *Father* Tupana" (Nóbrega 1955, 62, emphasis added). The Tupiniquim and

---

* This response, and all quotations (unless it is indicated in the references within it), was translated from Portuguese by Fabrício Henrique Meneghelli Cassilhas and Flávia Wanzeller Kunsch.

Tupinambá were not, therefore, the blank slate Nóbrega expected. Aside the failed attempt of cultural translation by using Tupã (Bosi 1992, 65–66), Nóbrega allows us to discern the indigenous policy in its absence of the One (Clastres 2013, 184–89): the first natives possess divine things, but not the Father's authority. The description of a religious phenomenon according to sorcery terms—"From such and such years some sorcerers come from afar, *pretending to bring sanctity*" (emphasis added)—was not enough to hide the type of society encouraged by the (nonfetishized) "human figure" of the calabash.

> When the sorcerer arrives bringing celebration to the place, he enters a dark house, and lays the calabash he brings, which has a human shape, on a place more convenient for his mistakes, and, changing his own voice to a boy's, and, with the calabash, tells them not to work, not to go to the plantations, that the provisions will grow by themselves, and you shall never want food, and the house will come by itself; and the hoes will dig, and the arrows will go to the forest to hunt for their master, and they shall kill many of their opponents and will tame many others for your eating. (Nóbrega 1955, 63)

Imbued, therefore, with an anthropophagous religiousness (and without any reification) constantly alert to ways of coercive power, the Tupiniquim and Tupinambá seem to live in their own original paradise: "Not a proper thing has what is not common, and what one has shall be shared with the others, especially if they are edible, of which not a single thing is saved for the next day, nor care for treasuring riches" (Nóbrega 1955, 65). Here is the apparent problem of the Jesuit missions and their civilizational project: how to preach the redemption for Adam and Eve before the fall? Nóbrega himself reveals its impossibility: "There are only a few terms to well declare our faith ... they are very much attached to sensual things. They have many times asked if God has a head, and a body, and a wife, if He eats, and what He wears, and many other similar things" (68). Given this structural incompatibility of the language—Nóbrega was not willing, after all, to redeem and re-create his own language (Pompa 2001)—it is not without reason that some years after the relatively optimistic letter from *Informação das Terras do Brasil*, Nóbrega also rewrote in 1556–1557 *O Diálogo da Conversão do Gentio* (see Hansen 2010, 141–66).

Tired of the first natives' resistance being "increasingly more open and pertinacious to the missionary work, or else in a deceitful acceptance that did not change their beliefs, rites, and costumes prior to the baptism"

(Beozzo 2009, 47), Father Manuel da Nóbrega gives up catechizing through pure translation and once and for all incorporates the Christian mission into the action of civil authorities. Under Mem de Sá and the auspices of the Portuguese Crown, his propositions of forced conversion reached the status of general policy of the colonial state[1] and the "Terras do Brasil"[2] entered, definitively, the history of the civilization of Christ and commodity. Facing this irreversible scenario, there would be no choice left for the Tupi. Montaigne's cannibals, by 1580, had already known that (Ginzburg 2007, 53–78).

* * *

For the Tupiniquim reader (i.e., a by-product of colonial projects called *brasileiro*), a response to articles on biblical studies about the Freudo-Marxian articulation (or not) will be—to honor the Tupi tradition and Oswald de Andrade's *Manifesto* in 1928—necessarily anthropophagous: "tupi or not tupi, that is the question" (Andrade 1972, 13). As a modern *mestiço*, son of a new-people (Ribeiro 1970, 105–9) who has always lived with modernity and with mercantile/industrial/financial capitalism, it is reasonable that I recognize the neuroses of Occidental thought. Anthropophagy, however, implies "the permanent transformation of the taboo into a totem" (Andrade 1972, 15). Perhaps because of this specific characteristic of Tupi ritual cannibalism, I have other ways to swallow Marx, Freud, the (so-called) postcolonial, and the Bible.

The title of my response suggests, in itself, the anthropophagous process. The sentence belongs to Freud's *The Future of an Illusion* (1978), and it might as well be one of the taboos to be transformed into a totem in a Tupiniquim biblical criticism—a tropical reading (Cavalcanti 1993, 201–18) that reveals itself at the crossroad of sin (Vainfas 2014, 27–66). In a frank polemic about the value of the religious ideas, Freud reproduces an excerpt from the 1844 poem *Deutschland, ein Wintermärchen* by Heinrich Heine, Marx's friend and an "anthropophagous poet avant la lettre" (Vallias 2011, 20), and claims, as a civilizational task, "an education for reality"

---

1. For readers of English interested in more deeply evaluating the early days of Portuguese colonization in America, I suggest Metcalf 2005.

2. "In the absence of gold and silver, or even cloves and cinnamon, the Portuguese were able to find some use for these 'Indians,' making them fell trees. Thus the natives were named as 'brasil,' for the brazilwood was what mattered" (Gambini 2000, 43).

(Freud 1978, 123). Free from the "neurotic relics" of religious teachings, Freud bets on a "reconciliation between men and civilization" (118). It is true that psychoanalysis of religion in the Occidental civilization, being limited in its reception of a profound suspicion toward illusions, could release the desire for eros of only one part of humankind. It seems to me, however, that Freud had already dreamed of the anthropophagic risks of his bet against the "intellectual atrophy" when he writes, "But it is already another thing with the big mass of the noneducated and the oppressed, who possess all the reasons to be enemies of civilization. While they do not discover that people do not believe in God anymore, everything will be fine. But they will discover it, infallibly" (114).

Curiously (or not), Freud identifies, in this same text, an element of the psychic justification of the illusionist religion that connects him to the famous (and not always well explained) Marxian sentence, "religion is the opium of the people" (Marx 2010, 145). Freud (1978, 122) writes, "That the effect of religious consolation can resemble the effect of a narcotic is a fact well illustrated by what is happening in the United States." How not to comprehend Freud's civilizational polemic against the United States, "God's Own Country" (99)? Or perhaps more precisely: how not to recognize the neoimperial capitalist reasons of North America's civilizational impossibility? For the Tupiniquim anthropophagy of civilization, the combination of Marx and Freud suggests a criticism of religion and the market as combined illusions. This time Marx (2010, 146) will say, "The criticism of religion is, therefore, *in embryo*, the *criticism of that vale of tears* of which religion is the *halo*" (emphasis original).[3]

Precisely by germinating the criticism of history's vale of tears (see Heine 2008, 212), the idea of the fetish in Marx (Marx 1996) seems to be more helpful, in terms of universality, than the one in Freud (1972, 1996). Even if both have understood the illusory character of the repressive civilization of happiness, Marx in his criticism of commodity—that complex thing, "abounding in metaphysical subtleties and theological niceties" (Marx 1996, 197)[4]—establishes once and for all the hermeneutics of suspicion toward the fetishist religious form of the capitalist economy project. Freud does not do so. By transferring the term *fetish* to the domain

---

3. English text is accessible at the Marxists Internet Archive, http://tinyurl.com/SBL0684i.

4. English text is accessible at the Marxists Internet Archive, http://tinyurl.com/SBL0684j.

of erotic perversion, he keeps himself inside the field of bourgeois illusion of the private kingdom of the masculine domestic space. Hence "the logic by which Freud privileges the penis in the scenario of fetishism is by itself fetishist" (McClintock 2010, 285), and "the Freudian theory is also part of the sacerdotal empire of this cult. It was conceived inside totally capitalist molds" (Benjamin 2013b, 22; cf. Bloch 2005, 54–67). If this is the case, my fear is that the articles gathered here may, at some measure, still be entangled by the *feitiços* of the postcolonial capital through a "psychoanalytic mediation" that neither admits nor addresses ("I know it well, but nevertheless…") the ambiguity of fetishism in its historical performance (McClintock 2010, 276). Would this be the case of Roland Boer's articles?

When evaluating some anti-imperial biblical studies, especially those produced in the North American context ("the belly of the imperial beast," according to Boer), the bet in the reinstatement of imperial fetishism seems right, especially with the conceptual combination of Marx and Freud regarding the fetish. "Gorged with devotion," as Freud (1978, 122) would have said, the confessional tone of anti-imperial biblical studies from North America results in a truly shallow comprehension of the biblical text. Actually, at this point, I need to praise Boer's equally critical analysis of Latin American studies. In fact, when addressing idolatry—and not fetish—as the first category in its critique of capital, Latin American theological production (also) found itself domesticated by the laws of the market (see, above all, Althaus-Reid 2005, 35–54). However, how may one be interested "in the fetish transfer itself, in the attribution of power to an object that comes at the expense of human relations" and, at the same time, grants so much power to the phallus through the scene of castration? As it is well warned by Anne McClintock (2010, 275), "the phallic theory reduces the fetishism to a privileged poetics of sexual difference and does not admit class or race as crucially formative categories." After all, if in his theory Freud made the nanny abject, why would not Boer—even embracing castration—do the same with Brigitte Kahl and make her abject in his evaluation of Richard Horsley's edited volume?

Even qualifying the crucial difference of Kahl's (2008) article in the volume edited by Horsley, Boer prefers to invest in the fear of castration of the overwhelming majority of men who contributed to *In the Shadow of Empire*. Would his final suggestion of accepting castration and interrupting the fetishist transference imply, eventually, Kahl and her refusal of homogeneity of the fetishized biblical text as the *history of faithful resistance*? Effectively, Kahl's name seems to open Boer's text—almost reluctantly—to other anti-imperial biblical readings held in the *same* belly of the imperial beast. The recognition of this ambiguity seems fundamental to me, first of all, in order to avoid easy cases of homogenization that serve only to protect the theoretic coherence previously formulated and, second, to encourage a global theory of the place of interpretation, in which the global critique of capital and its fetishes is "generated locally by indigenous peoples, in the concrete and etymological senses of this last word" (Viveiros de Castro 2015b, 16). By the way, would not this procedure be important for not overestimating the Chinese competition for the succession to the imperial throne?

Aware of the dangerous effects of the global domestication of the market also reaching the discipline of biblical studies, the prohibition of images proposed by Boer as a way of blocking the merchandising of criticism is coherent to his acceptance of castration and suggests, accurately in my view, the ineffectiveness of the erection of (old or new) idols with easy answers in such critical times (Nandy 2015, 89–124). In fact, to deliver his proposition more radically—moving, unquestionably, from the critique of idolatry to that of fetish—it would be indispensable to amplify his generous orientation toward the indecent *porteña* wisdom of Marcella Althaus-Reid (2000, 193): "It is time to break the capitalist-heterosexual symmetry that produces clones" (see Althaus-Reid 2005, 272; Anzaldúa 2007, 106–7). Without prescribing rehashed utopias but (re)formulating adequate theoretical questions (Adorno 2003, 131–37), can we still be ambitious in our "reflections on vision and task" (Segovia 2015, 24; cf. Santos 2015)?

I am convinced that it is still possible to find "fellow unbelievers" (Freud 1978, 123) in the United States: "A thing is called sacred and Divine when it is designed for promoting piety, and continues sacred so long as it is religiously used: if the users cease to be pious, the thing ceases to be sacred" (Spinoza 1891, 1:167; cf. Spinoza 2008, 198). Once the North American imperial "metaphysical subtlety" is clearly identified (Tolbert 1995, 267–68), we could propagate (and not conceal) the studies that denounce, locally, the global fetish of the new type of empire, namely, the one of North American financial capital and of the multinational corporation in search of the free market. Erin Runions's (2006) nonconfessional analysis of the messianic-apocalyptical speeches of the Bush administration is an evident example of the possibility of global anti-imperial criticism at the imperial place itself. As Tina Pippin's article in this volume seems to allude to Runions's article, it would be expected that the "desire for the end of the world" of Hollywood films—such as the "desire for war" of Bush's speeches—fetishizes, in itself, economic desires in a biblical-apocalyptic language proper for the end of history (without redemption). Nevertheless, I am afraid that this was not necessarily the way taken by "Psychoapocalypse" in its appreciation of North American dystopic and apocalyptical art/commodity.

In her proposition to investigate "some psychological interweavings of the fantastic narratives," Pippin reserves to herself a daring task: How to understand the holy depth of the universe of the film *2012*? Does the power of the film really "reside in its obscenely direct staging of embarrassingly intimate fantasies" (Žižek 2011, 320; cf. 2012, 60)? How does the repressed desire ("for some utopian or dystopian future worlds," in Pippin's words) constitute the principle of its own performance in the film? And the most important—again, in Pippin's words—"in what ways does fantasy open up doors to change"? These are all questions answered by Pippin. However, in my view, she does that only partially. For Pippin, the fantasy seems to open a space of revelation to the *real desire*. But what would characterize this desire? The "embarrassingly intimate fantas[y]" itself? How do we negotiate desire's *real* meaning with the film if the film itself entangles us in its phantasmagoria?

In fact, it would be reasonable that the fantastic was the most appropriated place for the return of the repressed to civilization; after all, the fantasy seemed to be the only way for mental activity that "would remain free from the domain of reality's principle" (Marcuse 2010, 35). Not anymore, for what it seems. Even the space of the fantasy seems to have been colonized—by ghosts—in the universalization process of the fetishist phenomenon and of the mass society of contemporary capitalism. While watching the commodity *2012*, for example, it is not hard to see indistinctly the *feitiços* of modern capitalism, especially its fundamental "mystic regression" that forces a fake totalization. Pippin noticed well the imperial fetishes;[5] nonetheless, she has not truly exploded the apocalyptic

---

5. I would make one observation only, relatively obvious for a Tupiniquim anthropophagist from the former Portuguese Empire: the cosmic resolution of the apocalypse in the Cape of Good Hope (in the movie frames) may find a slightly more complex reason than the mere projection of the dream of colonizing Africa. In fact, the Cape historically represents the concrete possibility of globalization of the fetishist and mercantile modernity: "In 1482 the *feitoria* of São Jorge da Mina was established on the Guinea coast, and by 1488 Bartolomeu Dias has rounded the Cape of Good Hope. It was this event which conclusively dispelled the Ptolemaic belief that the Indian Ocean was a landlocked sea, and subsequently opened the way for Portuguese

narrative—à la Carmen Miranda, "The Lady in the Tutti-Frutti Hat" (and her 1938 song "E o mundo não se acabou")—as in a *profane illumination*: "The most trivial can contain the surprising, the miraculous, the moment of rupture, of revolution" (Matos 2000, 102). Instead, she preferred the terms of the narrative's negotiation as if apocalyptic narrative really directs some kind of revelation about desire for life. Maybe—and just maybe—for not having acknowledged, in the principles of reality, the psychological effects of the apocalyptic "state of exception" that is inherent to the imperial capitalism (such as using cheap Third World labor force to construct an ark for the "holy seed" to survive the end of the world). Maybe—and just maybe—*les damnés de la terre* from Cho Ming Valley, still in the year 2010, had already known that.

Facing this ghostly and dismal scenario, how can one resist the seductive postcolonial proposition proposed in the articles by Jione Havea and Jeremy Punt? Is it possible that a location supposedly peripheral to the global financial empire (with no formal colonies) makes them, a priori, vaccinated against the fetishes and ghosts of capital? Or is the "postcolonial" itself one more "metaphysical subtlety" of the mercantile and imperial voyeurism (see Huggan 2001)? Anne McClintock (2010, 30) is incisive: "The post-colonial scene happens in a historical suspension, as if the definite historical events had happened before our time and were not happening now."

If that is the case, it is not hard to understand the islander hermeneutic procedure adopted by Havea, such as the reason why we feel, as we read the article, immediately transported to the adventures of the *Argonauts of the Western Pacific* by Malinowski (1984). Truthfully, the *kula* scene, parallel to the *talanoa* one, seems to refer to an anthropologic postevolutionist strategy that refuses to the Others their entrance in the "universal history" (see Buck-Morss 2009) by situating them in the anachronistic space of the imperial fetish itself. Not by chance, the circular existential method of the "natives" from Oceania—as a comprehension device that refuses a preconceived agenda—ends up being turned into a commodity to be negotiated to interpret psychological dramas from the Bible (and its civilization).

It is evident that after the long era of the British missionary empire, the biblical psychological dramas also belong to its ex-colonies (Sugirtharajah

---

involvement in the proliferation of trading networks which stretched from the eastern coast of Africa to the islands of Indonesian archipelago" (Brotton 1997, 58–59).

2008). In this regard, one cannot deny that the *talanoa* of Havea shows—in a dialogue with 1 Sam 28 and Fanon—an exemplary appreciation, without concealment, of the psychological pathologies developed in colonial contexts. Nonetheless, different from Saul in his search for a cure from the executioner himself during the night, would it not be the moment to unveil—at the *talanoa* controlled by the narrator in daylight (Yee 2003)— the theological reasons for the maintenance of the "dependence complex"? Facing the strengthening of the biblical-destructive metaphysics of capital, does not the Fanonian task of "politicization of the masses" (Fanon 2005, 210) and of "putting an end to a vicious circle" (Fanon 2008, 27) make itself even more indispensable to biblical criticism as a *medium* toward the purpose of liberation from the imperial agenda?

To move forward in this direction, Punt—in "Conversations in Africa"—could have dedicated more than one vague footnote to the gestated materialist contribution in the Cape of Good Hope. I am obviously referring to the courageous doctoral dissertation by Itumeleng Mosala (1987). Elaborated at the height of modernity's barbarism, Mosala noticed, in a transparent way, the dangers of the Bible as a fetish to the new colonized peoples.

> What then is meant by the Bible as the "Word of God"? The ideological import of such theological statement is immense, because the "Word of God" can presumably (by definition) not be the object of criticism. Furthermore, the "Word of God" cannot be critiqued in the light of black experience or any other. The only appropriate response is *obedience*. (Mosala 1987, 5, emphasis original)

Did the (anachronistic) space and the (panopticon) time of Punt's texts and contexts end up surprising history? It is well known that South Africans (i.e., a by-product of colonial projects) are far from finding a solution to the theological legacy of Apartheid (Maluleke and Nadar 2004). It is true that there is an open path to a South African integration in the Brazilian style (Marx 1998, 273), but does the local experience of a "racial democracy" need to be repeated in a global scale to show its failed format of human reconciliation? If I can make any recommendation based on the tragic Brazilian experience, I would insist that the conversations in South Africa do not give up so easily the pedagogical construction of an emancipatory hegemony, in which the biblical psychology of obedience is universally denounced. Actually, such denunciation would be the first step to make the emancipatory hegemony feasible, after all, as Paulo Freire (2005, 201) already knew, "in order to be united the oppressed ones need to cut the umbilical cord—which is magic and mythical—through which they are connected to the world of oppression." Otherwise, the post-Apartheid promises to be very Brazilian: the Universal Church of the Kingdom of God will monopolize and provide "all answers" (Van Wyk, 2015).

By the way, we should pay more attention to the "liberation of theology" promoted by Bishop Edir Macedo since the 1990s in the land of brazilwood (Arenari 2013, 88–115). By filling the presumed *local* vacuum with a more purposive pedagogical agenda (in political terms) from the classic liberation theology in the neoliberal era (Gerstenberger 1995, 77; Löwy 2000, 176–202; Cardoso Pereira 2012, 162–66), the theology liberated from the Universal Church seems to meet the fetishist interests of the market (especially the touristic one at *Templo de Salomão* "rebuilt" by the church in downtown São Paulo), causing evident damage to the national politics (Dantas 2011). With its many pedagogical resources (e.g., the telecommunication of mass society, which in Brazil includes the soap operas), the Universal Church spreads the biblical theology of its bishop: the Bible is a canonical gathering of experiences in which the God from the Old Testament (desirous for absolute obedience) unites with the figure of Jesus in the New Testament by offering a "new" possibility of evangelical interpretation of history (Macedo 1993, 81–86).

Macedo's (1993, 20) biblical study does not give up on history, because it knows that "the heated discussions on the points of view, interpretation of the Scriptures, exegesis and eschatology can produce nothing profitable … regarding helping our fellow human beings that are walking obscurely through the life paths with no one to take them a message of faith, of love." How can we deny the fetishist effectiveness of Macedo's ingenious articulation? Not fearing to enter history (and recognizing its barbarism), the Universal Church of the Kingdom of God will preach till it reaches the last condemned on earth. It is a way out but one that is still stuck to the imperial fetish: obeying God's rules in the name of the prosperity of market theology (Coleman 2000, 27–39). At this moment of imminent danger, as it is adverted in Walter Benjamin's thesis 6 (2012, 11–12), has Tat-siong Benny Liew been able to "remove tradition from the sphere of conformism which is ready to conquer it"?

By approaching (1) the "messianic secret" in Mark and (2) the "dream of death" in John, Liew opens up profitable spaces for a profane illumination of the gospels in the devastating psychological context of the Roman

Empire. Facing the same colonial scene of *pax Romana*, the evangelists seem to offer, in different mobilizations of the horror itself and its ghosts, therapeutic processes of healing to colonial traumas (see Taussig 1993). The good news from Mark and John tries to deal with the real-life wishes repressed by the reality of death through the language of resurrection. Resurrection is, therefore, a traumatic resolution. The text of Mark invests in this trauma as silence: silence of the women disciples, silence of the conclusion, silence of the paratactic Greek. On the other hand, the text of John prefers to embrace the horror of death and subvert the trauma. How to choose between these two therapeutic proposals? Which one of them can overcome the vicious circle of the oppressor's pedagogy?

By digging and recollecting the gospels as *traumatic memory*, Liew ends up highlighting, in the present space, the exact place where he saves the things from the past (Benjamin 2013a, 101). However, he does not explicate it. If the psychological effects of *pax Americana* and its fantasy (and, therefore, utopia) were even more exposed (Schüssler Fiorenza 2007, 35–69), Liew may not have preferred to revive John's dead in order to create a different future. Ironically, it is the women's, the Greek's, and the end of Mark's text's silence that the Messiah is announced "not only as the redeemer, but as the one that will overcome the Antichrist" (Benjamin 2012, 12). By deconstructing the messianic scene—would this be its pedagogical secret?—Mark's text does not reinscribe the "theological nicety" of messianic authority as the text of John does. Contrariwise, "Mark provides an interpretation radically different from Jesus's messianism, in which the most obvious meaning remains hidden. Mark seems to suggest that we can know the Messiah by joining the messianic practices—listening, observing, praying, and watching" (Gunjević 2015, 224; see also Belo 1974).

Let us listen to the silences.

* * *

Newly released in Brazil, *The Falling Sky: Words of a Yanomami Shaman* (Kopenawa and Albert 2010) is a sharp attempt to break the silence and the failed orality of the words of a shaman from the extreme north of the Brazilian Amazon. Davi Kopenawa—shaman and spokesperson for the Yanomami—is certain about this project with the French anthropologist Bruce Albert: "I asked you to set them on this paper in order to give them to the white people who will be willing to know their lines. Maybe then they will finally lend an ear to the inhabitants of the forest's words and start thinking about them in a more upright manner?" (Kopenawa and Albert 2013, 13; cf. Kopenawa and Albert 2010, 13). Through Kopenawa's drawn words we have the single chance to listen to the traumatized memories of the Yanomami in their encounter with what the shaman classifies—to Marx's jealousy—as "people of merchandise" (Kopenawa and Albert 2013, 549 n. 1; cf. Kopenawa and Albert 2010, 549 n. 1). In this shamanic memory rests especially the trauma from the missions of those "people of Teosi ["God"]": "The missionaries talked to us about Teosi while showing us pictures, saying: 'These are the Bible's words!'.... Their words led our thought astray and left us worried" (Kopenawa and Albert 2013, 190; cf. 2010, 190).

Target of the "New Tribes Mission" in the 1960s—precisely the inaugural moment of the disastrous Brazilian dictatorial modernization (Prado and Earp 2009)—Davi (!) and his people did not take long to confront the frequent psychological reprimand of Teosi's "image skins about the people of Israel and about Sesusi": "To us, all these white people's words about Teosi are in vain.... We do not remain locked up all the time in our little houses *pretending to talk to Teosi* and eating alone, the way the missionaries do!" (Kopenawa and Albert 2013, 208–9, emphasis added; cf. 2010, 208–9). We should not be surprised that in 1972 the mission of investigation run by the "Aborigines' Protection Society" in Tootobi reported how the missionaries complained about the Indian's lack of will to save and work to accumulate wealth (Brooks et al. 1973). From the original land of the Universal Church of the Kingdom of God, Kopenawa's shamanic voice denounces—maybe as one of the last messages from the forest—the Bible fetishes of the people of merchandise.

Works Cited

Adorno, Theodor. 2003. "A filosofia muda o mundo ao manter-se como teoria." *Lua Nova* 60:131–38.
Althaus-Reid, Marcella. 2000. *Indecent Theology: Theological Perversions in Sex, Gender and Politics*. London: Routledge.
———. 2005. *La teología indecente: perversiones teológicas en sexo, género y política*. Barcelona: Bellaterra.
Andrade, Oswald. 1972. "Manifesto antropófago." Pages 11–19 in *Do Pau-Brasil à Antropofagia e às Utopias*, vol. 6 of *Oswald de Andrade, Obras completas*. Rio de Janeiro: Civilização Brasileira.
Anzaldúa, Gloria. 2007. *Borderlands/La Frontera: The New Mestiza*. San Francisco: Aunt Lute Books.

Arenari, Brand. 2013. *Pentecostalism as Religion of Periphery: An Analysis of Brazilian Case*. PhD diss., Humboldt Universität.
Belo, Fernando. 1974. *Uma leitura política do Evangelho*. Lisbon: Multinova.
Benjamin, Walter. 2012. *O anjo da história*. Belo Horizonte: Autêntica.
———. 2013a. *Imagens de pensamento: sobre o haxixe e outras drogas*. Belo Horizonte: Autêntica.
———. 2013b. *O capitalismo como religião*. São Paulo: Boitempo.
Beozzo, José Oscar. 2009. "O Diálogo da Conversão ao Gentio: a evangelização entre a persuasão e a força." Pages 43–78 in *Conversão dos cativos: povos indígenas e missão jesuítica*, by Paulo Suess et al. São Bernardo do Campo: Nhanduti.
Bloch, Ernst. 2005. *O princípio esperança*. Vol. 1. Rio de Janeiro: Contraponto.
Bosi, Alfredo. 1992. *Dialética da colonização*. São Paulo: Cia das Letras.
Brooks, Edwin, et al. 1973. *Tribes of Amazon Basin in Brazil, 1972: Report for the Aborigines Protection Society*. London: Knight.
Brotton, Jerry. 1997. *Trading Territories: Mapping the Early Modern World*. London: Reaktion.
Buck-Morss, Susan. 2009. *Hegel, Haiti and Universal History*. Pittsburgh: University of Pittsburgh Press.
Cardoso Pereira, Nancy. 2012. "Paper Is Patient, History Is Not: Readings and Unreadings of the Bible in Latin America (1985–2005)." Pages 149–66 in *The Future of the Biblical Past: Envisioning Biblical Studies on a Global Key*. Edited by Roland Boer and Fernando Segovia. Atlanta: Society of Biblical Literature.
Cavalcanti, Tereza. 1993. "Social Location and Biblical Interpretation: A Tropical Reading." Pages 201–18 in *Reading from This Place: Social Location and Biblical Interpretation in Global Perspective*. Edited by Fernando Segovia and Mary Ann Tolbert. Minneapolis: Fortress.
Clastres, Pierre. 2013. *A sociedade contra o estado: Pesquisas de antropologia política*. São Paulo: Cosac Naify.
Coleman, Simon. 2000. *The Globalization of Charismatic Christianity: Spreading the Gospel of Prosperity*. Cambridge: Cambridge University Press.
Dantas, Bruna Suruagy do Amaral. 2011. *Religião e política: ideologia e ação da "Bancada Evangélica" na Câmara Federal*. PhD diss., Pontifícia Universidade Católica de São Paulo.
Fanon, Frantz. 2005. *Os condenados da terra*. Juiz de Fora: Editora UFJF.

———. 2008. *Pele negra, máscaras brancas*. Salvador: EDUFBA.
Freire, Paulo. 2005. *Pedagogia do oprimido*. Rio de Janeiro: Paz e Terra.
Freud, Sigmund. 1972. "Três ensaios sobre a teoria da sexualidade." Pages 119–62 in vol. 7 of *Edição standard das obras psicológicas de completas de Sigmund Freud*. Rio de Janeiro: Imago.
———. 1978. *O futuro de uma ilusão*. São Paulo: Abril Cultural.
———. 1996. "Fetichismo." Pages 151–60 in vol. 21 of *Edição standard das obras psicológicas de completas de Sigmund Freud*. Rio de Janeiro: Imago.
Gambini, Roberto. 2000. *Espelho índio: a formação da alma brasileira*. São Paulo: Axis Mundi.
Gerstenberger, Erhard S. 1995. "Teologias da Libertação em Transformação: O testemunho do Antigo Testamento e o caminho dos cristãos latino-americanos depois da 'virada.'" *Estudos Teológicos* 35:67–83.
Ginzburg, Carlo. 2007. "Montaigne, os canibais e as grutas." Pages 53–78 in *O fio e os rastros: Verdadeiro, falso, fictício*. São Paulo: Companhia das Letras.
Gunjević, Boris. 2015. "Rezai e observai: a subversão messiânica." Pages 205–26 in *O sofrimento de Deus: Inversões do Apocalipse*, by Slavoj Žižek and Boris Gunjević. Belo Horizonte: Autêntica.
Hansen, João Adolfo, ed. 2010. *Manuel da Nóbrega*. Recife: Fundação Joaquim Nabuco; Editora Massangana.
Heine, Heinrich. 2008. "Alemanha, um conto de inverno (Caput I)." *Artefilosofia* 5:209–14.
Huggan, Graham. 2001. *The Postcolonial Exotic: Marketing the Margins*. London: Routledge.
Kahl, Brigitte. 2008. "Acts of the Apostles: Pro(to)-imperial Script and Hidden Transcript." Pages 137–56 in *In the Shadow of Empire: Reclaiming the Bible as a History of Faithful Resistance*. Edited by Richard A. Horsley. Louisville: Westminster John Knox.
Kopenawa, Davi, and Bruce Albert. 2010. *A queda do céu: palavras de um xamã yanomami*. São Paulo: Companhia das Letras.
———. 2013. *The Falling Sky: Words of a Yanomami Shaman*. Translated by Nicholas Elliott and Alison Dundy. Cambridge: Belknap Press of Harvard University Press.
Löwy, Michael. 2000. *A guerra dos deuses: Religião e política na América Latina*. Petrópolis: Vozes.
Macedo, Edir. 1993. *A libertação da teologia*. Rio de Janeiro: Editora Gráfica Universal.

Malinowski, Bronislaw. 1984. *Argonautas do Pacífico Ocidental: Um relato do empreendimento e da aventura dos nativos nos arquipélagos da Nova Guiné melanésia*. São Paulo: Abril Cultural.
Maluleke, Tinyiko, and Sarojini Nadar. 2004. "Alien Fraudsters in the White Academy: Agency in Gendered Colour." *JTSA* 120:5–17.
Marcuse, Herbert. 2010. *Eros e civilização: uma interpretação filosófica de Freud*. Rio de Janeiro: LTC.
Marx, Anthony. 1998. *Making Race and Nation: A Comparison of South Africa, the United States, and Brazil*. Cambridge: Cambridge University Press.
Marx, Karl. 1996. *O capital: Crítica da economia política—o processo de produção do capital*. São Paulo: Nova Cultural.
———. 2010. *Crítica da filosofia do direito de Hegel*. São Paulo: Boitempo.
Matos, Olgária Chain Féres. 2000. "A cena primitiva: Capitalismo e fetiche em Walter Benjamin." Pages 87–104 in *Pensar a República*. Edited by Newton Bignotto. Belo Horizonte: Editora UFMG.
McClintock, Anne. 2010. *Couro imperial: Raça, gênero e sexualidade no embate colonial*. Campinas: Editora da Unicamp.
Metcalf, Alida. 2005. *Go-Betweens and the Colonization of Brazil, 1500–1600*. Austin: University of Texas Press.
Mosala, Itumeleng. 1987. *Biblical Hermeneutics and Black Theology in South Africa*. PhD diss., University of Cape Town.
Nandy, Ashis. 2015. "Em direção a uma utopia terceiro-mundista." Pages 89–124 in *A imaginação emancipatória: Desafios do século 21*. Edited by Lucia Rabello de Castro. Belo Horizonte: Editora UFMG.
Nóbrega, Manuel da. 1955. *Cartas do Brasil e mais escritos*. Coimbra: Universidade de Coimbra.
Prado, Luiz Carlos Delorme, and Fábio Sá Earp. 2009. "O 'milagre' brasileiro: crescimento acelerado, integração internacional e concentração de renda (1967–1973)." Pages 207–41 in *O Brasil Republicano: o tempo da ditadura*. Edited by Jorge Ferreira and Lucilia Delgado. Rio de Janeiro: Civilização Brasileira.
Pompa, Cristina. 2001. "Profetas e santidades selvagens: missionários e caraíbas no Brasil colonial." *Revista Brasileira de História* 21.40:177–95.
Ribeiro, Darcy. 1970. *As Américas e a Civilização*. Rio de Janeiro: Civilização Brasileira.
Runions, Erin. 2006. "Desiring War: Apocalypse, Commodity Fetish, and

the End of History." Pages 112–28 in *The Postcolonial Biblical Reader*. Edited by R. S. Sugirtharajah. Oxford: Blackwell.

Santos, Milton. 2015. *Por uma outra globalização: Do pensamento único à consciência universal*. Rio de Janeiro: Record.

Schüssler Fiorenza, Elisabeth. 2007. *The Power of the Word: Scripture and the Rhetoric of Empire*. Minneapolis: Fortress.

Segovia, Fernando. 2015. "Criticism in Critical Times: Reflections on Vision and Task." *JBL* 134:6–29.

Spinoza, Baruch/Benedictus de. 1891. *The Chief Works of Benedict de Spinoza*. Translated by R. H. M. Elwes. 2 vols. London: Bell & Sons.

———. 2008. *Tratado teológico-político*. São Paulo: Martins Fontes.

Sugirtharajah, R. S. 2008. *Troublesome Texts: The Bible in Colonial and Contemporary Culture*. Sheffield: Sheffield Phoenix.

Taussig, Michael. 1993. *Xamanismo, colonialismo e o homem selvagem: um estudo sobre o terror e a cura*. São Paulo: Paz e Terra.

Tolbert, Mary Ann. 1995. "Reading for Liberation." Pages 263–76 in *Reading from This Place: Social Location and Biblical Interpretation in the United States*. Edited by Fernando Segovia and Mary Ann Tolbert. Minneapolis: Fortress.

Vainfas, Ronaldo. 2014. *Trópico dos pecados: moral, sexualidade e inquisição no Brasil*. Rio de Janeiro: Civilização Brasileira.

Vallias, André. 2011. *Heine, Hein? Poeta dos contrários*. São Paulo: Perspectiva/Goethe-Institut.

Van Wyk, Ilana. 2015. "All Answers: On the Phenomenal Success of a Brazilian Pentecostal Charismatic Church in South Africa." Pages 136–62 in *Pentecostalism in Africa: Presence and Impact of Pneumatic Christianity in Postcolonial Societies*. Edited by Martin Lindhardt. Leiden: Brill.

Viveiros de Castro, Eduardo. 2015a. *Metafísicas canibais: Elementos para uma antropologia pós-estrutural*. São Paulo: Cosac Naify.

———. 2015b. "Prefácio—o recado da mata." Pages 11–41 in *A queda do céu: Palavras de um xamã yanomami*. Edited by Davi Kopenawa and Bruce Albert. São Paulo: Companhia das Letras.

Yee, Gale A. 2003. *Poor Banished Children of Eve: Woman as Evil in the Hebrew Bible*. Minneapolis: Fortress.

Žižek, Slavoj. 2011. *Living in the End Times*. London: Verso.

———. 2012. *Vivendo no fim dos tempos*. São Paulo: Boitempo.

Contributors

Roland Boer is professor of literary theory at Remin University of Beijing, China, and research professor at the University of Newcastle, Australia. His main area of research concerns Marxism and religion. To that end, he has recently published the monographs *In the Vale of Tears* (Brill, 2014), *Lenin, Religion and Theology* (Palgrave Macmillan, 2014), and *The Sacred Economy of Ancient Israel* (Westminster John Knox, 2015).

Fernando Candido da Silva is professor of ancient history/religion studies at Federal University of Santa Catarina in Brazil. His work connects liberationist struggles with biblical hermeneutics. With Lieve Troch, he edited the *Body and Color: Reflections in Gender and Religion* issue of the Latin American journal *Mandrágora*. He is also author of "An Abominable and Perverted Alliance? Toward a Latin-American Queer Communitarian Reading of Deuteronomy," in *Exodus and Deuteronomy*, ed. Athalya Brenner and Gale Yee, Texts@Contexts (Fortress, 2012).

Jione Havea is a native Methodist pastor from Tonga who is primary researcher at the Public and Contextual Theology Research Centre, Charles Sturt University in Australia and visiting scholar at Trinity Methodist Theological College in Auckland, Aotearoa/New Zealand. Havea is the author of, among others, *Elusions of Control: Biblical Law on the Words of Women* (Brill, 2003) and "Lazarus Troubles," in Ken Stone and Holly Toensing, eds., *Bible Trouble: Queer Reading at the Boundaries of Biblical Scholarship* (Society of Biblical Literature, 2012).

Theodore W. Jennings Jr. is professor of biblical and constructive theology at Chicago Theological Seminary, where he also helped initiate the gay and lesbian studies program. He has also served as a local pastor, taught for three years at the Methodist Seminary in Mexico City, and served as a consultant with the United Methodist Church on issues related to commitment to the poor. Among his numerous publications are *The Insurrection of the Crucified* (Exploration, 2003), *Jacob's Wound: Homoerotic Narrative in the Literature of Ancient Israel* (Bloomsbury, 2005), *Reading Derrida/ Thinking Paul: On Justice* (Stanford University Press, 2005), *The Man Jesus Loved* (Pilgrim, 2009), and *Outlaw Justice: The Messianic Politics of Paul* (Stanford University Press, 2013).

Tat-siong Benny Liew is Class of 1956 Professor in New Testament Studies at the College of the Holy Cross (Worcester, MA). He is the author of *Politics of Parousia* (Brill, 1999), and *What Is Asian American Biblical Hermeneutics?* (University of Hawai'i Press, 2008). In addition, he is the editor, with Gale Yee, of the *Semeia* volume *The Bible in Asian America* (Society of Biblical Literature, 2002); *Postcolonial Interventions* (Sheffield Phoenix, 2009); with Randall Bailey and Fernando Segovia, *They Were All Together in One Place?* (Society of Biblical Literature, 2009); and *Reading Ideologies* (Sheffield Phoenix, 2011). Liew is also the executive editor of the journal *Biblical Interpretation* (Brill) and series editor of the *Sheffield Phoenix Guide to the New Testament*.

Christina Petterson is research associate at the School of Humanities and Social Sciences at the University of Newcastle, Australia. She works in the fields of New Testament and eighteenth-century European history and has most recently completed a book on the body of Jesus in John's Gospel titled *From Tomb to Text: The Body of Jesus in the Book of John* (Sheffield Phoenix, 2016).

Tina Pippin is the Wallace M. Alston Chair of Bible and Religion at Agnes Scott College. She is an activist educator involved in the Agnes Scott Living Wage Campaign, and she teaches in the areas of biblical studies, ethics and social justice, gender and wymyn's studies, and human rights. Publications include *Death and Desire: The Rhetoric of Gender in the Apocalypse of John* (Westminster John Knox, 1992) and *Apocalyptic Bodies: The Biblical End of the World in Text and Image* (Routledge, 1999). She is also editor, with Cheryl Kirk-Duggan, of *Mother Goose, Mother Jones, Mommie Dearest: Biblical Mothers and Their Children* (Society of Biblical Literature, 2010).

Jeremy Punt is professor of New Testament in the Theology Faculty at Stellenbosch University, South Africa. His works on New Testament hermeneutics, past and present, and focuses in particular on cultural studies and critical theory in relation to New Testament interpretation. He has recently published *Postcolonial Biblical Interpretation: Reframing Paul* (Brill, 2015) and regularly contributes to academic journals and book publications.

Erin Runions is associate professor in the Department of Religious Studies at Pomona College. She explores the intersections of biblical interpretation and political philosophies, with their multiple impacts on subjectivity, gender, sexuality, sovereignty, empire, and biopolitics. She is author of *Changing Subjects: Gender, Nation, Future in Micah* (Sheffield Academic, 2001), which puts the work of Homi Bhabha into conversation with Marxist literary criticism and biblical criticism; *How Hysterical: Identification and Resistance in the Bible and Film* (Palgrave Macmillan, 2003), which reads film and text through psychoanalysis and deconstruction; and most recently, *The Babylon Complex: Theopolitical Fantasies of War, Sex and Sovereignty* (Fordham, 2014).

Ancient Sources Index

Hebrew Bible		15:35–16:13	83
		19:19–24	198
Genesis		28	7, 82, 89, 91, 93–95, 205
12:1–4	90	28:2	83
		28:3	83
Exodus		28:3–25	105
4–14	88	28:5	82
20	65, 72	28:6	84
20:3–6	67	28:7	84–85
23:20	119	28:9	86
		28:11	87
Numbers		28:12	90
22–24	88	28:15	95
		28:18	92
Deuteronomy		28:19	91–92
5	65	28:20	95
5:7–10	68–69, 72	29:2	83
Joshua		2 Samuel	
2–6	88	13:1–22	88
17:1–12	85		
24	88	1 Kings	
		1:1–4	82
Judges			
13–16	82	2 Kings	
		4:8–10	82
1 Samuel			
2:28	90	Isaiah	119
8	83	24:19–20	178
8:20	92	40:3	119
9:1–3	83	40:19–20	67
9:17	83	41:6–7	67
10:1	83	42:17	67
15:24	93	44:6–7	69
15:26	83	44:9–20	67

ANCIENT SOURCES INDEX

Isaiah (cont.)
45:16–17 — 67
46:1–2 — 67
46:5–7 — 67

Malachi
3:1 — 119

Ancient Jewish Writers

Josephus, *Antiquitates judaicae*
18.55–59 — 157
18.60–62 — 138
18.261–283 — 157
20.2–4 — 139
20.97–98 — 139
20.105–122 — 138
20.113–114 — 139
20.118–122 — 139
20.120 — 134
20.125–133 — 139
20.167–178 — 139
20.188 — 139

Josephus, *Bellum judaicum*
2.457–468 — 139
2.487–498 — 139
5.446–451 — 139
6.403–406 — 139
6.418–420 — 139
7.23–24 — 139
7.37–40 — 139
7.96 — 139
7.142–157 — 139
7.407–419 — 139
7.443–446 — 139

Philo, *In Flaccum*
6.41–43 — 138
8.53–57 — 138
10.73–75 — 138
10.81–85 — 138
10.83 — 116

New Testament

Matthew — 208
8:22 — 163
15:21–28 — 105

Mark — 8, 99–122, 199–200, 207–9, 220–21
1:1 — 118, 120
1:1–3 — 119
1:2 — 119
1:9 — 112
1:14 — 112
1:15 — 118
1:16 — 112
1:39 — 112
1:44 — 100
3:7 — 112
5:42 — 103
6:45–52 — 106
7:24 — 116
7:24–30 — 105, 107
7:31–37 — 107
7:36 — 100
7:36–37 — 100
9:6 — 199
12:1–11 — 121
14:3–9 — 106
14:28 — 116
15 — 115
15:39 — 106
15:45 — 103
16:1–6 — 112
16:1–8 — 106
16:5–7 — 112
16:6 — 103
16:7 — 100, 113, 116, 118
16:7–8 — 99
16:8 — 99, 102, 113, 118

Luke
9:60 — 163

John	8–9, 121, 199–201, 206, 209, 220–21	5:24–29	147
		5:37	160
1:1–18	142	5:39	150
1:4	150	6:1–15	141
1:4–5	149	6:15	141
1:9	149, 161	6:15–25	153
1:12–13	160	6:22–35	141
1:14	140	6:25–27	155
1:18	160	6:27–68	150
1:19–12:50	142	6:35	155
1:29	141	6:35–64	161
1:36	141	6:39–40	147
1:38	153	6:44	147
2:1–11	141	6:46	160
2:3–4	160	6:49–50	141–42
2:4	131, 142	6:54	147
2:13–22	141, 143	6:55	141
2:19–22	147	6:58	141–42
3:1–8	151	7:1	142–43
3:3–8	161	7:1–11	153
3:14	149	7:19	142–43
3:14–15	147	7:25	142–43
3:15–16	150	7:30	131, 153
3:18–21	161	7:37–39	155
3:31	160–61	7:39	153, 157
3:35	161	7:44	153
3:36	150	8:12	149, 161
4:1–14	155	8:20	131
4:8	141	8:20–22	153
4:9	157	8:21	151
4:14	150	8:21–22	158
4:24	160	8:23	160
4:31–34	141	8:23–24	161
4:31–38	155	8:24	151
4:34	156	8:28	149
4:36	150	8:31–32	160
4:39–42	157	8:32	148
4:46–54	143	8:37	142, 143
4:47	141–42	8:40	142, 143
4:49	141–42	8:44	146
5:13–14	153	8:48	157
5:20	161	8:51	147, 160
5:21	142, 147	8:53	141
5:21–26	150	8:57	132
5:24	142	8:59	142–43, 153

John (cont.)

9:1–5	161	12:24	148
9:1–41	141	12:25	148
9:5	149	12:27	131
9:12	153	12:32	149
9:22	150	12:35–36	149
9:35	153	12:36	153
10:1–18	161	12:42	150
10:9	153	12:44–50	161
10:10	150	12:46	149
10:10–18	141–42	13:1	131, 152
10:17	161	13:1–19:42	141
10:17–18	149	13:1–20:31	142
10:18	161	13:10–30	155
10:28	150	13:21–26	149
10:31	143	13:27–30	149
10:31–33	142	13:34–35	156
10:32–33	143	13:36–38	141
10:39–40	153	14:2	152
10:40–11:16	152	14:6	149, 150
11	143	14:15–27	153
11:1–6	153	14:15–15:11	160
11:1–44	141	14:19	147
11:4	143, 152	14:19–23	161
11:7–8	143	14:25–26	150
11:7–10	161	14:25–31	150
11:9–10	149	14:26	157
11:11	152	14:30	150
11:13–14	143	15:1–16:4	161
11:16	143	15:9–11	161
11:17	143	15:12	156
11:21	143	15:13	161
11:25	150	15:14	161
11:32	143	15:17	156
11:39	143	15:17–16:3	156
11:44	143, 155	15:26	150, 153, 157
11:46–53	143	16:2	150
11:46–57	153	16:5	152
11:47–53	144, 146	16:7	152–53
11:49	158	16:13	157
11:51–52	157, 159	16:13–15	150
12–20	146	16:16–22	153
12:9–11	143	16:26–27	161
12:10–11	152	17	154
12:23	131	17:1–26	153
		17:2–3	150

ANCIENT SOURCES INDEX

17:6–9	160	21:18–23	143, 155, 162
17:14	156	21:18–24	157
17:20–26	161	21:20–23	141
18:3	149	21:22	143
18:4	149, 153	21:24	162
18:4–5	149	21:24–25	157
18:6	149	21:25	162
18:7	153		
18:7–8	149	Romans	
18:8	159	1:21	67
18:10–11	149	1:23	67
18:14	144	1:25	67
18:31–32	144, 146		
19:6	144	Philippians	132
19:7–16	144		
19:8–11	160	Revelation	171–89, 207
19:10	144, 146	21–22	187
19:11	160	21:2–5	185
19:12	162	21:11	176
19:12–22	144		
19:13–16	141	Greco-Roman Literature	
19:15	162		
19:21	157	Appian, *Bella civilia*	
19:25–27	137	2.102	136
19:25–28	153–54		
19:28–30	155	Cicero, *Orationes philippicae*	
19:31–37	141	10.20	144
19:38–39	153		
19:38–42	137	Dio Cassius, *Historiae romanae*	
20:14	152	43.23.3–6	136
20:15	153	68.32	139
20:19	153	69.12–15	139
20:19–28	162		
20:22	153, 157	Justinian, *Digesta*	132
20:26	153	1.5.4.2–3	135
20:30	157		
20:30–31	163	Juvenal, *Satirae*	
20:31	150	10.66–67	136
21	155		
21:1–14	147	Lucan, *Pharsalia*	
21:4	152	2.306–325	144
21:9–17	141, 155		
21:15	155	Lucian, *De luctu*	
21:15–19	155, 161	24	147
21:18–19	141		

Martial, *Spectacles*
    5.65   137

Plato, *Phaedo*, 138
    64a   138
    80e   138

Plato, *Symposium*, 196

Pliny the Younger, *Epistulae*   8
    8.18.1   153

Polybius, *Historiae*
    6.15.7–8   136
    6.54.1–4   144

Pompeius Festus, *De verborum*
    significatione   133

Seneca, *Epistulae*
    7.3–5   137
    26.6   153
    95.33   137

Sophocles, *Antigone*
    1256   102

Suetonius, *Divus Julius*
    39.4   136

Tacitus, *Agricola*
    30   114

Tacitus, *Annales*   153

Tacitus, *Historiae*
    5.13   139

Modern Authors Index

Abraham, Nicolas 119
Adorno, Theodor 3, 6–7, 10, 45, 59, 65, 70–76, 197, 216
Agamben, Giorgio 8, 132–36, 138, 140, 146, 150–51, 158, 160–61, 164, 199, 205–6
Ahmad, Aijaz 2, 22, 24, 26–27, 29–30, 205
Ahmed, Sara 105, 114
Albert, Bruce 221–22
Alexiou, Margaret 102
Althusser, Louis 3–4, 36, 53
Althaus-Reid, Marcella 215–16
Anderson, Warwick 3
Andrade, Oswald 213
Anzaldúa, Gloria 216
Anthias, Floya 31, 38
Anyidoho, Kofi 95
Apter, Emily 49
Arenari, Brand 220
Ashton, John 149
Assmann, Hugo 56
Assmann, Jan 60, 145
Badiou, Alain 4
Bailey, Randall C. 134
Balasopoulos, Antonis 185
Baldwin, James 156
Barthes, Roland 24, 25, 153
Bartolovich, Crystal 3
Bate, David 3
Baudrillard, Jean 151, 159
Beam, Joseph 156
Belo, Fernando 221
Benjamin, Walter 56, 74, 110, 121, 215, 220–21

Benyamini, Itzhak 4
Beozzo, José Oscar 213
Berger, James 108
Bernstein, Michael André 118
Berquist, Jon L. 31, 46
Berrigan, Daniel 91
Bersani, Leo 4
Bhabha, Homi K. 3, 8, 26, 30, 36, 104, 205, 208
Bhaskar, Roy 35
Binz, Stephen J. 118
Blanco, María del Pilar 105
Blanton, Ward 1
Bloch, Ernst 215
Boer, Roland 1–2, 6–7, 21, 22, 29, 196–97, 201, 203, 206, 209, 215–16
Boheemen-Saaf, Christine van 3
Bonhoeffer, Dietrich 201
Borch-Jacobsen, Mikkel 113, 132
Borgman, Paul 93
Bosi, Alfredo 212
Bosteels, Bruno 2
Bould, Mark 183
Bourdieu, Pierre 145, 147
Boyarin, Daniel 165
Brennan, Teresa 105
Brett, Mark G. 20, 26, 31, 46
Brittain, Christopher 70–1
Brogan, Kathleen 117
Bronfen, Elisabeth 163
Brooks, Edwin 222
Brooks, Peter 145
Brosses, Charles de 49, 54, 57
Brotton, Jerry 218
Brown, Raymond E. 115

MODERN AUTHORS INDEX

Brueggemann, Walter 46
Buck-Morss, Susan 218
Bultmann, Rudolf 132
Buchholz, René 71
Butler, Judith 94
Butler, Octavia 176
Callinicos, Alex 30, 35
Campbell, Jan 3
Cardoso Pereira, Nancy 220
Carey, Greg 46
Carlson, Carl C. 188
Carter, Warren 46, 104
Carusi, Annamaria 20–21, 27–29
Caruth, Cathy 110–11, 113
Castelli, Elizabeth A. 159
Cavalcanti, Tereza 213
Césaire, Aimé 23
Chan, Jeffrey 101
Chang, Juliana 104, 114, 119, 208
Cheng, Anne Anlin 133
Cheung, King-kok 101
Chibber, Vivek 2–3
Chin, Frank 101
Cho, Grace M. 3, 105
Choi, Jin Young 106–8
Chow, Rey 101, 205
Chrisman, Laura 22, 32, 35
Clough, Patricia Ticineto 3
Cobb, John 56
Coleman, Kathy M. 137
Coleman, Simon 220
Collins, John J. 172
Collins, Adela Yarbro 172
Comte, August 48
Conway, Colleen M. 142
Countryman, L. William 144
Crossan, John Dominic 46, 115
Croy, Clayton 118
Culpepper, R. Alan 129–31, 145
Dantas, Bruna Suruagy do Amaral 220
Davidson, Steed 2, 205
Davis, Mike 186
Day, John 68
De Man, Paul 164
Delaney, Carol 109
Deleuze, Gilles 29
Derrida, Jacques 8, 24, 28–29, 33, 37, 89, 105–18, 131–32, 142, 152–53, 163, 200–201
Dinkler, Michal Beth 102
Dirlik, Arif 2, 205
Dixon, Wheeler Winston 175, 177
Donaldson, Laura E. 2, 105
Du Bois, W. E. B. 145
Dube, Musa W. 2, 161
Dufourmantelle, Anne 131
Duling, Dennis C. 118
During, Simon 25
Durkheim, Emile 158–59
Durrant, Sam 3
Dussell, Enrique 56
Dwyer, Timothy 103
Eagleton, Terry 26, 28
Earp, Fábio Sá 222
Edwards, Catherine 137, 142, 144, 147, 151, 153, 155, 159, 160, 163
Elliott, Neil 46, 104
Eng, David L. 119
Engels, Friedrich 2, 52, 197
Evans, Craig A. 115
Evans, C. Stephen 56
Fanon, Franz 3, 23, 32, 40, 88, 95, 135, 137, 144, 149, 156, 196, 204–5, 219
Feldman, Louis H. 139–140
Fenichel, Otto 112
Feuerbach, Ludwig 54, 75, 196
Figiel, Sia 82, 86
Floyd, Kevin 3
Freire, Paulo 220
Freud, Sigmund 3, 5–10, 22, 32–39, 45, 48–51, 56–59, 65–71, 76, 89, 103–5, 108–12, 118–21, 145, 147, 173–75, 195–97, 201, 208, 213–16
Frier, Bruce W. 131–32
Gadamer, Hans-Georg 163
Gallagher, Susan VanZanten 31
Gambini, Roberto 213
Garland, Robert 115
Garnsey, Peter, 137
Gandhi, Leela 24–28, 30–1
Gilroy, Paul 3, 135
Ginzburg, Carlo 213

Glancy, Jennifer A.	134, 137	Jackson, Rosemary	177
Gomo, Mashingaidze	95	Jameson, Fredric	32, 36, 72, 173–76
Gordon, Avery F.	8, 105–13, 117–18, 121	JanMohamed, Abul R.	8, 134, 140, 145, 149–52, 158, 162, 206
Goss, Jasper	24	Jay, Martin	6,
Gottwald, Norman K.	1, 46	Jenson, Deborah	3
Green, Barbara	90, 96	Jobling, David	2, 85, 89, 96
Gregg, Melissa	105	Jolly, Rosemary	25
Gugelberger, Georg M.	23	Kahl, Brigitte	46, 215
Gunjević, Boris	221	Kapoor, Ilan	38
Gunn, David M.	83	Keller, Nora Okja	119
Gwyther, Anthony	175	Keller, Richard C.	3
Habermas, Jürgen	29	Kelly, Christopher	131
Halberstam, J.	148	Kessler, Rainer	4
Halliday, W. R.	114	Khanna, Ranjana	3
Halperin, David J.	4	Kim, Uriah Y.	2
Han, Shinhee	119	Kipnis, Laura	3, 36–7
Hanh, Thich Nhat	91	Klauck, Hans-Josef	115–16, 137, 153
Hansen, João Adolfo	212	Klein, Naomi	189
Hardt, Michael	34, 47	Kloppenborg, John S.	137
Harrill, J. Albert	135	Koban, Craig J.	180
Havea, Jione	7, 198, 204–5, 207, 218–19	Koester, Craig R.	140, 144, 147, 149, 152
Hawley, John C.	39	Kojève, Alexandre	141
Hegel, Georg Wilhelm Friedrich	24, 38, 63, 132, 135, 141	Koosed, Jennifer L.	105
Heidegger, Martin	132, 154, 161	Kotrosits, Maia	101, 106–8, 114, 118, 120–21, 207–8
Heine, Heinrich	213–14	Krell, David Farrell	163
Hinkelammert, Franz J.	56	Kristeva, Julia	24–25, 28–29, 33, 102, 140, 201
Hirsch, Marianne	119		
Hochschild, Arlie Russell	3	Kyle, Donald G.	136–37
Holland, Sharon Patricia	133–34, 141, 154	Lacan, Jacques	3–4, 8, 22, 29, 32–34, 36–38, 50, 113–14, 129, 132, 172, 187, 199, 201
Holloway, Karla F. C.	134–35, 138, 147, 157–58, 206		
		LaCapra, Dominick	119
Homer, Sean	113	Laclau, Ernesto	3
hooks, bell	182	Lardinois, André	102
Horkheimer, Max	73–75	Lazarus, Neil	3
Horsley, Richard A.	46–47, 104, 215	Levinas, Emmanuel	154, 161, 200
Howard-Brook, Wes	175	Liew, Tat-siong Benny	2, 8–9, 199–201, 205–9, 220–21
Huggan, Graham	218		
Hurtado, Larry W.	99–101, 103–4	Lifton, Robert Jay	174
Hutcheon, L.	30	Lincoln, Andrew	99
Huxley, Aldous	183	Lindsey, Hal	188
Hyman, Gavin	32, 38–39, 42	Lischer, Richard	56
Inada, Lawson Fusao	101	Loraux, Nicole	154, 159
Isaac, Benjamin	134	Lowe, Lisa	3

Löwy, Michael 56, 220
Loy, David 56
Luepnitz, Deborah 129
Lukács, Georg 55, 71
Lyall, Sarah 173
Lyotard, Jean François 37, 159
Macedo, Edir 220
Macey, David 205
Macy, Joanna R. 174
Mailer, Norman 140, 142, 145
Malinowski, Bronislaw 218
Maluleke, Tinyiko 219
Marchal, Joseph A. 19
Marcuse, Herbert 3, 217
Marin, Louis 208
Marriott, David 135, 138, 156
Martin, Dale B. 102
Marx, Anthony 219
Marx, Karl 2–3, 5–6, 8, 10, 22, 24, 27, 31, 33, 48–9, 52–9, 72, 75, 111, 176, 196, 201, 213–15, 222
Matos, Olgária Chain Féres 218
McCane, Byron R. 116
McClintock, Anne 3, 215, 218
McClure, Laura 102
McGuckin, Eric 23, 29, 38
McKay, Niall 24, 32
Meeks, M. Douglas 56
Metcalf, Alida 213
Michaud, Ginette 163
Miéville, China 9, 171–74, 176
Miklitsch, Robert 3
Mills, Sara 33
Milz, Sabine 20, 29, 38
Miranda, Carmen 218
Miranda, José Porfirio 1
Moala, Kalafi 82
Mokoena, Michael 22
Monk, Daniel Bertrand 186
Monleón, José B. 185
Moore, Stephen D. 2, 43, 104, 129–31, 135, 144, 158, 160, 162
Morrison, Toni 147
Morton, Donald 37, 38
Mosala, Itumeleng J. 1, 21, 219
Moule, Charles F. D. 100
Mufti, Aamir 3
Murray, Stuart 32, 42
Nadar, Sarojini 219
Nandy, Ashis 4, 25, 216
Negri, Antonio 34, 47, 75, 196
Nicole, Robert 91
Nietzsche, Friedrich 33, 65, 164, 197
Nigam, Aditya 31
Nilges, Mathias 180
Nóbrega, Manuel da 211–13
O'Brien, Suzie 20
Økland, Jorunn 1
Oliver, Kelly 135
Orchard, Helen C. 149
Parham, Marisa 105
Parry, Benita 2, 22, 25, 27, 29–31, 34
Patterson, Orlando 150
Petersen, Norman R. 149
Pietz, William 48–49, 51
Pigott, Susan M. 85, 92, 96
Pippin, Tina 9, 197, 207, 216–18
Plass, Paul 136, 159
Pompa, Cristina 212
Pontalis, J. B. 145
Posnock, Ross 164
Prado, Luiz Carlos Delorme 222
Prakash, Gyan 3
Pritchard, Elizabeth A. 71
Punt, Jeremy 2, 5, 195–96, 203, 205–6, 208, 218–19
Quinby, Lee 184
Radhakrishnan, R. 119
Rambo, Shelly 113, 118, 121
Rashkow, Ilona 4, 32, 34, 37–38
Reed, Randall W. 1
Reinhartz, Adele 150
Ribeiro, Darcy 213
Ricoeur, Paul 195
Rieger, Joerg 36, 121
Roberts, Dorothy 154
Robinette, Nick 27, 39
Rogers, Annie G. 110
Rohrbaugh, Richard L. 204

Rose, Jacqueline	134	Szeman, Imre	20
Royalty, Robert M., Jr.	175	Taussig, Hal	101, 106–8, 114, 118, 120–21, 207–8
Runions, Erin	172, 185, 216		
Said, Edward	4, 27, 134, 145, 164	Taussig, Michael	147, 221
San Juan, E., Jr.	2	Taylor, Mark C.	38
Sanders, E. P.	47	Taylor, Astra	180
Santner, Eric L.	119	Thatcher, Tom	129, 145
Santos, Milton	216	Thiemann, Ronald F.	56
Scarry, Elaine	114	Todorov, Tzvetan	188
Schäfer, Peter	156	Tolbert, Mary Ann	99–100, 102, 216
Schüssler Fiorenza, Elisabeth	221	Tolkien, J. R. R.	173, 183
Schwab, Gabriele	105	Tomkins, Silvan S.	105
Scott, David	3	Tomsic, Samo	3
Scott, James C.	117	Torok, Maria	119
Scott, Peter	56	Trible, Phyllis	88
Sedgwick, Eve, Kosofsky	105–6	Tuhkanen, Mikko	3
Segovia, Fernando F.	2, 19–20, 22, 23–24, 27, 34, 134, 216	Vainfas, Ronaldo	213
		Vallias, André	213
Seigworth, Gregory J.	105	Van Wyk, Ilana	220
Seshadri-Crooks, Kalpana	3	Vandermeersch, Patrick	4
Shohat, Ella	3	Verheyden, Joseph	39
Siddiqi, Yumna	120	Victorino, Maria Gemma	118
Silva, Daniel F.	3	Viveiros de Castro, Eduardo	211, 216
Sloyan, Gerard S.	115	Walker, Alice	88–89
Smith, Anne-Marie	102, 110	Wan, Sze-kar	30–31
Smith, D. Moody	121	Wendt, Albert	96
Smith, Linda Tuhiwai	91	Wengst, Klaus	104
Sobrino, John	56	West, Gerald O.	2, 21
Sontag, Susan	179, 181–82	Wiegman, Robyn	111
Soyinka, Wole	92	Willemen, Paul	181
Spencer, Neville	27, 39	Willett, Cynthia	156
Spillers, Hortense J.	130, 140, 145–46, 153–54, 161	Williams, Joel F.	99, 103, 118
		Williams, Raymond	108, 110–11
Spinoza, B.	211, 216	Wilson, Andrew P.	117
Spivak, Gayatri Chakravorty	3, 94, 101, 107, 161	Wolfenstein, Eugene Victor	4
		Wong, Shawn	101
Staten, Henry	142, 158	Wrede, William	101–2, 120–21
Stendahl, Krister	47	Wright, Richard	134, 138
Stibbe, Mark W. G.	153	Yee, Gale A.	1, 219
Stoler, Ann Laura	104–5	Young, Robert J. C.	3, 24
Strozier, Charles B.	181	Zeligs, Dorothy F.	4
Suda, Max Josef	56	Žižek, Slavoj	3, 33, 36, 38–39, 45, 50–51, 103, 172, 176, 180, 182, 186–87, 199, 201, 208, 217
Sugirtharajah, R. S.	2, 21, 218		
Sung, Jung Mo	56		
Suvin, Darko	173, 176–77		

www.ingramcontent.com/pod-product-compliance
Lightning Source LLC
Chambersburg PA
CBHW020647300426
44112CB00007B/267